A CONCISE HISTORY

OF

FOREIGN BAPTISTS

TAKEN FROM THE NEW TESTAMENT, THE FIRST FATHERS, EARLY WRITERS, AND HISTORIANS OF ALL AGES;

Chronologically Arranged;

Exhibiting their distinct Communities, with their orders in various Kingdoms, under several discriminative appellations from the establishment of Christianity to the present age.

WITH CORRELATIVE INFORMATION, SUPPORTING THE EARLY AND ONLY PRACTICE OF BELIEVERS' IMMERSION:

ALSO

OBSERVATIONS AND NOTES

ON THE ABUSE OF THE ORDINANCE,

AND THE RISE OF MINOR AND INFANT BAPTISM THEREON.

INTENDED FOR

JUVENILE BRANCHES OF THEIR CHURCHES.

By G. H. ORCHARD,

Baptist Minister, Steventon, Bedfordshire.

"In *all things* that I said unto you, be circumspect."—Exod. xxiii. 13.
"Now I praise you, brethren, *that ye keep the ordinances,* as I delivered them to you."
—1 Cor. xi. 2.

"Logical arguments, and controversial reasonings, cannot be well adapted to every understanding; but historical facts, and the consequences thence deducible, are to the meanest understanding plain and obvious."—Bowers's Lives of the Popes.

London:

GEORGE WIGHTMAN, PATERNOSTER ROW.

1838.

Republished 2019 by
The Old Paths Publications, Inc.
www.theoldpathspublications.com
ISBN: 978-1-7341927-4-2

The cover picture is the church Dr. John Clarke founded and remains active as a Reformed Baptist Church and carries the name of United Baptist Church, John Clarke Memorial in honor of its founder.

ADVERTISEMENT.

My Young Christian Friends,

The reason for the following work is soon assigned. While on a visit to a friend in Somersetshire, in 1823, a minister of the Independent persuasion panegyrized Dr. Carey to me and others, as the individual who raised the Baptists out of obscurity; and further remarked, that "they had no existence before the days of the Commonwealth." The respectability and age of the minister did not allow me, a young man, and unacquainted as I was with our history, to negative his assertion, only by a relieving hint, "' that from the days of John the Baptists, *until now*,' I believed our denomination had had an existence." I was resolved to be satisfied on this subject, particularly since this assertion has appeared in print; but there was no volume to which I could be directed, that would meet the inquiries and solicitude of my mind. Mr. Ivimey's work was of the English Baptists; Mr. Crosby's was of the same character; Mr. Danvers enters into the question, but gives no historic connexion. I wrote to Mr. Jones, author of the History of the Christian Church, and his work (on his recommendation) I procured; and this valuable history gave me *the clue to the church of God.* I had now to ascertain the views the different parties advocated, which cost me very considerable application, and the result fully satisfied my inquiries. After some years' reading, and making extracts from authors, on the subject of my investigation, I resolved on throwing my materials into chronological order, to exhibit the feature of a connected history. This done, I became fully satisfied; and established the proof of what Robinson conjectured, that " the English Baptists, contending for the sufficiency of Scripture, and for Christian liberty to judge of its meaning, can be traced back in authentic documents, to the first Nonconformists and to the Apostles."

In the course of my reading, materials so accumulated on my hands, as to enable me to furnish facts sufficient to make a compendious history of the Baptists in various provinces; from their rise, to their being scattered or extinguished; and which facts are submitted in the following pages. Nor do I fear contradiction, since I have taken the most accredited historians, and have preferred, in most instances, the testimonies of men *hostile to our communion.*

The ensuing facts, with *many* more, were selected to satisfy my own inquiries; but when I had placed them in a connective form, I thought they might be useful to others similarly circumstanced, and might render some aid to inquiring youths in our churches, conducing, perhaps, to the removal of a portion of that visible ignorance, as to the early features of our denomination; particularly, since it has been said, that "the Baptists may be considered as the only Christian community which has stood since the times of the Apostles; and as a Christian society, which has preserved pure the doctrines of the gospel through all ages." This statement we consider to be proved in the following pages, where authors are quoted, supporting these facts.

It is stated in the most satisfactory manner, that *all* Christian communities during the first three centuries were of the Baptist denomination, in constitution and practice. In the middle of the third century, the Novatian Baptists established separate and independent societies, which continued till the end of the sixth age; when these communities were succeeded by the Paterines, which continued till the Reformation. The oriental Baptist Churches, with their successors, the Paulicians, continued in their purity until the tenth century, when these people visited France, resuscitating and extending the Christian profession in Languedoc, where they flourished till the crusading army scattered, or drowned in blood, one million of unoffending professors.

The Baptists in Piedmont and Germany are exhibited as existing under different names, down to the Reformation; these churches, with their genuine successors, the Mennonites in Holland, are connectedly and chronologically detailed to the present period, for proof which, see the body of the work.

The writer is aware that Dr. Stennett *collected* materials for this very object, and Mr. B. Stinton *commenced* a History of the Baptists; but both of these excellent men were removed by death, before they had made any progress in the work. The deficiency was felt in the connexion, and our London ministers directed the attention of Mr. Robert Robinson to the subject, requesting his services in this department. "After the labour of years, and wading through loads of books," he issued the *History of Baptism*, which satisfied no one but himself. His Ecclesiastical Researches were published after his death. This work is valuable, and its importance would have been increased, had not his aversion been so prominent to the evangelical party, and the innocency of mental errors so frequently justified. Mr. Allen in his "Junius," made many extracts from early writers, but produced no history. In the Baptist Magazine, some very valuable extracts have been exhibited from Allen's Junius and early writers, but nothing of a clear, connected history has been produced by any. A History of the Baptist Denomination was still a *desideratum*.

Free admission to the extensive libraries of Earl Spenser and the Duke of Bedford, is gratefully acknowledged; from which sources the writer has drawn some portion of the denominational materials now submitted.

The ground of unity and denominational claim to the people whose Christian characters are detailed, is not the harmony of their creeds or views; this was not *visible or essential in the first age*: but THE BOND OF UNION, *among our denomination in all ages, has been* FAITH IN CHRIST; *and that faith* PUBLICLY EXPRESSED, *by a voluntary submission to his authority and doctrine in baptism.* Wherever this conduct is evident, we claim the disciple as belonging to our communion and of primitive character, at the same time leaving his mind in the full enjoyment of his native and purchased freedom; and in establishing this association, we feel no difficulty or dishonour, since almost every denomination has, from their honourable and holy characters, claimed affinity to them in faith and practice, though such claims are not supported by family likeness.

That the ordinance of baptism has been diverted from its original assignment and place in the Christian church, has been allowed by the violators of the primitive order. It has been awfully abused, and its original simplicity obscured; but ultimately, TRUTH will prevail, and when its legitimate influence shall be allowed, and the remaining vestiges of papacy shall have been removed from the Christian church, it will be seen and admitted, that infant baptism has ever been *the bourn* to his reign and influence, who has been emphatically denominated, *the man of sin.*

Most *modern* historians have been of the Pædobaptist persuasion. These writers have, in a general way, suppressed in their details those evidences of *believers' baptism*, which abound in early writers. This omission in their histories was intended, that the modern practice may not be disturbed, and themselves condemned as innovators, by the records and practice of early churches. These writers, from the pope to the peasant, have united in suppressing and extinguishing *part of the truth;* consequently, it was necessary to collate writings, histories, and documents, before the dawn of the German Reformation, in order to get at *the whole truth;* and strange to say, while ministers of religion, for party purposes, have suppressed certain denominational features, Voltaire, Hume, Gibbon, and other infidel with deistical writers, have in these respects faithfully and openly recorded events, and have been more impartial in their details than many modern divines.

The author has found it necessary to use the specific names of the denomination more frequently in this history than might be agreeable to some readers. The reluctancy of some moderns to allow of the early and reputable existence of this class of Christians, made it necessary that the terms *Baptist*, Anabaptist, &c., should be often mentioned, to prevent misconstruction, and the more fully to establish *the object* the writer had in view.

He has also kept unadorned facts prominently forward. *These are the stubborn materials of history.* In many instances, he has copied the language of able historians, and here he acknowledges his obligations to Mr. Jones's invaluable writings on the Church of Christ. On controverted points he feared to alter statements or clothe ideas in his own language, lest cavilling readers should doubt his veracity. If more verbosity had been given, the work would have been more agreeable to some, but the writer feared weakening the evidence of his work, and of making a large book; he has, therefore, preferred crowding the materials together, to make his compilation, a reference book *in triumph*, rather than its contents should be questioned from any accommodating aspect. In its character, it may be considered a rough rampart, planted round the visible camp of the saints, within which fortification they may feel safe, while at the same time, they are furnished with those means of repelling attacks, made with *antiquated* weapons.

These facts do not invite the critic's eye; its humble aspect we conceive to be far below his envenomed shaft: nor are they submitted to the rich and the learned; such persons have the means and opportunity of procuring those works from which these records were drawn, and of going more fully into historic details. We apprehend the stubborn facts detailed, will awaken those to anger, whose craft is supported by the error exposed. Their defence will be taken from the stores of an *unholy alliance ;* but unscriptural and unsanctified weapons, with all the support of antiquated reproach, &c., &c., will best *prove* to the inquiring disciple, the absence of *all* precepts and examples for the rite, sought to be supported. We hope the following sheets are free from acrimony, and where censure is given, the palpable violation of truth and order merited severity; indeed, truth at times could not be detailed in its importance, if infamy were not attached to delinquency. However awful the characters of some early innovators were, we unhesitatingly assert that very many Pædobaptists *since* the Reformation have been, and still deservingly are, numbered among the excellent of the earth. We can and do respect them for their piety, but we cannot approve of their error; nor can they expect it, since many of their best men admit that pædobaptism had no place in the church in apostolic days, and some moderns are so tender on this point now, as to practise it in private. A refutation we do not fear; this would be a difficult task, since controverted facts are generally *given in the words of the historian,* and so far as the writer could, a Pædobaptist's testimony has had the preference. References could have been increased to a considerable extent, but the support of the statement by one respectable name was deemed sufficient.

Illness, and the claims of the ministry, have prevented an entire devotion to this object; and though truly conscious of his unfitness to do justice to the subject, yet he has been always happy in the employment. Whatever inadvertence or errors there might be, the writer's best efforts are here offered to the society of which he stands an unworthy member, and if he realizes their approbation, he shall consider it next to the smiles of his Master, and feel remunerated for fifteen years' labour; at the same time, his desire, prayer, and efforts, are for the promotion of *the truth, the whole truth, and nothing but the truth;* and his hope is, that this heavenly principle will soon universally prevail: then the precepts of men, traditionary services, and compulsory religion shall be *swept away* from the church of God; truth then, in all its legitimate and unrestrained influence, shall have *free course*, unadorned by human fancy, unchecked by human laws, unaided by human device; then, reinstated in its native dignity, *truth* shall be found like the beams of the sun alighting and regulating the inhabitants of the world, dispelling darkness and ignorance, conferring on the benighted the blessings of a gospel day, exhibiting their moral condition, awakening new sensations, requiring the north to give up, the south to keep not back; bring my sons from far, and my daughters from the ends of the earth; then shall we see eye to eye, Jerusalem shall be the joy of the whole earth, and our God shall bless us.

Yours to serve in the kingdom of Christ,

THE AUTHOR.

Steventon, Jan. 1, 1838.

HISTORY OF THE BAPTISTS.

CHAPTER I.

Section I.

PRIMITIVE BAPTISTS.

"From the days of John the Baptist till *now*, the kingdom of heaven suffereth violence, and the violent taketh it by force."—*Matt.* xi. 12.

1. ECCLESIASTICAL history must ever prove an interesting subject to every true lover of Zion. Not only does every saint feel personally interested in her blessings, but he solicitously wishes and prays for their diffusion, as widely as the miseries of man prevail. Psal. lxxiii. 19. Feelings of holy jealousy are awakened within the bosom of each of Zion's offspring, for the success and purity of that cause, in which all his soul is enlisted: emotions, therefore, of pain or pleasure, will accompany all his discoveries in historic details, in proportion as he views his adorable Lord honoured or dishonoured, by the obedience or disobedience of his professed followers.

2. Among those duties clearly revealed, and which the New Testament enjoins on the disciples of our Redeemer, BELIEVERS' BAPTISM, holds a very conspicuous place. This ordinance was particularly regarded in the

days of the Redeemer and his apostles with their successors, and no satisfactory reason can be assigned for its perversion or neglect. Its importance has occasioned some kind of attention from the general body of professed Christians in every after age, though its scriptural character has been observed and perpetuated by *one class or branch* of the professing church, while other sections degenerated into the most unscriptural customs and heathenish rites. In ancient and modern times, it has been the apple of strife, as to its place and importance in the divine economy. By the great body of disputants, it has been diverted from the subject to which the Scriptures assigned it (Acts viii. 37, and xviii. 8,) from various motives, all which have made it to convey *the essentials* of purity and spiritual life. Yet it has a scriptural aspect and import, for which we contend; and our desire is, to be found succeeding in spirit, views, and practice, those Christians who, under different names, and in various parts of the world, contended earnestly from apostolic days. Our design is, to trace and record the existence and practice of those Christian societies, which scripturally administered the ordinance, and this we hope to do, from the *Jewish* Jordan to the *British* Thames.

3. The first mention of this divine ordinance is found in Matthew the third. John, the son of Zechariah; is allowed to have been the first administrator of it. The way of John's administering the ordinance occasioned his being called THE BAPTIST.[1] The novelty of

---

[1] The word *baptist*, as distinguishing now a class of Christians, was given to express the act of John in administering the ordinance, and this term left by the Holy Spirit, without translating, is the only scriptural cognomen for that sacrament, and which has been through all ages, used to distinguish those who followed the first example. M‘Knight, Gill on Matt. iii. 1. *The Koran*

John's ordinance, with the prevailing expectation among the Jewish community of his sustaining some important embassy, rather than the doctrines he preached, attracted the attention of multitudes inhabiting Judea.[2] Many were reformed by John's ministry, and agreeably to his terms were admitted to his baptism. "And there went out unto him all the land of Judea, and they of Jerusalem, and were all baptized of him in the river Jordan, confessing their sins," Mark i. 5. Some Pharisees became candidates for this ordinance, when John inquired into their motive, assuring them, that their parents' holiness would *now* avail them nothing, neither could he confer the ordinance on account of any promise made to their believing father; but that each candidate must bring forth the fruits of repentance, as an indispensable qualification for the New Testament dispensation ordinance. John's extraordinary proceedings occasioned some inquiry among the leaders of the nation, seeing he had introduced *a new* ordinance into society of a religious aspect, John i. 25. The deputation from the Sanhedrim made inquiries of John, who assured them he received his commission from heaven.

A.D. 26

---

has rendered the word *to dip*; and total immersion is frequently enjoined in the Mahometan code. See Sale's Koran, vol. i., sec. 4, p. 138, &c. Pococke's Description of the East, vol. ii., b. 2, chap. 8, p. 120. Pitt's Relig. and Manners of the Mahometans, pp. 80—82. The word *baptize* is rendered in all ancient versions of the Scriptures *to dip*. See Greenfield's Def. of the Seramp. Marrh. version, pp. 39—44. Dr. Ryland's Candid Statement: notes at the end. [2] Some have asserted that immersion could not have been practised in Judea from scarcity of water; but, " the Lord thy God bringeth thee into a good land, *a land of brooks of water, of fountains and depths,* that spring out of the valleys and hills, Deut. viii. 17. Ezek. xix. 10. Joseph. Wars, b. 1, c. 16, b. 5, c. 4, which confutes the objector, since Judea was to be different to Egypt in this very point, Deut. xi.

John i. 21 ; Matt. xxi. 25.³ That his ordinance was appointed to make the Messiah and his adherents *mani-fest* to Israel. John i. 31. He also required of the deputation an acknowledgment of its heavenly origin by their obedience, and in order to express their desire of escaping the wrath to come, Matt. iii. 7, which they refusing, excluded themselves from the privileges of the gospel kingdom, Luke vii. 30.

4. John, having exercised his ministry about six months, was visited by Jesus of Nazareth, who came as a candidate for baptism. John hesitated, but when he understood that the ordinance constituted part of "*the righteousness*" in the new dispensation, they both descended into the river Jordan,[4] and John became the

10.   ³ Had Jewish proselyte baptism been in use at this period, this inquiry would not have been made, nor would the rulers have felt any difficulty in answering the Redeemer, Matt. xxi. 25. Some of the rabbins speak of John as being the innovator of this rite, and affirm the newness of its character. When proselyte baptism came into use, is not known: the proselyte *dipped himself*, but *his posterity* was not subject to the rite; no repentance, faith, or belief was required. If it existed, there is no part of scripture for the practice ; and if it belonged to the Jewish dispensation, all ceremonies were abrogated by Christ's death. Yet this rite is said to be the " basis of infant baptism." Many able divines, as Owen, Jennings, Benson, &c., declare the absence of such rite in the Jewish church. See this ably handled in Gale's Reflect. on Wall, and Appendix. edit. 1820.   ⁴ The river Jordan is an interesting object. It was divided by divine power for Israel, Elijah, and Elisha. By dipping in this water, Naaman was cured. It was the place of John's ministry, and of attesting the Messiah's character. "Some stripped and bathed themselves in Jordan, others cut down boughs from the trees; every one employed himself to take a memorial of this famous stream : the water was turbid and too rapid to be swam against. For its breadth, it might be about twenty yards over : and in depth, it far exceeded my height."—Maundrell's Journey, &c. p. 111. Madden's Travels in Syria, &c., vol. ii., lett. 38, p. 307.

administrator. John and Jesus exercised their ministry for a short time to the same people, and during the same period both administered the ordinance, John iv. 1. But the multitudes which attended John's ministry awaken in Herod's mind apprehensions of a revolt, he consequently shut up John, to prevent any political disturbance,[5] or rather, as the evangelists say, his reproving Herod of incest, occasioned his duresse, and afterwards he removed him by decapitation.

5. It had been predicted that John should make ready a people for the Lord. The Saviour declared John as the harbinger of the new dispensation, and that his ministry had virtually terminated "the law and the prophets," Luke xvi. 16, and commenced the gospel kingdom, Mark i. 1. The instruction given by John to those persons whom the Saviour chose to discipleship, plainly fulfilled those predictions, Acts i. 21. These disciples went forth by his authority to preach and baptize during the Saviour's personal ministry; and after his resurrection, they were invested with authority to preach the gospel to all nations, baptizing those who acknowledged themselves willing disciples to his doctrines.[6] On the day of Pentecost they became fully qualified, by the outpouring of the Holy Spirit, for rightly understanding and correctly executing

---

[5] Josephus' Antiq. b. 18, c. 7. [6] The first order given to the eleven to make converts, to baptize and to teach, was not confined to the ministers or apostles, but extended to *all* capable of rendering aid to the Christian interest. That this was the construction then put upon that charge, receives support from the subsequent part of the history; Philip, the Eunuch—Ananias at Damascus, could equally teach and baptize, though these were not apostles. Campbell's Lect. on Ecc. Hist., p. 68, lect. 4. This view of the Commission was taken by early dissidents, and the difficulty of baptizing by immersion, 3000 or 10,000 in one day, finds an easy solution.

their Lord's will. It will be our pleasure to accompany them while in the discharge of their sacred trust, and to observe carefully for *our guidance* how they fulfilled their commission.

6. The extraordinary circumstances on the day of Pentecost, occasioned many Jews congregating where the apostles and disciples met, at which time Peter opened to the Jews the gospel system of salvation. Three thousand felt the force of truth, and confessed themselves convinced of the dignity and authority of Christ as the Messiah; and as a proof of their sincerity, and the submissive state of their minds to his commands, they arose, were baptized, and washed away their sins; and the same day were added unto the church. To which number, in a few days, were added five thousand more: so that the word of the Lord prevailed, and the number of the disciples multiplied in Jerusalem greatly, and a great company of the priests were obedient to the faith. "So mightily grew the word of the Lord and prevailed," and "Jerusalem was filled with the doctrine; and the multitude of them that believed were of *one heart* and *one soul*, and great grace was upon them all."

7. This church of Jerusalem was composed of those only who " gladly received the word and were baptized." Their *unity of spirit* was their " *beauty of holiness*." This church so constituted is the acknowledged pattern or model[7] by which other Christian churches were formed,

---

[7] Hierarchalists, with others, say, the New Testament presents *no settled form of church government*. But the Judean churches were considered as models by Paul, who praised the Thessalonians for following their example: nor were the customs of different people allowed to influence churches in different provinces, but the teachers of religion throughout the world were to follow Paul's example. This model imitated, occasioned a harmony in

1 Thess. ii. 14: since "the law was to go forth out of Zion, and the word of the Lord from Jerusalem." This community of Christians was also the arbitrator in spiritual affairs during apostolic days, and must be allowed still to be the standard of doctrine and practice to every Christian church, aided as it was by all the wisdom of inspired teachers; and particularly since no promise is found in the Scriptures, allowing us to expect those extraordinary aids, to qualify any men in forming *any other* church than the New Testament presents. This Christian assembly as it was the first, so it is the mother church in the Christian dispensation.

8. All the apostles and teachers emanating from this community sustained the character of holy faithful men. Their knowledge of divine things was regulated by an unerring guide. They all agreed in doctrines, duties, and discipline, so that from their teaching there was no *schism in the body*. However various their talents, into one spirit they had been made to drink, and by that spirit were all baptized into one body. A divine spirit actuated the whole community of Christians and teachers, so that all spoke and taught the same things,

---

practice for 100 years. If there is no form, then the Scriptures cannot be a perfect rule of faith and practice; each province, town, or society, may legislate without giving offence to the King of Zion; and consequently every age, from new customs, might have a new form of church government. Yet Jesus Christ has forbidden any thing to be added to his word; and one feature of the *man of sin* is, that he should "change laws in God's temple;" but every plant not of scriptural authority shall be taken away, and every innovator in Christ's kingdom will meet with his displeasure. The unity enjoined, the discipline established, the example left, and the accountability of each servant for his conduct in the service of God, prove there is a settled law for our guidance. See Maclean on the Commission, and Glass's King of Martyrs.

1 Cor. iv. 17. This oneness of views about doctrines, duties, and discipline, admitted the different epistles written by the apostles, to be of general use to the churches situated in various provinces of the Roman empire; which has not been the case, since a diversity of opinions on duties have been adopted by different communities, and distinctions pleaded, as to essential and non-essential things.

9. Stephen the deacon, taught with such force of evidence in his public preaching, that the enemies of the gospel, incapable of repelling conviction, resolved on his death. A severe persecution ensued, which drove many of the disciples from Jerusalem into other cities and provinces. These cruel proceedings against the church were strongly supported by one Saul of Tarsus, who afterwards, while on a journey for this express purpose, was arrested by divine interposition, when near Damascus,[8] and thus became an eminent disciple and apostle. In this scattered condition, the disciples went every where preaching the word. Their efforts were attended with remarkable success. From their labours, with those of the apostles, many souls were converted, and Christian communities extensively established. Among those assemblies on record, it is said of the church of Samaria, "They believed Philip's preaching the kingdom of God and the name of Jesus, and were baptized, both men and women." At Philippi, "Lydia's heart was opened, she and her household were baptized

[8] See a description of this city and its waters, with the coffee-houses, where visitors are entertained on sofas in a circular court, in the midst of which court is a basin of water, fountain, &c. &c. This city is said to stand on the Eden of antiquity, Dr. Pococke's Descrip. of the East, &c. v. ii. b. 2, ch. 8, p. 113, &c., and a sketch in Robinson's Hist. of Baptism, ch. 40, p. 614. Pococke gives a description of the baptistry in the Mosque.

and *comforted*," Acts xvi. 40. The jailer, Crispus, Cornelius, and their households believed, and were baptized; with the eunuch in the wilderness,[9] Saul at Damascus, the Corinthians, Acts xviii. 8; the Ephesians, Acts xix. 5, all which instances prove believers' baptism.[10]

10. The apostles, in writing to different churches, make their appeal only to responsible persons, nor do they ever allude *to any* having received baptism, but such as knew its spiritual import. Those addressed are termed "saints, sanctified, justified, God's building, habitation, temple, Christ's body, spouse," &c. Paul says to the Romans, " know ye not, that *so many of us* as were baptized into Jesus Christ, were baptized into his death? Therefore we are buried with him by baptism into death: that, *like as Christ* was raised up from the dead by the glory of the Father, even *so we* also should walk in newness of life." He said to the churches formed throughout the province of Galatia, " For as many of you as have been baptized into Christ, have put on Christ." The church at Colosse was formed of those who were " buried with Christ in baptism, and *were raised* again through the faith of the operation of God." The Corinthian community was composed of a diversity of persons; but, " whether Jew or Gentile, bond or free, they had all been made to drink into one Spirit, and by

---

[9] See a description of the fountain in which the eunuch was baptized in Pococke, v. ii., b. 2, c. 11. p. 45. and the sufficiency of water in some parts of the wilderness, Deut. x. 7. [10] "The covenant of peculiarity was national; but now every one of you distinctly must be baptized in the name of the Lord Jesus, and transact *for himself* in this great affair."—Henry, on Acts ii. 38. " As God has appointed saints to be the seal and subject of the ordinance, having granted the right of them, *to them alone.*—Dr. Owen's New Test. Worship, p. 103."

that one Spirit were all baptized into one body." The apostles having taught the same things in every place, and composed the churches of similar materials in every province, the same conclusions enforce themselves on the mind of every inquirer, that *those only* who had fellowship in the spirit of the gospel, were the *only subjects* interested in gospel ordinances.

11. At an early period, abuses crept into Christian churches, which occasioned apostolic correction. The Judaizing teachers required the converts to Christianity, from among the Gentiles, to be circumcised. Now, if the ordinance of baptism had come into the place of circumcision, the apostles would most certainly have explained such things to the Christian churches; and their instruction on this point of discipline, would have prevented the Jewish rite being *added to baptism*, and practised for some time with a New Testament ordinance. When the mixture of rites was discovered, the apostles, Paul and Barnabas, were not capable of deciding the point in dispute, so as to rectify the evil, and satisfy the contending parties, without calling their brethren together. The Redeemer had assured his disciples, during his ministry, that their decisions should abrogate any previous ordinance, or if they imposed new precepts they should be obligatory. The disputed point occasioned the elders and disciples to assemble at Jerusalem. After some consultation, they very solemnly, and by divine direction, put an end to the covenant which God had made with Abraham and his posterity; annulling federal holiness, national distinctions and privileges; securing a glorious liberty to believers of all nations. This decision cancelled the seal, *circumcision*, and left the Jewish people without a covenant or a promise.

12. Predictions held forth, that the Jews should be

without their privileges many days, Hos. iii. 4. And that God would *break* the covenant *with all the people*, Zech. xi. 10. John the Baptist told the Jews that the axe was laid to their national privileges, and consequently, refused to admit them to gospel privileges, from relative considerations. These features of God's intentions were repeated by Christ, John xv. 2. The synod at Jerusalem had declared the covenant with Abram void, and circumcision nothing. But while the Jews could assemble in the temple, a rivalship on their part was maintained, and a disposition constantly evinced to persecute the followers of the Lamb. The violent conduct of the Jews, engaged the emperor's attention, and required all Nero's cruel policy to manage. These commotions of the Jews allowed the Christians to realize a respite from persecution, which the emperor had commenced for his diversion.

A contest had some time existed between the Jews and Syrians, about Cæsarea, which city stood on the confines of both kingdoms, and was claimed alike by both. The dispute was referred to Nero, who decided in favour of Syria; on the report of this decision, the Jews flew to arms, butchered Romans and Syrians, which conduct drew on their countrymen dwelling in foreign cities and provinces, a retaliating vengeance.

The combined armies of Rome and Syria subdued the Jews, and after a seige of five months, during which the sufferings of the beseiged were unparalleled, the temple and city of Jerusalem were destroyed. Eleven hundred thousand lives were lost, and ninety thousand persons were led into captivity.[1] The destruction of the city and temple, after 1500 years existence, effectually terminated Jewish distinctions.

[1] Myers's Hist. of the Jews, c. 53.

13. After the destruction of the Jewish capitol, the Christian church enjoyed for several years outward peace. Its inward harmony was often disturbed during this century by advocates of unscriptural doctrines, whose austerity of manners, and apparent sanctity of conduct, gave force to their doctrines upon the unwary.[2] These circumstances occasioned dissidents, yet at this period, each party tenaciously held the name of Christian, and had strong aversions to any other.[3] At the close of the century, the cruel edicts of Domitian changed the aspect of affairs towards the church.

96

14. We now turn to the writings, next in importance to the sacred oracles, in order to ascertain the views encouraged by the early fathers on baptism.

45 BARNABAS, Paul's companion, (Acts xiii. 2.) and like him sound in the faith.[4] This worthy minister says on baptism, "Consider how he hath joined both the cross and the water together; for this he saith, Blessed are they who putting their trust in the cross, descend into the water." * * Again, "We go down into the water, full of sin and pollutions, but come up again bringing forth fruit; having in our hearts the fear and hope which is in Jesus."[5]

95 HERMES, whom Paul salutes in the church at Rome, (Rom. xvi. 14.) writing about A.D. 95, speaking of baptism and backsliders, says, "They are such as have heard the word, and were willing to be baptized in the name of the Lord; but when they call to mind what holiness it required in those who professed the truth, withdrew themselves." Again, "Before a

---

[2] Gibbon's Rom. Hist. c. 15.   [3] Bingham's Antiq. of the Chris. Ch. b. 1. c. 1. s. 6.   [4] Toplady's Hist. Proof, v. i. p. 125.   [5] Catholic Ep. of Barnabas, § 11. p. 292, Dr. Wake's translation.

man receives the name of the Son of God, he is ordained to death; but when he receives that seal, he is freed from death, and delivered unto life: now that seal is water, into which men descend under an obligation to death, but ascend out of it, being appointed unto life.[6]

96   CLEMENS asserts, "that they are right subjects of baptism, who have passed through an examination and instruction."[7]

IGNATIUS was a disciple of John, and acquainted with Peter and Paul. He was an elder in the church at Antioch. In a discourse on baptism, he says, "That it [baptism] ought to be accompanied with faith, love, and patience, after preaching."[8]

15. We will now subjoin a few extracts from the most accredited historians on the same subject.

"The Son of God was dipped in the waters of Jordan, by the hand of John the Baptist. Philip baptized the eunuch in a river. It seems also, that Lydia and her household at Philippi, were baptized in a river, at which prayers were usually made."[9] The same historians tell us, "they baptized only the adult or aged, whether Jews or Gentiles:" they also say, "the manner of baptizing was by dipping or plunging in water, in the name of the Trinity," so agreeably to the sense of the word, and also by the allegory of death, burial, and resurrection, to which the apostle alludes.[10]

Dr. Mosheim says, "Whoever acknowledged Christ as the Saviour of mankind, and made a solemn profession of his confidence in him, was immediately baptized and received into the church." Again, "The sacrament of

---

[6] Stennett's Ans. to Russen, p. 143.   [7] See Jacob Morningus, in his Hist. of Bap. p. 2, out of Clem. Epis.; also, Dutch Martyrol., cent. 1.   [8] Dutch Martyrol. c. 1.   [9] Magdeb. Cent. c. 1. l. 1. c. 4.   [10] Id. p. 497 in Danver's Hist. of Bap. p. 58.

baptism was administered in this century without public assemblies, in places appointed and prepared for the purpose, and was performed by the immersion of the whole body in the baptismal font." He also states, that "no persons were admitted to baptism, but such as had been previously instructed into the principal points of Christianity, and had also given satisfactory proofs of pious dispositions and upright intentions:" and now arose the different names of catechumen and believers, the first being under instruction, in order to receive baptism, the other had received baptism, and were members in communion.[1]

"It is plain," says Dr. F. A. Cox, "from the writers of this century, who will be allowed to have been the *earliest* next to the apostles, as Barnabas, Hermes, Clement of Rome, Ignatius, and Polycarp, and yet *not one* of these speaks of baptism being administered to infants."[2]

16. One evidence that the religion of the New Testament was from God, is derived from the progress the cause of truth made when it was first propagated.[3] This progress, and consequently, the evidence upon which it is suspended, *entirely depends* on the class of persons initiated into its community. If children were in any way admitted to the ordinance, *a great part* of those numbered amongst the adherents or converts to Christianity, in this century, must be *subtracted*, as being from their minority incapable of judging of its merits. This dilemma we leave with Pædobaptists. But the account, given by Luke in the Acts, of various churches collected by the first preachers, are details of communities made up of persons *whose convictions of the truth*

---

[1] Hist. c. 1. § 8.   [2] Bapt. p. 155.   [3] Benson's Hist. of the first planting of Christianity.

decided their choice; and such converts only, establish the full force of the evidence, that Christianity was divine, and the triumphs of its truths, rational. This evangelist declares, chap. i. 3, that he had perfect understanding of all things, from the very first; and in Acts i. 1, says, his gospel stated "*all* that Jesus began both to do and to teach, until the day in which he was taken up." Yet no allusion is made to the infant rite; we cannot, therefore, assert its existence in the church in his day, without impeaching Luke's veracity. The historian Gibbon has endeavoured through his work to weaken the evidences brought forth in favour of the gospel, manifesting a solicitude to lessen the number of the first converts. Had he been able to have established the point, that children were admitted into Christian communities,[4] he would have employed effectually, that circumstance to lower the triumphs of the cross. But this, Gibbon could not do, for want of evidence. At an after period, he discovered children and slaves in Christian churches, consequently he records their characters, to exhibit the sublimity of the Saviour's cause, and its rivalship in numbers with Pagans. Thus pædobaptism in all ages has aided infidelity, by lessening the evidences of the gospel,[5] and compounding the church of opposing materials, conferring a spiritual rite on an irrational subject, and allowing a comparison of its merits and success, with the enterprise of Mahomet, who enlisted subjects by force, and embraced members without virtue![6]

[4] The following item would have suited Gibbon, " We have 900 baptized, and candidates for baptism, and about *forty members* in our church." W. Ellis's Mem. of his Wife; Missionary to the Sandwich Is. p. 91.   [5] About the middle of the last century, a work was published, " *Christianity irrational from Pædobaptism,*" several pædobaptists replied to it, New Evangelical Mag. 5, 210.
[6] Gibbon's Hist. c. 15. v. ii. pp. 302 and 309.

17. There was no difficulty in administering baptism by immersion. Mr. Horne remarks, that " the bath was always agreeable to the inhabitants of the East; and it is not at all surprising, that it should have been so, since it is cooling and refreshing. The bath is frequented by eastern ladies, and may be reckoned among their principal recreations. It was one of the civil laws of the Hebrews, that the *bath* should be used; Lev. xiv. 8, 9. We may, therefore, consider it as probable, that public baths, soon after the enactment of this law, were erected in Palestine, of a construction similar to that of those, which are so frequently seen at the present day in the East."[7] The Greek *baths* were usually annexed to the gymnasia, of which pastimes they were considered as part. The Roman *baths* were generally splendid buildings. It is said that at Rome there were eight hundred and fifty-six public baths; and according to Fabricius, the excessive luxury of the Romans appeared in nothing more visible than in their baths. Seneca complains, that the baths of the plebeians were filled by silver pumps; and that the freedmen trod on gems. Agrippa built 160 places for bathing, where the citizens might be accommodated either with hot water or cold, free of expense. The baths of Nero had salt water brought into them. Those of Caracalla were adorned with two hundred marble columns, and furnished with sixteen hundred seats of the same materials. Lipsius assures us, the baths were sufficiently large for 1800 persons to bathe at the same time. But the baths of Dioclesian surpassed all the rest in magnificence; 140,000 men were employed many years in building them.[8] The rich had baths at home, and frequently

[7] Intro. to the Crit. Study, &c., v. iii. p. 434.   [8] Howard's Roy. Ency. v. i., Art. Baths. Potter's Antiq. of Gr. b. 1. c. 8. &c Fosbroke's Ency. of Antiq. vol. i., p. 46.

very magnificent ones. In Italy, and in the east, baths on a large scale are still seen.9 In Modern Turkey, as well as among the ancients, bathing makes part of diet and luxury; so that in every town and in every village, there is a public bath.10 The baths in Persia consist of three rooms for the accommodation of bathers. The Persians are obliged to immerse, when they would cleanse themselves from any legal pollutions. Persons of distinction have their own baths in their own houses.1

It is thus made plain to the unlettered, that no difficulty existed in the east in performing baptism by immersion.

Section II.

PRIMITIVE BAPTISTS CONTINUED.

"Fulfil ye my joy, that ye be like-minded, having the same love, being of one accord, of one mind."—*Phil.* ii. 3.

1. THE death of Domitian, in 97, introduced Nerva, a tolerant emperor, to the throne. In 98, Trajan became possessed of the sceptre, whose prejudices were very strong against the followers of the Lamb. Persecuting edicts were issued, and the commencement of the cen-

---

[9] Lon. Ency. Art. Baths. Adam's Rom. Antiq. pp. 375—81. Penny Cyclo. Art. Bath. Robinson's History of Bap. c. 9—11.
[10] Lon. Ency. Art. Bathing. [1] Millar's New Geograph. v. i., p. 27, col. 2, fol. Sandys's Travels in Turkey, &c. Tooke's Russia. Pococke's View of the East.

tury was the beginning of fresh trials to the professors of the gospel. Pliny, the governor of Pontus and Bithynia, inquired of Trajan what policy he should pursue towards Christians, as he felt convinced their destruction would nearly annihilate the inhabitants of those provinces under his governance.[1] Trajan replied, they should not be sought for as heretofore; but if any were known openly to profess Christianity, "let them be punished." Under this emperor, many Christians suffered death, and numbers, even of the female sex, were racked, to occasion their criminating each other. Adrian rather improved the condition of Christians. Titus Antonius Pious succeeded, and proved himself a mild prince; but when Marcus Aurelius Antoninus ascended the throne, he issued his cruel measures, and Polycarp, with many in Asia and France, were called to martyrdom. In 180, Commodus became head of the government, and the condition of Christians became tolerable; but on Severus succeeding, the aspect was changed towards the churches: Asia, Gaul, Egypt, and other provinces, were dyed with Christians' blood.

2. All historians speak of the Christian church sustaining, to an eminent degree, the character of a *pure virgin*, for above one hundred years. The severity of the times would check insincere persons taking a profession; the examples of the apostles and their successors were still kept in view; besides, the churches were composed of obscure persons in the estimation of the world; nor did learning adorn her ministers, so as to awaken any fears of rivalship among the philosophers or literati of the day. Yet their obscurity, with their

---

[1] Lib. 10, Epis. 97.

"excess of virtue,"[2] was no guard to their lives or property. It was a maxim with the Romans, to tolerate the religions of those nations they conquered: but this indulgence they extended *not* to the professors of the gospel. Various reasons and motives combined to occasion an alteration in their wonted policy, though the true grounds are assigned by Paul. Rom. viii. 7. Gal. iv. 29.

The first Christians were poor; and their benevolence towards each other was calculated to keep them free of worldly incumbrances, yet it is equally evident they were numerous, and the success of the gospel enraged the pagan priests, who reported to the govenor the vilest accusations against them.[3] Those vile reports were ably refuted by apologists, whose works were persented to the emperor.[4] The insinuations of the enemy were but too credulously regarded, and often regulated the policy of the presiding governor. The priests lived by the altars. In the public games, merchants, tradesmen, mechanics, servants, and the rustic who sold the sacrifices, were all *interested* in maintaining the pagan worship. Hence that popular ridicule, contempt, and persecution, which government sometimes durst not, or could not, control. Whenever religion influenced the heart, whether of parent or child, it proved a kind of restless leaven, which attempted, by every silent and lawful means, to impregnate the whole body with which it stood connected, so that, Christianity was often accused of disturbing the previous harmony of families, and of infusing sectarian principles into the inhabitants

---

[2] Gibbon's Hist. c. 15. [3] Some causes assigned for these calumnies by Mr. Robert Turner, are supported neither by reason nor evidence, particularly on Christians eating their own offspring, c. 4. [4] W. Reeve's Apologies of the Fathers.

of towns and provinces. Nor did Christianity feel in her proper station, in standing at a distance, and surveying the region of misery with philosophic apathy; but its advocates boldly advanced into the very centre of infection, and endeavoured to apply the only remedy provided for its cure: yet such was the nature and desperate state of the disease, that it urged the infected to aim the destruction of every benefactor. " Beside, all other people professed a national religion, and the multitude looked on each other's idols with indifference; but Christianity formed *a sect* of distinct and separate character."[5] " It did not confine itself to the denial or rejection of every other system: it carried on its forehead all the offensive character of a monopoly, which, when understood, spread an alarm over the Roman empire for the security of its establishments."[6] Every awakening providence, as earthquake, famine, drought, plague, &c., was, by pagans, attributed to the anger of their gods against the followers of the Cross; this view of things being impressed on the minds of the multitude, often occasioned the rabble to demand the blood and lives of valuable men.

Christianity was observed to give dignity, composure, serenity, and confidence, to its possessor, which was supposed by heathens to be confirmed obstinacy,—which many consequently resolved to subdue. The religion of the Cross has, in all ages, formed a bond of union among its disciples, to which no heathen superstition made pretensions. The enemies of the Lamb, being totally unacquainted with the genius and spirit of Christianity, and the objects of its followers in uniting together in social worship, misconstrued their motives, attributed

---

[5] Gibbon's Hist. c. 15.   [6] Chalmers's Evid. of Christianity, c. 4, p. 105.

to them revolting crimes, and that their love and unity led to associations of a political character formed against the government.

It was also seen, that Christianity ever maintained an uncompromising character; it forbade its friends "to partake of other men's sins," or to pour out libations, or throw a grain of incense on the pagan altars: and this unsociable, uncommunicable temper, in matters of religion, could be regarded, by the best of the heathens, in no other light, than arising from an aversion to mankind.[7] From these circumstances, the pagans would never be destitute of materials for misconstruction. As Christians would not themselves bow to pagan rites, so they were alike careful to prevent any character, however exalted, realizing the privileges of their communion, without a strict conformity, in spirit and conduct, to the requirements of divine revelation. They, consequently, at times, became the objects of the most unrelenting fury, for maintaining, in their ecclesiastical community, *purity of principle*, and *purity of practice*.

3. The Christian societies, instituted in the cities of the Roman empire, were united only by the ties of faith and charity. Independency and equality formed the basis of their internal constitution;[8] and they were in every way corresponding to churches of the Baptist denomination at the present day, in the admission of members, discussing affairs, dismissing brethren, or excluding offenders.[9] Though the churches sustained a primitive character for more than one hundred years, yet, during this century, and particularly towards its

---

[7] Jones's Ecc. Lect. v. i., p. 193. [8] Gibbon's Hist. c. 15.
[9] Mosh. Hist. C. 2, p. 2, c. 2, § 4. Robin. Res. p. 123. Campbell's Ecc. Lect. p. 122. Jones's Ecc. Lect. v. i., p. 299.

close, the scriptural simplicity of the institution became obscured, from the introduction of various rites borrowed from the Old Testament; and baptism was now supposed to convey some peculiar advantages to the receiver.[10] There being persons of narrow capacities, the teachers of religion thought it advisable or expedient to instruct such in the essential truths of the gospel, by placing those truths, as it were, before their eyes, under visible objects or images.[1] By these and other *expedients*, the purity of the original institutions became sophisticated; and when once the ministers of religion had departed from the ancient simplicity of the gospel, and sullied the native purity of divine truth by a motley mixture of human inventions, it was difficult to set bounds to this growing corruption.[2]

4. We shall now refer to the writers of this century on the subject of Baptism; and the first we notice is JUSTIN MARTYR, who was born of pagan parents, but became a proselyte to the Jewish religion. Dissatisfied with his profession, he embraced Christianity. His character is obscured by his mixture of systems, and his figurative style was calculated to lead astray. He taught, through natural objects, to view spiritual things, viz., "The cross, according to the prophet (Moses), was the great characteristic of his power and government; almost every thing we see resembles a cross;" the yards of a ship, the head of a plough, the handle of a spade, &c.—"nay, man erect with his arms extended forms the cross."[3] He retained the leading features of Christianity, and wrote ably in its defence.

In giving an account to the emperor, Justin says, " I

---

[10] See Wall and Bingham.   [1] Mosh. Hist. C. 2, p. 2, c. 4, § 6.   [2] Id. C. 6, p. 2, c. 3, § 1.   [3] Justin's Apol. § 72. Reeve's trans. v. i., p. 96.

shall now lay before you the manner of dedicating ourselves to God, through Christ, upon our conversion; for should *I omit this*, I might not seem to deal sincerely in this account of our religion. As many as are persuaded and believe that those things which are taught by us are true, and do promise to live according to them, are directed first to pray, and ask God, with fasting, the forgiveness of their sins: and we also pray and fast together with them. Then we bring them to some place where there is water; and they are *regenerated* by the same way of regeneration by which we were regenerated: for they are washed in the name of the Father, &c. After he is baptized, and becomes one of us, we lead him to the congregation of the brethren, where, with great fervency, we pour out our souls together in prayer, both for ourselves and for the person baptized, and for all other Christians throughout the world. Prayer being ended, we salute each other with a kiss. Bread, and a cup of wine and water, are then brought to the president or bishop, who offers up prayer and thanksgiving in the name of the Lord Jesus, the people concluding with a loud amen. The deacons distribute the elements to those who are present, and carry them afterwards to the absent members.[4] This food we call the eucharist, of which none are allowed to be partakers, but such only as are true believers, and have been baptized in the laver of regeneration for the remission of sins, and live according to Christ's precepts.[5]

---

[4] Wall's Hist. of Inf. Bap. p. 1, c. 2, § 3. [5] Justin's Apol. § 79, 85, 86, Reeve's trans. Justin's Apology to the emperor describes the dedication of believers in religion, but not of infants! In § 36, he deplores the way the heathens trained their children; and § 18, alludes to believers discipleing their offspring to Christ. He does not refute the charge of infanticide, by asserting that Christians dedicated their children to Christ by baptism, though

On this statement Dr. Wall observes, this is the most ancient account of the way of baptizing, next the Scriptures, and shows the plain and simple manner of administering it. The Christians of these times had lived, many of them at least, in the days of the apostles.[6]

Justin's use of the term *regeneration*, instead of baptism, with other figurative language, led the simple and unlettered to conclude, that the import of the word was conveyed in the ordinance. Too much dependence was, at this period, placed on the eucharist; as is evident, in its being carried to absent members *after it had been prayed over*. So the simplicity of the supper was departing, by the mixture of water with the wine: though the church still retained, in its members and discipline, all the essentials of its original constitution.

180 IRENÆUS, pastor of a church at Lyons. He was a Greek by birth, and liberally educated. Before he accepted the pastorate of Lyons, he lived at Smyrna, under the religious instruction of Polycarp, one of John's disciples. During his residence at Lyons, the Christians were called to realize death in every form. A creed is still extant bearing his name, and much of early simplicity.[7] The following passage from his writings is supposed by some to allude to the ordinance: "Christ passed through all ages of man, that he might SAVE all by himself: all, I say, who by him are *regenerated to God*—infants, and little ones, and children, and youths, and persons advanced in years:"[8] but so favourable an opportunity offered; at the same time, he evinces an anxiety *not to omit* to his imperial majesty any circumstance or practice that would lessen the force of prejudices against Christians. Justin has committed an unpardonable fault in omitting the infant rite; unless, *as was the case*, pædobaptism was unknown.

[6] Wall's Hist. ubi sup. [7] Le Clerc's Ecc. Hist. and Jortin's Rem. on Ecc. Hist. v. ii., b. 2, p. 2, p. 25. [8] Facts opposed to Fiction, p. 17.

these words refer to *salvation*, not *baptism*. The word *regeneration* cannot, in this passage, be understood to signify baptism, without attaching too much importance to that ordinance. The same pious father regrets the conduct of some " who thought it needless to bring the person to the water at all; but mixing oil and water together, they pour it on the candidate's head."9 How deeply would Irenæus grieve, did he live *now!*

190 CLEMENT, the schoolmaster and innovator, presided over a school at Alexandria, to whom we shall again refer. He observes, on the ordinance, "The baptized ought to be children in malice, but not in understanding; even such children who, as the children of God, have put off the old man with the garments of wickedness, and have put on the new man."10

5. Although unwarrantable customs and ceremonies began to prevail at the conclusion of this century in some churches, yet the ordinances of religion were not diverted or altered from their scriptural subject, which is supported by the best historians, as, "It does not appear by any approved authors, that there was any mutation or variation in baptism from the former century."1

"During this century, the sacrament of baptism was administered publicly twice a year, at the festivals of Easter and Whitsuntide. The persons to be baptized, after they had repeated the creed, confessed, and renounced their sins, particularly the devil and his pompous allurements, were immersed under water, and received into Christ's kingdom, by a solemn invocation." After baptism, various ceremonies ensued.2 Immersion

---

9 Wall's Hist. part 1, p. 406. 10 Epis. III. in Bap. Mag. v. i., p. 166. 1 Mag. Cent. c. 2, in Danver's, p. 59. 2 Mosh. Hist. c. 2, p. 2, c. 4, § 13.

universally prevailed, since all the ancients thought that burying under water did more lively represent the death, burial, and resurrection of Christ.[3]

The absence of infant baptism, during the two first centuries, is fully acknowledged by so many of the most learned among the Pædobaptists, that it is quite unnecessary to copy their assertions.[4]

Justin Martyr, Athenagoras, Theophilus of Antioch, Tatian, Minucius Felix, Irenæus, and Clement of Alexandria, constitute the Christian writers of this second century; who so far from *directly* speaking of infant baptism, *never once* utter a syllable upon the subject.[5]

Section III.

PRIMITIVE BAPTISTS CONTINUED.

"After my departure shall grievous wolves enter in among you, not sparing the flock."—*Acts* xx. 29.

1. The tragical conduct of Severus towards the disciples of Jesus has been mentioned. His son and successor, Caracalla, was mild in his measures. Several emperors followed in rather hasty succession, whose clemency admitted of an increase of professors to the doctrines of the cross. Many persons in the employment and in the public offices of government professed the Christian religion; privileges also

211

---

[3] Bingham's Antiq. of the Christian church, b. 11, c. 11, sec. 1.
[4] Booth's Pedo. Exa., C. 4, p. 78; and c. 9, p. 194.   [5] Dr. F. A. Cox on Bap., p. 156.

were increased to them, and several provinces were considered favourable to Christianity. While these tolerant features existed in the government, the profession of Christianity was considerably extended; but at the same time its character *was not* that enjoined in the New Testament code. In 249, Decius, coming to the throne, required all without exception to embrace the pagan worship on pain of death.

249

Professors were not in a state to meet sufferings, and apostasy to an alarming extent ensued, as measures of the severest kinds were adopted to bring all to acknowledge pagan rites. Many realized cruel martyrdoms. Varied circumstances attended the churches through the remainder of the century. At the close of this age we may discover the expiring order of gospel worship, and the extinction of that simplicity which characterized apostolic institutions.

2. The officer formerly known by the name of elder, bishop, or presbyter (terms exactly synonymous in the New Testament) became now distinguished by the elevation of the bishop above his brethren, and each of the above terms was carried out into a distinction of places in the Christian church.[1] The minister, whose congregation increased from the suburbs of his town and vicinage around, considered the parts from which his charge emanated, as territories marking the boundary of his authority; and all those presbyters sent by him into surrounding stations to conduct evening or other services, acknowledged the pastor of the mother interest, as bishop of the district: this view of the pastor, connected with his charge of the baptistery, gave importance to his station and office which entailed an

---

[1] See Lord Barrington's Essay on the distinction between the apostles, elders, &c. vol. i. pp. 61 and 252; and vol. ii. p. 4.

evil.² Associations of ministers and churches, which at first were formed in Greece, became common throughout the empire. These mutual unions for the management of spiritual affairs, led to the choice of a president, which aided distinction amongst ministers of religion.³ In those degenerating times, aspiring men saw each other in varied elevations; consequently jealousy, ambition, and strife ensued, and every evil work followed. The minister having the largest interest under his superintendence; another whose usefulness in the Christian interest had been evident; and a third whose popular declaiming talents had raised him into general approbation; led to distinctions and superior stations, which at last became vested in the metropolitan minister. Places of distinction to which ministers were eligible, prompted the ambitious to use every device to gain the ascendant position; and every part of the word of God, with every scriptural example to support such distinctions and proceedings, was quoted, enforced, and practised. The learning of the philosopher contributed to popularity, and where the suffrages of the community were to be taken, this acquisition was important to the aspirant; while the Jewish distinctions of ministers gave force and example to place and power. It was some time before the bishops, presbyters, and deacons, now very distinct classes of men, could persuade the people *that they* succeeded to the character, rights, and privileges of the Jewish priesthood. So far as those ministers were successful they opened a door to the adoption of every abrogated rite; and one evidence of success soon appeared, in the *abundance of wealth* conferred on the clergy.⁴

² Camp. Lect. pp. 72 and 148 ; Lect. 4 and 8.   Robins. Hist. Bap., p. 346.   ³ Camp. Lect. 9, p. 163.   ⁴ Lond. Ency., v. xi. p. 286. c. 2, History.

3. The bishops, says Mosheim, now aspired to higher degrees of power and authority than they formerly possessed; and not only violated the rights of the people, but also made gradual encroachments on the privileges of the presbyters. That they might cover their usurpations with an air of justice and appearance of reason, they published new doctrines concerning the nature of the church, and episcopal dignity. One of the principal authors of this change in the government of the church was CYPRIAN, Bishop of Carthage (A.D. 254), who pleaded for the power of the bishops with more zeal and vehemence than had ever been hitherto employed in that cause. The change in the form of government was soon followed by a train of vices, which dishonour the character and authority of those to whom the administration of the church was committed. For though several yet continued to exhibit to the world illustrious examples of primitive piety and Christian virtue, yet *many were sunk* in luxury and voluptuousness, puffed up with vanity, arrogance, and ambition, possessed with a spirit of contention and discord, and addicted to other vices, that cast an undeserved reproach upon the holy religion, of which they were the unworthy professors and ministers. The bishops assumed in many places princely authority; particularly those who had the greatest number of churches under their inspection, and who presided over the most opulent assemblies. They appropriated to their evangelical functions *the splendid ensigns of imperial majesty.* A throne surrounded with ministers, exalted above his equals, *was* the servant of the meek and humble Jesus: and sumptuous garments dazzled the eyes and the minds of the multitude into an arrogant veneration for their arrogated authority. The examples of the bishops was ambitiously imitated by the presbyters, who, neglecting the sacredness of

their station, abandoned themselves to the indolence and delicacy of an effeminate and luxurious life. The deacons, beholding the presbyters deserting their functions, boldly usurped their rights and privileges; and the effects of a corrupt ambition were spread through every rank of the sacred order.[5] The duties of the sanctuary consequently devolved on new officers, and menials were appointed to do the work of idle bishops and presbyters; ceremonies were added by bishops to please the multitude, or the immediate possessors of power; and a disposition prevailed to accommodate the religion of Jesus *to the taste of heathens.*[6]

4. During the rise and growth of these corruptions, the churches for three centuries remained as originally formed, independent of each other, and were united by no tie but that of charity:[7] while they were so constituted, corrupt practices did not prevail in some to the same extent as in others, particularly in those communities situated in the country, where objects stimulating ministers to rivalship, seldom presented themselves. Nor are we to conclude that all those persons forming Christian societies in cities, yielded to the ambitious projects of city ministers, and to the glaring and retrograding customs proposed. A certain portion of societies leaves all choice to the leader; but in all periods, some persons in every free community have appeared, who opposed innovation, and such dissidents in the church have adhered to "the law and the testimony. It is impossible to trace the first secession from a professing interest on scriptural grounds. At the conclusion of the last century, Tertullian withdrew from one society on account of its corruptions, and

---

[5] Eccl. Hist. C. 3, p. 2, c. 2, § 4, 5.   [6] Lond. Ency., v. xi. p. 286. Campbell's Lect., No. 8.   [7] Robinson's Res., pp. 55 and 123.

united with another on the grounds of purity of communion. It is evident that many individuals remonstrated with ministers, and that efforts were used to reform the degenerated churches; but those dissidents, finding a corrupt ministry and interest an overmatch for them, and seeing no room to hope for a restoration of purity and primitive simplicity, constantly withdrew and worshipped God, in public or private, as circumstances allowed. That such a course of conduct must have been pursued by numbers, all through the early part of the century, is most evident, since by the middle of this age, 250, *many of the old churches were reduced to a pitiable state;*[8] *while Italy was full of dissidents*[9] *who never were in communion with Rome, which is beyond all contradiction.*[10] The deformity of the old churches we have made apparent. To be dissidents in such societies—to separate from such bodies, bishops, presbyters, deacons, and menials, who polluted every sacred appointment, and abused the benefactions of the people—to dissent, was *the proof of existing virtue*, and to such nonconformists we shall turn.

If the features of nonconformity can be thus traced in Italy, no doubt other provinces contained persons of corresponding characters, particularly in the East, where the old interests were in a deplorable condition.[1]

5. We shall now subjoin the views and testimonies of the writers of the third century, on the subject of baptism.

195 to 216 TERTULLIAN was born of pagan parents at Carthage. He was brought up to the law. His learning was considerable, and his style of writing acquired him the title of the first of the

[8] Campb. Lect. 7. p. 124, &c.   [9] Rob. Res., p. 121.   [10] Rob. Res. p. 440.   [1] Campb. ib.

Latin Fathers. He wrote an able and bold defence of the Christian religion. He was evidently a man of extraordinary genius: his piety was warm and vigorous, with some features of austerity; but a degree of superstition accompanying his profession, prevents our relying on his judgment. Tertullian's writings prove, that he as a baptist stood between contending parties; he explained duties to some, enforced them on others, while some of his instructions gave a check to the innovations of the times.

His views of the ordinance were, that "those who are desirous to dip themselves holily in this water, must prepare themselves for it by fasting, by watchings, by prayer, and by sincere repentance for sin."[1] And "that adults were the only proper subjects of baptism, because fasting, confession of sins, prayer, profession, renouncing the devil and his works, are required from the baptized."[2] "The soul is sanctified, not by washing, but by the answer of a good conscience—baptism is the seal of faith; which faith is begun and adorned by the faith of repentance. We are not therefore washed that we may leave off sinning, but because we have already done it, and are already purified in our hearts."[3] "There is no distinction between the catechumens and believers, they all meet together, they all pray together, they all hear together."[4] "To begin with baptism, when we are ready to enter into the water, and even before, we make our protestations before the minister and in the church, that we renounce the devil, all his pomps and vanities; afterwards we are plunged in the water three times, and they make us

---

[1] Dupin's Eccl. Hist., 3d. Cent. p. 80. [2] De Baptismo, Bap. Mag., v. i., p. 210. [3] De Pœniten., c. 6. Gale's Refl. 410. [4] Rob. Hist. Bapt., p. 245.

answer to some things which are not specified in the gospel." [5]

Some persons at this period gave undue importance to places, as to the waters of Jordan. To such Tertullian asserts, "It is all one whether a person is washed in the sea or in a pond, in a fountain or in a river, in standing or in running water: nor is there any difference between those whom John baptized in Jordan, and those whom Peter baptized, unless it be supposed that the eunuch, whom Philip dipped in the water, obtained more or less salvation."[6] On which observation Bingham remarks, "So that the first ages all agree in this, that whether they had baptisteries or not, the place of baptism was always without the church, and after this manner baptisteries continued till the sixth century."[7]

Others felt disposed to forego baptism, because salvation had been realized without. Tertullian says to those, "Whereas it is an acknowledged rule that *none* can be saved without baptism." He further argues, from Christ's words, John iii. 5, to prove the necessity of obeying and conforming; and asserts, "that all believers from thenceforth [from the giving of the above words] were baptized."[8] He adds, "That men's minds were hardened against baptism, because the person [to be baptized] was brought down into the water without pomp, without any new ornament or sumptuous preparation, and dipped at the pronouncing of a few words."[9] See churches in Africa.

---

[5] De Coronâ Militis, Dupin, 3d Cent. p. 82. [6] De Bapt., c. 4.
[7] Antiq. of the Christian Church, b. 8, c. 17, § 1. [8] Wall's Hist. p. 1, p. 40. [9] De Bapt., c. 2; see African Churches.

185 to 252 Origen was born at Alexandria, of Christian parents. He became a very learned man. His education being guided by Clemens, proved injurious to his views of truth; and his after eminency in the school and the church, was exceedingly pernicious to the cause of pure and undefiled religion. On baptism he observes, "They are rightly baptized who are washed unto salvation. He that is baptized unto salvation, receives the water and the Holy Spirit: such baptism as is accompanied with crucifying the flesh and rising again to newness of life, is the approved baptism."[10]

254 Dionysius of Alexandria, writing to Sextus, Bishop of Rome, testifies, that it was their custom to baptize upon a profession of faith.[1]

280 Arnobius, Professor of Rhetoric at Sicca, says, "Thou art not first baptized, and then beginnest to affect and embrace the faith; but when thou art to be baptized, thou signifiest unto the minister thy desire, and makest thy confession with thy mouth."[2]

6. The most respectable historians affirm, that no evidence exists as to any alteration in the subject or mode of baptism during the third century.

"We have no testimony as to any alteration as to the rites of baptism."[3]

"They baptize with some ceremonies those that were well instructed in their religion, and who had given satisfactory signs of their sincere conversion; they generally dipped them thrice in water, invoking the name of the Holy Trinity."[4]

---

[10] Homily on Ezek. xvi. 4, and on Rom. vi.; see African Churches.   [1] Danver's Hist. Bap. p. 63.   [2] Danver's Treat. 66.   [3] Mag. Cent. c. 3. Danv. p. 62.   [4] Dupin's Hist. Cent. 3.

"There were, twice a year, stated times when baptism was administered to such as, after a long course of trial and preparation, offered themselves as candidates for the profession of Christianity."[5]

"The severity of ancient bishops exacted from the new converts a novitiate of two or three years."[6]

"The historians of this period do none of them mention any thing concerning infant baptism."[7]

While the government was pagan, infants could not receive baptism, without being involved with their parents in persecuting edicts; but there is no evidence extant of this. Though Tertullian delicately alludes to this consequence, if minors were baptized; which we shall refer to hereafter. "In the first three centuries, no natural infants appear in any writings, either authentic or spurious."[8]

Not one natural infant, of any description, appears to have been baptized in the Church of Rome during the first three centuries, and immersion was the only method of administering the ordinance.[9]

The Pædobaptists say, that, "On infant baptism, as well as *other* subjects, the study of antiquity is an inextricable maze; and to consult what is called the Fathers, is to ask counsel at an oracle, whose response is usually of an ambiguous import."[10]

7. During the first three centuries, Christian congregations, all over the East, subsisted in separate independent bodies, unsupported by government, and consequently without any secular power over one another. ALL THIS TIME THEY WERE BAPTIST CHURCHES; and though all the Fathers of the first four ages down to

---

[5] Mosh. Hist. C. 3, p. 2, c. 4, § 4.   [6] Gibbon's Hist. c. 20.
[7] Wall's Hist. p. 1, c. 21, § 4, p. 411.   [8] Rob. Res. pp. 131, 362.   [9] Jones's Ecc. Lect. v. i. pp. 277, 324.   [10] Bogue and Bennett's Hist. of Diss., v. i., p. 144.

Jerome were of Greece, Syria, and Africa—and though they give great numbers of histories of the baptism of adults, yet there is not one record of the baptism of a child till the year 370, when Galetes, *the dying* son of the emperor Valens was baptized, by order of a monarch, who swore he would not be contradicted.[1]

Section IV.

PRIMITIVE BAPTISTS CONTINUED.

"Many walk, of whom I have told you often—who mind earthly things."—*Phil.* iii. 18.

300   1. The fourth century commenced with outward peace to the church; but the pagan priests wrought so effectually on the fears of *Diocletian*, as to **303**   obtain from him, in 303, an edict to pull down the sanctuaries of Christians, to burn their books and writings, and to take from them all their civil rights and privileges, to render them incapable of any honours or civil promotion. Other orders were issued of a more sanguinary character; the magistrates employed all kinds of tortures, and the most unsupportable punishments were invented, to force Christians to apostatize—and the ministers of religion were in particular the objects of the emperor's aversion. The severity and indecent measures adopted, with their continuance for two years, were likely to have proved fatal to the Christian interest.

[1] Robin. Resear. p. 55.

306 In 306, Constantine, surnamed the Great, was saluted emperor by the army, and the aspect of affairs towards the Christian church was soon changed;
325 and in 325, the old corrupt interests were incorporated by an act of the emperor's, from which union we dissent.

2. In 251, there were forty-four Jewish Christian congregations in Rome. Till the time of Sylvester, the Christians had baptized either in private baths, or in subterranean waters, or in any place without the city. The emperor Constantine gave Bishop SYLVESTER the imperial mansion for a sort of parsonage-house: and here was erected the first artificial baptistery in Rome. From this period, at proper seasons of the year, all their catechumens went to be baptized at the Lateran baptistery. Other churches looked to the bishop, who presided over the Lateran congregation and the baptistery; consulted him about the times of baptism, or administering the ordinance, and the regulation of other ecclesiastical affairs. This mode of proceeding in consulting the bishop, led to the destruction of civil and religious liberty, and ruined the independency of the churches.[1]

3. It might appear to some readers, that the testimonies of early baptisms, as adduced above, are few in number for three centuries; many more allusions to the ordinance could be given, yet it should be remembered, that while there existed an harmony among the churches, on the mode and subject of baptism, and all parties were regulated by the scriptures, there was no necessity for the churches to record their views of baptism; but when the ordinance became diverted from the believer, we find an increase of witnesses, recording the ancient way, and testifying against the innovation.

[1] Wall's Inf. Bap. vol. ii., p. 352. Robin. Hist. Bap. p. 345.

It is in the fourth century our testimonies increase; and the following plain and consecutive declarations are *no obscure* evidence as to the period when infant baptism assumed *a decided* station in Christian assemblies. This evidence is corroborated by the first recorded fact of a youth's baptism: Galetes, the dying son of Valeus, A.D. 370, already mentioned.

4. The following testimonies of the Fathers have outlived the ravages of time; no doubt thousands of voices were raised against the incoming abuse, and many things were said and written on baptism, that had only an ephemeral existence. Some of the subjoined writers advocated baptismal regeneration; and those views led to baptize youth and minors, with infants, at a later period.

360 HILARY, bishop of Poictiers, in France, prayeth, "O living Lord, preserve my faith, and the testimony of my conscience; so that I may always keep what I have confessed in the sacrament of my regeneration, when I was baptized in the name of," &c.[2]

360 ATHANASIUS, bishop of Alexandria, says, "Our Lord did not slightly command to baptize; for first of all he said, teach, and then, baptize, that true faith might come by teaching, and baptism be perfected by faith."[3]

370 EPHRAIM SYRUS relates that, in his time, "It was the custom, when any one was baptized, to declare they did forsake the devil and all his works, adultery," &c.; also, that "the baptized used to confess their sins, and testify their faith, before many witnesses."[4]

378 JEROM or HIEROM, a presbyter in Dalmatia, observes on Matt. xxviii. 19, "They first teach

---

[2] Danver's Treat., p. 65.   [3] Ib.   [4] Bap. Mag., v. i., p. 212.

all nations, then, when they are taught, they baptize them with water; for it cannot be, that the body should receive the sacrament of baptism, unless the soul have before received the true faith."[5] He declares, "that in the eastern churches, the adult only were baptized;" also, "that they are to be admitted to baptism to whom it doth belong: viz., those only who have been instructed in the faith."[6] He also appealed to his auditory, and remarked, "When you were baptized, did you not swear allegiance to Christ, and that you would spare neither father nor mother for his sake?"[7]

378 BASIL, bishop of Cæsarea, addresses his hearers with, "Do you demur, and loiter, and put off baptism, when you have been from a child catechized in the word—are you not acquainted with the truth?"[8] He declares, "One must believe first, and then be sealed with baptism."[9] "Must the faithful be sealed with baptism? Faith must needs precede, and go before." Again, "None is to be baptized but the catechumens, and those who are duly instructed in the faith."[10] He observes, "Faith and baptism are two means of salvation nearly allied, and *inseparable;* for faith is perfected by baptism, and baptism is founded on faith : * * * and the confession which leads us to salvation goes before, and baptism, which seals our covenant, follows after."[1]

Dr. Wall remarks on the address of Basil to his auditory, "Part of Basil's auditory at this time were such as had been from their childhood instructed in the

---

[5] Wall's Hist. p. 2, c. 1, p. 7. [6] Danver's Treat. p. 67.
[7] Morris's Biog., v. i., 377. [8] Wall's Hist., p. 1, c. 12, p. 148. [9] Id. p. 2, c. 1, p. 7. [10] Danver's Treat., p. 65.
[1] Stennett's Answer to Russen, p. 90.

Christian religion, and consequently in all probability born of Christian parents, and yet not baptized."[2]

The emperor Valens sent for Basil, in 370, to baptize his *dying* son, Galetes: the ground of the request was the *illness* of the youth. The above extracts from Basil's works show he could not confer the ordinance without a profession of faith: and, from Fox's account, it appears he did not baptize the child, but that the rite was administered by an Arian bishop.

---

[2] Inf. Bap., p. 1, c. 12, p. 148. Basil was a great advocate for trine immersion, a custom which prevailed in the church for centuries. Baronius Ann., v. viii., p. 30, fol. Wall's Hist. 2, 384. Bingham's Antiq., v. i., b. 10, c. 3, § 4. Baptism was so much in vogue in the early ages, that one class of professors, the Hemerobaptists, religiously dipped themselves every day: Gale's Reflec., p. 136. Mosh. Hist., v. iii., p. 189. Robinson's Bap. 33. Modern Pædobaptists assert, that baptism by immersion cannot be proved to have been the early mode.—Evan. Mag., v. xxii., p. 104; Congre. Mag., 1824; Alb. Barnes's Notes on Rom. vi. 4. We would ask those persons who are so hardly driven to maintain their rite, *what* proof they require? Scripture is supported by authenticated facts for ages; yet all evidence on this point, with them, amounts to nothing. The opposers of the Bible are constantly demanding *proof* of those miracles recorded, of a Providence, &c. Errors of all degrees *borrow* the same weapons! It is to be regretted, Pædobaptism lends its aid in so *many ways* to the opposers of vital religion, and unites in destroying the testimonies of the most accredited historians, weakens the authority of Scripture, and endeavours to lessen the creature's fealty to his Saviour. All early churches immersed; the Grecians, Russians, Armenians, Prussians, Abyssinians, &c. &c., do so to this day, and thousands of incidental and correlative circumstances on record, with the direct statements of early and modern historians, and the concessions of later writers, which will be detailed, PROVE, if any fact admits of proof, that believers, before admitted to fellowship in any early primitive church, *were immersed* once or thrice, on a profession of faith; and that there is no trace of infant baptism in early scriptural communities.

CH. I. § 4.] TESTIMONIES OF THE FATHERS. 41

380 CHRYSOSTOM, bishop of Constantinople, asserted that "the time of grace was the time of baptism, which was the season the three thousand, in the second of Acts, and the five thousand afterwards, were baptized." Again, "To be baptized and plunged into the water, and then to emerge or rise out of it again, is a symbol of our descent into the grave, and of our ascent out of it; and, therefore, Paul calls baptism a burial, when he says we are buried with him."[3]

384 SIRICIUS, bishop of Rome, declares, "that those only should be admitted [to baptism] who have given in their names forty days or more before Easter, and have been cleansed by exorcisms, and daily prayers, and fastings, to the end that that precept of the apostle may be fulfilled, of purging out the old leaven that there may be a new lump."[4]

385 CYRIL, bishop of Jerusalem, exhorts his auditory, "not to go to baptism as the guest in the gospel who had not on the wedding garment; but having their sins first washed away by repentance, they might be found worthy at the marriage of the Lamb.[5] You must prepare yourselves by purifying the conscience, and not consider the external baptism, but the inward grace that is imparted by it, for the water is sanctified by invocation. The water washes the body, but the Spirit sanctifies the soul; and being thus purified, we are made meet to draw near to God. If any one be baptized without having the Holy Spirit, he receives not the grace of baptism; and if any one receive not baptism, he cannot be saved. Candidates," he says, "are first anointed with consecrated oils; they are then

---

[3] Stennett's Ans., p. 145. *Chrysostom* baptized youths with their parents, all in a state of nudity. Wall's Inf. Bap., p. 2, c. 9, § 3. Bing. Antiq., v. i., b. 11, c. 11, § 1. [4] Wall's Hist., p. 1, c. 17, p. 250. [5] Baptist Mag., v. 1, p. 211.

conducted to the laver, and asked three times if they believe in the Father, Son, and Holy Ghost; then they are dipped three times into the water, and retire out of it by three distinct efforts."⁶

386 GREGORY, Bishop of Nazianzen, says, "Baptism consists in two things, the *water* and the *Spirit;* that the washing the body with water represents the operation of the Spirit in purifying the soul." He asserts baptism to be, "a compact which we make with God, by which we oblige ourselves to lead a new life." He remarks, "there are three different classes of persons that receive baptism, and there are three sorts who do not receive baptism;—the impious and vicious, who have no relish for it; others delay for liberty to sin; the last are those who cannot receive it, either because of *their infancy,* or some accident."⁷ He asserts, "the baptized used in the first place to confess their sins, and to renounce the devil and all his works, before many witnesses;" and "they were prepared for baptism, by watchings, fastings, prayer, alms-deeds, restitution of ill-gotten goods;" and that, "none were baptized of old, but they that did so confess their sins." He shows also, the necessity of keeping the baptismal vow, and that "the most acceptable posture, or preparation to receive it, is a heart inflamed with a desire for it."⁸ Again, "We are buried with Christ by baptism, that we may also rise again with him; we ascend with him, that we may also be glorified together."⁹

388 GREGORY, Bishop of Nyssa, asserts, "In baptism, there are three things which conduct us to immortal life, *Prayer, Water, and Faith.* That the re-

---

⁶ Dupin's Ec. Hist., c. 4, v. ii., pp. 109—113.   ⁷ Dupin, c. 4, p. 171.   ⁸ Wall's Hist., v. i. c. 11, p. 112.   Orat. in Bapt Mag., v. i. p. 212.   ⁹ Stennett's Ans. p. 144.

generation wrought in baptism ought not to be attributed to the water, but to a divine virtue; that by dipping the person under water three times, the death and resurrection of Jesus Christ is represented; that without baptism no man can be washed from sin.[10]

390 AMBROSE, Bishop of Milan, speaking of baptism, says, "there were three questions propounded, and three answers or confessions made, without which none can be baptized;"[1] * * * " at last you are introduced into the place where the sacrament of baptism is administered, you are obliged to renounce the devil and all his works, the world, and all its pomps and allurements. You found in this place the water and a priest who consecrated the waters; the body was plunged into this water to wash away sin; the Holy Ghost descended upon this water; you ought not to fix your mind upon the external part of it, but to consider in it a divine virtue."[2] He asserts, "Thou wast asked, Dost thou believe in God the Father Almighty? thou saidst, I do believe, and wast dipped, that is, buried. Thou wast asked again, Dost thou believe on our Lord Jesus Christ, and his crucifixion? thou saidst, I believe, and wast dipped again, and so wast buried with Christ. Thou wast interrogated the third time, Dost thou believe in the Holy Spirit? thou answeredst, I believe, and wast dipped a third time.[3]"

395 EPIPHANIUS, Bishop of Salamis, wrote on 80 heresies in the Christian church; he speaks of faith, as a disposition necessary to the receiving of baptism. He does not charge any class of professors with the error of conferring the ordinance without a pro-

---

[10] Dupin, c, 4, p. 178.
[2] Dupin, c. 4, p. 214, &c.
[1] Morris's Biog. v. i. p. 356.
[3] Stennett's Ans. p. 144, and Cox on Bap. p. 48.

fession of faith.⁴ Epiphanius, with others, does not mention any thing concerning infant baptism.⁵

400 Augustin, or Austin, Bishop of Hippo, in Africa, says, "It is evident that men who still persevered in sins, desired to be baptized; and there were those who supported their unreasonable wishes, and thought it sufficient to teach them *after baptism* how they ought to live, still holding out a hope to their minds, that they might be saved as by fire, because they had been baptized. True saving faith works by love; that the instruction of catechumen includes morals as well as doctrines; that the labour of catechising is exceeding profitable to the church; and *that persons ought to be catechized before they receive baptism*, that they may know how vain it is to think of being saved without holiness: as in the case of the eunuch who was catechized before he was baptized.⁶

Augustin's view of original sin led many to inquire how it could be taken away from those who could not believe; the answer was, that sin was removed in baptism: consequently, this view of baptism drove him into pædobaptism, and infants became as eligible in his view, as minors and youths had been for the last century. Augustin, to enforce his views of infant salvation by water, called an assembly, of which we shall speak hereafter.⁷

5. We here subjoin a few extracts from those early assemblies of ministers, commonly called *councils;* and the rules they adopted called *canons*.

305 The council of Elvira, or Granada, enjoins a delay of baptism if the catechumi act worldly:

⁴ Dupin, c. 4, p. 234, &c. ⁵ Wall's Hist., p. 1, c. 21, p. 411, § 4. ⁶ Miln. Hist. of the Ch., C. 5, c. 7. ⁷ Rob. Bap. c., 23.

also adultery and intermarriages should be checked, and ministers of religion should not have strange women with them.[8]

315
The council of NEOCESSAREA, in the sixth canon, saith, "That confession and free choice were necessary to baptism.[9]

365
The council of LAODICEA required notice from the person who intended to be baptized, and resolved all should be instructed before they received it;[10] and determined that the baptized should rehearse the articles of the creed.[1]

383
The council of CONSTANTINOPLE decreed that certain persons should remain a long time under scriptural instruction, before they receive baptism.[2]

397
The council of CARTHAGE, in canon 34, declares, that "sick persons shall be baptized, who cannot answer any longer, when those who are by them testify that they desired it." Again, "those who have no testimonials, and do not remember that they were baptized, shall be baptized anew."[3]

398
The council of CARTHAGE, in canon 85, enjoins, that catechumens shall give in their names, and be prepared for baptism. That the clergy should not cohabit with strange women; that they should not go to fairs; that those ministers shall be degraded who are traitors, and those who speak lascivious words be removed; that those be reprimanded who swear by the creature![4] These clergy prepare us for the next declaration.

401
The fifth council of CARTHAGE, in canon 76, declares children ought to be baptized.[5]

[8] Dupin's Hist. c. 4, p. 242. [9] Magde. Cent. in Danver's, p. 68. [10] Dupin, c. 4, p. 262. [1] Magd. Cent. in Danver's, p. 68. [2] Dupin, c. 4, p. 273. [3] Id. p. 279. [4] Id. p. 282.
[5] Id. p. 288.

416 The council of MELA, in Numidia, in Africa, enjoin Christians to baptize their infants[6] for forgiveness of sin, and curse all who deny the doctrine.[7]

517 At GIRONA, in Spain, seven men of different provinces made the *first* European rule for infant baptism.[8]

789 Charles the Great, in 789, issued the *first law in Europe* for baptizing infants.[9]

6. To strengthen those testimonies as to the early subjects and mode of baptism, we shall merely run through some miscellanies, confirmatory of our practice.

The Greek word baptize, regulates all the Grecian and eastern churches in dipping. The Mahometans baptize by immersion, and have every conveniency for that purpose. References to rivers at an early period, imply the way of administering the ordinance among Christians. Many paintings are extant, representing the act of immersion. The extensive and beautiful buildings erected, with their apartments and apparatus, prove the mode to have been dipping, and the subjects, men and women. The clothes worn, and the officers in attendance on these occasions, support the same views. Records mention persons and youths having been drowned in baptisteries; and immersion in those places has been attended with those casualties which are too delicate to record, and circumstances which would now be deemed reproachful. The canon law required for ages trine immersion, with creeds and rituals, which expressed the subject and described the mode. Sermons were addressed to all catechumens, after

---

[6] Rob. Bap. p. 216.   [7] Wall's Hist., p. 1, c. 19, § 37, p. 372, &c.   [8] Rob. Hist. of Baptism, p. 270.   [9] Id. p. 283, ch. 26.

long preparation; and orations were delivered to candidates, with homilies expressive and confirmatory of the same things. Inscriptions, mottoes, and poetry, convey the same information. The earliest reformers scripturally administered the ordinance; while the German and other revivers of religious knowledge, with every respectable historian, admit, on record, the early practice to have been believers' immersion, and dipping is now continued by all those nations not subject to the authority of the pope.

7. The record of children born of Christian parents, and yet not baptized during infancy, we next subjoin.

300 to 400

BASIL, son of Basil, bishop of Nicene, and his wife, Eumele, whose grandfather was a martyr, was tenderly educated like a second Timothy, under his gracious mother. He became a learned man, and a great preacher, and was baptized in Jordan, by Maximinus, a bishop.[10] Also Chrysostom, Jerom, of Strydon, Theodore, the emperor,[1] Gregory Nazianzen, Augustine, Ambrose,[2] Polycrates,[3] Nectaries,[4] the emperor Constantine, with other nobles.

Dr. Field observes, on the histories of these great men,[5] "that very many that were born of Christian parents (in the fourth and fifth centuries), delayed their

---

[10] Danver's Treat. pp. 69—71. [1] Gibbon's Ro. Hist., c. 27, vol. v. p. 12. [2] Danver's Treat. 70. [3] Gale's Reflect. p. 407. [4] Danver's Treat. p. 72, and Rob. Hist. of Bap. Ch. 13, § 5, p. 67. [5] Since these names, with others which could be recorded, are some of the most distinguished for respectability, in the annals of history, *one plain evidence* enforces itself upon our attention, that *Pædobaptism* was unknown among royalty, courtiers, and respectable persons in Europe, at the period of these eminent men's births.

baptism for a long time, insomuch, that many were made bishops before they were baptized. The same views are supported by Beatus Rhenanus, and Mr. Den; the latter mentions Pancratius, Pontius, Nazarius, Tecla, Luigerus, Erasma Tusca, all offsprings of believers, and yet not baptized till aged. Similar observations are made by the learned Daille and Dr. Barlow.[6]

The great champion for infant baptism, Dr. W. Wall, remarks, "It seems to me that the instances which the antipædobaptists give, of persons not baptized in infancy, though born of Christian parents, are not (if the matter of fact be true) so inconsiderable as this last plea [the sayings of the Fathers] would represent. On the contrary, *the persons they mention are* so many, *and* such noted persons, that (if they be allowed) it is an argument that leaving children unbaptized was no unusual, but a frequent and ordinary thing. For it is obvious to conclude, that if we can in so remote an age trace the practice of *so many* that did this; it is probable that a *great many more* of whose birth and baptism we do not read *did the like.* This I will own, that it seems to me the argument of the greatest weight of any that is brought on the antipædobaptist side in this dispute about antiquity."[7]

We conclude this chapter with the words of CURCELLEUS, "Pædobaptism was not known in the world the two first ages after Christ, in the third and fourth it was approved *by few;* at length, in the fifth and fol-

---

[6] Danver's Treat., p. 72. Daille's Use of the Fathers, b. 2, ch. 6, Reas., 6, p. 149. [7] History of Inf. Bap., p. 2, § 16, p. 42. We admit sprinkling to be more ancient than John, Jesus, or Moses: see Robins. Hist. of Bap. c. 6. pp. 39—42.

lowing ages, it began to obtain in divers places; and, therefore, we (pædobaptists) observe this rite indeed, as an ancient custom, but not as an apostolic tradition. The custom of baptizing infants did not begin before the third age after Christ, and that there appears not the least footstep of it for the first two centuries.[8]

[8] Stennett's Ans., &c., p. 87.

CHAPTER II.

Section I.

CHURCHES IN ITALY.

Now I COMMAND you, brethren, in the name of our Lord Jesus Christ, that ye withdraw *yourselves from every brother that walketh disorderly.*—2 *Thess.* iii. 6.

1. WE have endeavoured to detail, in the previous pages, the features of the Christian churches generally. While the interests of religion retained their scriptural character, all were upon equality, and each society possessed its government within itself; so that, no one church originally can claim our attention more than another. *The churches, during this early period, were strictly Baptist, in their practice and constitution.*[1] These early interests stood perfectly free of Rome, and at after periods refused her communion. As churches rose into importance, contentions about offices were frequent, and tumults ensued; but having no secular aid, their rage against each other spent itself in reproaches, and often subsided into apathy. The disappointed, the disaffected, the oppressed, the injured, with the pious, had only to retire from the scene of strife, and they were safe; which evidently they did: and while the express command, 2 Thess. iii. 6, regulated dissidents, other causes and motives combined to increase their number, since by 250 they became very numerous, as already

---

[1] See above, ch. 1, s. 3, § 7.

stated. These dissidents, in small companies, or in more general associations, unostentatiously worshipped God under their own vine, and were not disturbed, unless the government adopted measures *involving all;* but as dissidents increased, political considerations regulated the governors.

2. The religion of the New Testament commenced with *Dissent.* John, Jesus, and his disciples were charged with innovations, both at Jerusalem, and in other cities, John i. 22; Luke xxiii. 2, 5; Acts vi. 28; xvii. 7; and xviii. 13. Their want of conformity was a crime in the eyes of the unthinking or secularizing multitude. The genuine spirit of religion has been and will be preserved by those *only,* who dissent from all establishments, derived by human policy.[2] Liberty of soul is the breath, the element, the existence of that religion inculcated in the New Testament, of which liberty, the Baptists have ever been the most open advocates.[3] "Ye have one master, even Christ, and all ye are brethren." The voice of Moses and the prophets, with Jesus and his apostles, urge on all *who fear God,* singleness of motive, blamelessness of character; and in their social stations, purity of communion. In obedience to these heavenly injunctions, men and women have "come out" of impure communities, and with such persons, actuated by divine motives, we now hope to associate.

249 3. When Decius came to the throne in 249, he required by edicts all persons in the empire to conform to Pagan worship. Forty years' toleration had greatly increased professors, and they were found in every department of the government. They had been so long unaccustomed to trials, that the lives of many

---

[2] Church records prove purity to have existed *only* out of establishments. [3] Robins. Resear. pp. 641, and 551, from Voltaire.

were unsuited to suffering. Decius's edicts rent asunder the churches, multitudes apostatized, and many were martyred. In two years the trial abated, when many apostates applied for restoration to Christian fellowship, and sanctioned their application by letters, written by some eminent Christians who had been martyrs during the persecution.[4] The flagrancy of some apostates, occasioned an opposition to their readmission. In the time of peace, many had entered the church without calculating on trials; and when persecution arose such persons revolted easily to idolatry, and on trials subsiding, gained but too easy admittance again to communion. One NOVATIAN, a presbyter in the church of Rome, strongly opposed the readmission of apostates, but he was not successful. The choice of a pastor in the same church fell upon *Cornelius*, whose election Novatian opposed, from his readiness to readmit apostates. Novatian consequently separated himself from the church, and from Cornelius's jurisdiction.[5]

4. Novatian, with every considerate person, was disgusted with the hasty admission of such apostates to communion, and with the conduct of many pastors, who were more concerned about *numbers*, than *purity* of communion. Novatian was the first to begin a separate interest with success, and which was known for centuries by his name. One *Novatus*, of Carthage, coming to Rome, united himself with Novatian, and their combined efforts were attended with remarkable success. It is evident that many persons were previously in such a situation, as to embrace the earliest opportunity of uniting with churches whose communion was scriptural. Novatian became the first pastor in the new interest,

---

[4] From this circumstance arose prayer to saints.   [5] Dupin's Hist., c. 3, p. 125, &c.

and is accused of the crime of giving birth to an innumerable multitude of congregations of puritans, in every part of the Roman empire; and yet, all the influence he exercised was, an upright example, and moral suasion: these churches flourished until the fifth century.[6]

5. There was no difference in point of doctrine between the Novatianists and other Christians. Novatian had seen evils result from readmitting apostates; he consequently refused communion to all those who had fallen after baptism. The terms of admission in those churches were, "If you wish to join any of our churches, you may be admitted among us by baptism; but observe, that if you fall away into idolatry or vice, we shall separate you from our communion, and on no account can you be readmitted among us. We shall never attempt to injure you, in your person, property, or character; we do not presume to judge the sincerity of your repentance, or your future state; but you can never be readmitted to the fellowship of our churches, without our giving up the securest guardian we have for *the purity of our communion.*"[7] "They considered," says Mosheim, "the Christian church, as a society where virtue and innocence reigned universally, and none of whose members, from their entrance into it, had defiled themselves with any enormous crimes; and, of consequence, they looked upon every society, which readmitted heinous offenders to its communion, as unworthy of the title of a true Christian church. On account of the church's severity of discipline, the example was followed by many, and churches of this

---

[6] Euseb. b. 6, c. 42. Dupin's Hist., c. 3, pp. 125, and 146. Mosh., c. 3, § 17, 18. [7] Robins. Res., pp. 127. Jones's Lect., 1, 306.

order flourished in the greatest part of those provinces which had received the gospel."[8] Many advenient rites had been appointed, and interwoven with baptism, with a threefold administration of the ordinance, in the old interests, which obscured the original simplicity and design of the institutor. To remove all human appendages, the Novatianists said to candidates, "If you be a virtuous believer, and will accede to our confederacy against sin, you may be admitted among us by baptism, or if any catholic has baptized you before, by rebaptism." They were at later periods called anabaptists.[9] The churches thus formed upon a plan of *strict communion* and rigid discipline, obtained the reproach of PURITANS; they are the first Protestant Dissenting churches, of which we have any account, and a *succession of them*, we shall prove, has continued to the present day. Novatian's example had a powerful influence, and puritan churches rose in different parts, in quick succession. So early as 254, these Dissenters are complained of, as having infected France with their doctrines,[10] which will aid us in the *Albigensian* churches, where the same severity of discipline is traced,[1] and reprobated.[2]

6. Learned men and historians have investigated the pretensions of these churches to puritanical character, and have conferred on them the palm of honour. Dupin says, "Novatian's style is pure, clean, and polite; his expressions choice, his thoughts natural, and his way of reasoning just; he is full of citations of texts of Scrip-

---

[8] Hist. c. 3, § 17. [9] Rob. Res., p. 127. Baronius' Ann., v. iii. 231. Chamb. Ency. Collier's Dict. Ency. Brit. Art. Anabap. Formey's Ecc. Hist., v. i. p. 64, and Mosh., ubi sup. [10] Mezeray's Hist., p. 4. Miln. Ch. Hist., c. 3, c. 13. [1] Allix's Pied., c. 17, 156. [2] Mosh. Hist., cent. 13, p. 2. c. 5, § 7, note.

ture, that are always to the purpose; and besides, there is a great deal of order and method in those treatises of his we now have, and he never speaks but with a world of moderation and candour."[3] "Their manners," says Dr. A. Clarke, "were, in general, simple and holy; indeed, their rigid discipline is no mean proof of this." We well know that those called Pietists in Germany, and Puritans in England, were in general, in their respective times, among the most religious and holy people in both nations.[4] "They were," says Robinson, "Trinitarian Baptists."[5]

7. These churches existed for sixty years under a pagan government, during which time, the old corrupt interests at Rome, Carthage, and other places, possessed no means, but those of persuasion and reproach, to stay the progress of Dissent. During this period, the Novatian churches were very prosperous, and were planted *all over the Roman empire.*[6] "They were very numerous," says Lardner, "in Phrygia," and a number of eminent men were raised up in the work of the ministry. It is impossible to calculate the benefit of their services to mankind. Their influence must have considerably checked the spirit of innovation and secularity in the old churches. Although rigid in discipline and schismatic in character, yet they were found extensive, and **306** in a flourishing condition, when Constantine came Aug.6. to the throne, 306. Their soundness in doctrine, evident unity among themselves, with their numbers, suggested to Constantine the propriety of uniting them

---

[3] Dupin, c. 3, pp. 125, and 146. [4] Suc. of Sac. Lit. Mosh. i. 222. Gill's Cause of God, &c., v. iv. pp. 57 and 131. Miln. Ch. Hist., c. 3, ch. 3 and 11. Neal's Hist. of the Puritans, v. i. pref. vii. [5] Robins. Res. p. 213. [6] Jones's Lect., v. i. pp. 305 and 436.

with the catholic church, but this comprehension they refused. These churches, with other dissidents, realized religious liberty in 313, from Constantine.[7]

In 331, he changed his policy towards these people, and they were involved, with other denominations, in distress and sufferings. Their books were sought for, they were forbidden assembling together, and many lost their places of worship.[8] The orthodoxy of the Novatian party, with the influence of some of their

---

[7] Constantine's father lived in Britain at the time of his birth, 271. He was not baptized during infancy, though his father was favourable to Christianity, if not a professor of it. When he came to the throne, he professed to receive the gospel, and many officers and servants did the same. He gave Bishop Sylvester his mansion, for a baptistery, and conferred freedom on those slaves who would receive baptism. He offered a reward to others, on their embracing Christianity, so that 12,000 men, besides women and minors, were baptized in one year. In 319, he relieved the clergy of taxes, and in 320, issued an edict against the Donatists. He abolished heathen superstition, and erected splendid churches, richly adorned with paintings and images, bearing a striking resemblance to heathen temples. Places were erected for baptizing, some over running water, while others were supplied by pipes. In the middle of the building was the bath, which was very large, (Dr. Cave.) Distinct apartments were provided for men and women, as are found in Baptist meeting-houses at this day. See Bing. Antiq. Robins. Hist. Bap. and Res. Gibbon's ch. 20. Campbell's Lect. No. 3, p. 35. Fosbroke's Ency. of Antiq., v. i. p. 103. Pilkington's Sac. Elucidations, v. 2, part 4. [8] Constantine's conduct *in the church*, has proved a kind of Pandora's box to the interest of religion, and *the hope* of deliverance has tried the faith of the godly to this day. The evils of splendid churches and pensioned bishops were soon seen in their persecuting ascendency, and in the ministers of religion, exhorting their congregations to crown their talents with clapping their hand, and loud applause.—See Lardner's Credibility of the Gospel History, v. 4, part 2, c. 70, p. 169.

ministers, is supposed to have procured some mitigation of the law. Constantine's oppressive measures prompted many to leave the scene of sufferings, and retire into more sequestered spots. Claudius Seyssel, the popish archbishop, TRACES the rise of the Waldensian heresy to a pastor named *Leo*, leaving Rome at this period, for the Valleys.⁹

352 The succeeding emperor, Constantius, embraced the Arian faith, and severely oppressed the orthodox. In the territory of Mantinium, a large district of Paphlagonia, the Novatianists were extremely numerous. Being involved in the massacre sanctioned by Constantius, a body of four thousand troops was sent to exterminate them, with other Trinitarians. The Novatian peasants, however, arming themselves with scythes and axes, fought the invaders of their homes in so desperate a manner, that they even vanquished and destroyed the disciplined soldiery.¹⁰ They lost several of their places of worship, but Julian on ascending the throne, required the Arians to rebuild and restore them. In 375, the emperor Valens embraced the Arian **375** creed. He closed the Novatian churches, banished their ministers,¹ and probably would have carried his measures to extreme severity, had not his prejudices and zeal been moderated by a pious man, named Marcion. During this severe trial, the benevolent feelings of the Novatianists became so apparent,

---

⁹ Facts opp. to Fict. p. 37. ¹⁰ Mosh. Hist. Cent. 4, § 14. J. R. Peyrin's Def. of the Vaudois, p. 362. It is said Liberius, Bishop of Rome, in 360, baptized 8,800 persons on one Saturday, and that a boy was drowned on the occasion. ¹ This Valens, who required baptism for his dying son, sent 80 ministers into banishment, but before the vessel had gotten far from land, it fired and all of them perished.

as to extort admiration from their enemies.
About this period, 380, Pacianus, Bishop of Barcelona, wrote some treatises against these people. He observes to Sempronianus, one of the Novatian ministers, "You have forsaken the tradition of the church, under pretence of reformation: likewise you say, that the church is a body of men regenerated by water and the Holy Spirit, who have not denied the name of Christ, which is the temple and house of God, the Pillar and Ground of truth: we say the same also."[2]

In 383, Theodosius assembled a synod, with a view to establish unity among churches. On the Novatianists stating their views of discipline; the emperor, says Socrates,[3] "wondered at their consent and harmony touching the faith." He passed a law, securing to them liberty, civil and religious, all their property, with all churches of the same faith and practice. While these Dissenting interests were in peace and concord, it is stated that discord prevailed in the national churches.

8. At the conclusion of this fourth century, the Novatianists had three, if not four churches, in Constantinople; they had also churches at Nice, Nicomedia, and Cotiveus, in Phrygia, all of them large and extensive bodies, besides which, they were very numerous in the Western empire. There were several churches of this people in the city of Alexandria, in the beginning of the fifth century. In 412, Cyril was ordained bishop of the catholic church in this city. One of his first acts, was to shut up the churches of the Novatianists,[4] to strip them of all their sacred

---

[2] Dupin, cent. 4, pp. 81—3. [3] Lib. 5, cap. 10. [4] Persecution in the first ages was confined to the edict of the Emperors; but in Cyril and Innocent's conduct, we see the spirit and rising power of the man of sin.

vessels and ornaments. One minister, Cyril deprived of every thing he possessed. They experienced very similar treatment at Rome, from Innocent, who was one of the first bishops to persecute the Dissenters, and rob them of their churches. This proceeding is easily accounted for. The clergy of the establishments were an idle and ignorant class of men, and unacquainted with the Scriptures. Innocent wrote many letters to various bishops, containing the rules of discipline in his church, plainly with the intention of establishing uniformity.[5] This uniformity could not be imposed on the Novatianists, nor would they receive his views on children's baptism and communion; they, consequently, became the object of his aversion. Another means of awakening the catholic prelates' anger, was *rebaptizing*. When this was first introduced, purity of communion, with a strict adherence to Zion's laws, was no doubt intended; but when the Arians arose, different creeds were formed, and the candidate's acquaintance with the creed was, in each church, the *sine qua non* for baptism. The catholic party, now accumulating power, saw, in other churches' rebaptizing, a virtual renunciation of the baptism they had conferred upon those who went over to the other party; as understood by the pædobaptists of the present day: consequently, a spirit of persecution was raised against *all those* who rebaptized catholics. In the fourth Lateran council, canons were made to banish them as heretics, and these canons were supported by an edict in 413, issued by the emperors, Theodosius and Honorius, declaring, "that all persons *re*baptized, and the *re*baptizers, should be both punished with death." Accordingly, Albanus, a zealous minister, with others, was punished with death, for re-

---

[5] Dupin, c. 5, pp. 195—8.

baptizing.⁶ The edict was probably obtained by the influence of Augustine, who could endure no rival, nor would he bear with any who questioned the virtue of his rites, or the sanctity of his brethren, or the soundness of the Catholic creed; and these points being disputed by the Novatianists and Donatists, two powerful and extensive bodies of dissidents in Italy and Africa, they were consequently made to feel the weight of his influence. These combined modes of oppression led the faithful to abandon the cities, and seek retreats in the country, which they did, particularly in the valleys of Piedmont, the inhabitants of which began to be called Waldenses.⁷

415   9. The Novatianists had hitherto flourished mightily in Rome, having a great many places of worship, and large congregations; but the rising power of the Catholic interest, its union with the sword, the ambitious character of its officers, with the tyrannical

---

⁶ Bap. Mag. vol. i. p. 256.   Circumstances become here apparent, and unite their evidence *to prove* WHEN infant baptism was publicly espoused. We have already noticed the writers who declared against the innovation. In 412, the Baptists were banished as heretics. In 413, Innocent sent letters of advice to various ministers. In the same year, the Baptists, for re-baptizing, were sentenced to death. In 416, a council at Mela, *accursed* all those who denied forgiveness to accompany infant baptism, and in 418, a council at Carthage enforced the same curse. Augustine, Cyril, Innocent, and others, concurred in its expediency, Rob. Res. 151. They borrowed the sword of the magistrate, to enforce what their arguments and views could not do, Wall, i. p. 111. The sword, and the infant rite, have always been companions, Rob. Bap. 438 and 450; and the early advocates *accursed* the parents who withheld the blessing from the child. Its support by the sword has called the Baptists to extreme sufferings, but they are additionally convinced of its origin from its companion and defence, and know that every rite defended by the sword shall perish by the sword.

⁷ Bap. Mag. ib.

spirit of its bishops, prompted them to crush every opposing interest. They, consequently, robbed the Novatianists of all their churches, and drove them into obscurity. About this time, some epistles appeared against them, written by different individuals,
425 which had a baneful influence at this period on the interests of this people. One individual, whose
432 hostility was felt by the Novatianists, was Celestines, one of Innocent's successors, A.D., 432. He took possession of all their churches in the city of Rome, and compelled them to worship in private houses,
455 in the most obscure places. A council was convened at Arles, and at Lyons, in 455, in which the views of the Novatianists on predestination were controverted, and by which name they were stigmatized.[8]

These holy people now retired from public notice; yet it is pretty manifest that, while some of them sought asylums in other kingdoms, many of these despised people continued in Italy, and a succession of them will be found under *another name*.[9]

476 In 476, on the 23rd of August, a period was put to all persecution in Italy, by the subjection of that kingdom to the Goths, whose laws breathed the purest spirit of equal and universal liberty. The state of religion out of the Catholic church is not made apparent. This civil and religious liberty continued for about *three centuries*, during which time the dissidents, no doubt, greatly increased.[10] The accounts given of the Novatianists, by Eusebius and Socrates in their histories, are decided proofs of their extensive influence.
575 That they subsisted towards the end of the sixth century, is evident from the book of Eulogius,

[8] Mezeray, p. 19, Clovis. [9] Mosh. Hist. cent. 12, p. 2, c. 5, § 4, note; and cent. 11, p. 2, c. 5, § 2, note; and cent. 11, p. 2, c. 2, § 13, note. [10] Rob. Res. ch. 8, pp. 151, 157.

Bishop of Alexander. Dr. Lardner remarks, "The vast extent of this sect is manifest from the names of the authors who have mentioned or written against them, and from the several parts of the Roman empire in which they were found. It is evident, too, that these churches had among them some individuals of note and eminence."

10. The rise of these puritans at so critical a period, their soundness in the faith, their regard to character and purity of communion, their vast extent, and long success, must have had a powerful influence in all the vicinity of their churches, in checking the ambition and secularity of the established clergy, and in shedding a moral auspice on benighted provinces. These sealed witnesses, Rev. vii. 3, were the first protestant dissenters from assuming hierarchies; and it is most gratifying to be able *to prove ourselves* the successors of a class of men, who first set the example of contending for the purity and simplicity of Christian worship, and a firm adherence to the laws of the King of Zion.[1]

Section II.

AFRICAN CHURCHES.

Now I BESEECH you, brethren, mark them which cause divisions and offences contrary to the doctrine which ye have learned, and avoid them, &c.—*Rom.* xvi. 17.

1. THE history of these churches *is not* to be understood as comprehending the whole of that immense

---

[1] Robins. Ec. Res. ch. 8. Jones' Lect., 25. See a detailed account of the Novatianists in Lardner's Credibility of the Gospel History, vol. iii. part 2. c. 47. p. 206—seq.

tract of land which extends from the Mediterranean Sea on the north, to the Cape of Good Hope on the south, but that part principally which runs parallel with, and borders on, the Mediterranean Sea. As to the extent and influence of Christianity on the interior nations of Ethiopia, we have now no means of ascertaining. It is not certain, by whom these people were first evangelized. The current opinion is, that the Eunuch first, and afterwards, Matthias, laboured in the part called Ethiopia: and that Mark in 39, with Simon and Jude, preached in Egypt, Memorica, Mauritania, and other parts of Africa.[1] It is recorded that Mark baptized Auzebius on a confession of his faith,[2] and that this Evangelist was martyred by the people of Alexandria. The hostility of the nations to the gospel, the unobtruding course of the first disciples, with the obscurity of those persons who formed the first communities, are probable reasons, why the materials are so few respecting the churches first planted. It is very evident that the churches of this province were introduced into notice and brought prominently into history, by their association with those learned men, whose names are recorded as some of the first corrupters of the gospel.

2. The first, and the most fatal of all events to the primitive religion, was the setting up of a Christian academy at Alexandria. Christians had been reproached with illiteracy, and this seemed a plausible method to get rid of the scandal. This school was first kept by Pantaenus, whom Clement first assisted, and then succeeded, as Origen did him.[3] In this school baptism was first associated with a

---

[1] Young on Idolatry, v. 2. p. 216, &c. Robins. Bap. p. 584.
[2] Vicecomes' Life of Auzebius. [3] Rob. Res. p. 51. Mosh. Hist. c. 2. p. 1. c. 1. § 12. and p. 2. c. 1. § 4.

learned education. Here minor baptism began with young gentlemen under age, and afterwards gradually descended to boys of seven years of age, where it stood for centuries in the hierarchies.[4] Here youths were first incorporated and became church members by baptism: before, baptism had only signified a profession of the religion at large. In this school human creeds were first taught and united with baptism.[5]

In apostolic days a simple expression of faith was required of each candidate, Acts viii. 37, but in after-periods, to accommodate the ignorance of catechumens, short sentences were drawn up for the candidate to utter.[6] These sentences were in this school improved into a creed or compendium of doctrines, a knowledge of which was thought essential to the catechumens, and the acquirement of which occasioned a delay, from forty days to uncertain years, and some put off the ordinance till the close of life.[7] "We know," says Dr. Wall, "that every one repeated the creed at his baptism, either by himself or his sponsors."[8] And as "abstinence, prayer, and other pious exercises, prepared persons for baptism; it was to answer for such persons, as offered themselves for baptism, having attended to these duties or exercises," observes Mosheim, "that sponsors were appointed."[9] These exercises of the candidates for baptism were afterward known by the term of *exorcising* him, or putting him to his oath."[10] From which oath probably the term sacrament had its rise.[1]

171 3. The evils attendant on the union of Christianity with Judaism, Paganism, and philoso-

[4] Rob. Bap. p. 155. [5] Id. p. 227. [6] Wall's Hist. p. 2. c. 9. § 10. [7] Rob. Bap. p. 239. Gibb. Rom. Hist. c. 20. [8] Hist. Inf. Bap. p. 2. c. 9. § 5. [9] Ecc. Hist. C. 2. p. 2. c. 2, § 15. [10] Wall's Hist. p. 2. c. 9. § 9. [1] Dr. P. Smith's Intro. Essay to Leighton on the Creed.

phy which was effected in this school, occasioned swarms of dissidents in Africa. Among those who were hostile to the Alexandrian school, is to be numbered *Montanus*. His aim evidently was to maintain or restore the scriptural simplicity and native character of the religion of the New Testament, with a constant reliance on the promised aid of the Holy Spirit. He consequently declared himself a mortal enemy to philosophy and religion. He adopted a severe discipline, and yet proved very successful in planting many churches, whose members were far from the lowest orders, over various provinces. He is reproached as a heretic by all state paid clergy, though it is very probable his attempts were designed to recover Christianity to its original *spiritual* character.[2]

4. When Pantaneus was called to fill a missionary station in the East, Clemens, who had been his assistant, succeeded to the office of catechist in the Alexandrian school. Clemens was born at Athens, and had realized the advantages of an early education. While he sustained the character of a schoolmaster, he directed his attention to the Gospel, with the newly arranged doctrines of Plato, and endeavoured, through these opposite sources, *to form* an imaginary coalition, in order to render learning more palatable to Christians, and to meet in part the prejudices of heathens. Presiding, as Clemens did, over the academy, he tinctured the fountain of knowledge with the poison of his system, which proved of the most serious consequences to the cause of Christianity. The boys under his superintendence were trained to sing his compositions; and a choir of those, who were supposed to be pious, was

---

[2] Mosh. Hist. c. ii. p. 2. c. 5. § 23-4. Jortin's Rem. on Ec. Hist. v. 2. pp. 1-3.

appointed in the church *resembling the heathen orgies*.³ During his filling this office, he wrote a book entitled "Pedagogue." Jesus was the pedagogue, and *all disciples were children*. To support this view he selected the words, child, children, little children, little ones, babes, &c. out of the Scriptures, to prove the character of true disciples. He calls the church of Alexandria "a Choir of Infants." For these infants his instructions were intended, as the book is a Christian's directory, and contains some plain admonitions to avoid the excesses visible in the world. The Egyptian symbols expressive of infancy were honey and milk; Clemens would have these symbols given to newly-baptized persons, to remind them of their *infancy in grace*.⁴ A door was now opened into the church for Jewish ceremonies, Egyptian images, Pagan rites, and oriental science, and the following schoolmaster perfects the system. "As there were many persons of narrow capacities, the Christian teachers thought it advisable to instruct such in the essential truths of the gospel, by placing those truths, as it were, before their eyes, under visible objects or images."⁵

198 5. Ammonius Saccas, who was born of Christian parents, because a very learned man, and a professor of the Christian religion. He also was a a teacher and became very popular in the Alexandrian school. He attempted to reconcile ALL PARTIES by those general truths *all parties held*, and by various subtleties in argument, supported by austerities of life, won too successfully on inquiring youths and the carnal multitude. Here we discover a broad entrance into the Christian profession, and it is not difficult to

---

³ Rob. Bap. 163.   ⁴ Mosh. Hist. C. 2. p. 2. c. 2. § 6. Wall's Hist. p. 2. c. 9.   ⁵ Mosh. Hist. ubi sup.

CH. II. § II.]   TERTULLIAN'S VIEWS.   67

discover the extensive and mixed company that entered, The infirmities of the weak and ignorant were to be accommodated by symbolic instruction. Symbols and images required some learning to explain them; besides ignorance was a disgrace in the Athens of Africa.

The learned men of the school, with the ministers and explainers of symbols, allegorized every thing, and darkened by figures the plainest truths. But what is learning, without gazing and admiring disciples? A system of extensive comprehension must establish the reputation of the deviser, and this stretch of charity and sagacity is awarded rightly to Saccas. Converted Jews came into this new system with their full attachment to the mint, anise, and cummin of their old economy. Heathens, alike converted, professed this Christianity, and at the same time, respected the *departed manes* of their ancestors. Others were equally accommodated on the ground of allowed truths, and all this motley group were held together by forbearance and charity: and to complete *this system of expediency* in Africa, the teachers declared, the employment of

200 falsehood in the cause of virtue was harmless!!![6]

202 6. Tertullian was a lawyer at Carthage. He became a Christian, and joined the church in that city. His views on baptism we have already mentioned. He was elected an elder, and wrote ably in

215 defence of the Christian religion. It was reputed in 215, that the tenth part of the inhabitants were Christians, and there were many congregations in other parts. Tertullian thought they had increased too fast, and lost in the crowd the simplicity of the Christian religion. Awhile he had endeavoured to

[6] Mosh. Hist. C. 2, p. 2, c. 1, § 6—11.

stem the torrent, by a strict scrutiny at the admission of members, and as several came to join the church, who had been, or pretended they had been baptized elsewhere, he insisted on re-examining and rebaptizing them, unless they could make it appear they had been baptized by churches in communion with that at Carthage.⁷

7. Tertullian was inquired of, by a rich lady named Quintilla, who lived at Pepuza, a town in Phrygia, whether infants might be baptized on condition, *they ask to be baptized*, and produce sponsors?⁸ In reply to Quintilla, Tertullian observes, "That baptism ought not to be administered rashly, the administrators of it

---

⁷ Rob. Hist. Bap. c. 22, p, 183.

⁸ When baptism was made to convey a saving influence, an inquiry was agitated in the eastern churches, "*What becomes of the unbaptized?*" The answer was, "None are saved without baptism." For penitents, martyrs, and others, therefore, dying unbaptized, the Greeks allotted a middle place, called by the Latins *Limbus Puerorum*. Wall, pt. i. p. 160. It was during the agitation of this question in the East, that Quintilla made this inquiry, and what might have encouraged her to submit her anxieties to Tertullian was, the report that in the African churches, particularly at Carthage and Alexandria, a great many infants were employed in the church *as readers*. Her inquiry amounts to this, " How early might children be baptized after they can speak so as to be understood?" Rob. Bap. ch. 21. p. 171. Mr. Robinson has proved that the words *infants, little ones*, &c. are terms too vague for argument, or *to ground* a rite upon. He has amply shown that these words, at this period, were expressive of *minors*: as infants were employed in the church service, are said to have composed hymns, willed away property, erected churches, were made bishops, and presbyters, suffered martyrdom; various ages expressive of minority were inscribed on tombs; as Menophylus, *an infant*, who lived eight years and five months. Also it is said infants married, &c. &c. So that the terms in early days among these churches, were expressive of youths under legal responsibility. Hist. Bap. c. 19.

know. Give to him that asketh? every one hath a right, as if it were a matter of alms? yea, rather say, Give not that which is holy to dogs, cast not your pearls before swine, lay hands suddenly on no man, be not partakers of other men's sins. If Philip baptized the eunuch on the spot, let us remember that it was done under the immediate direction of the Lord.... the eunuch was a believer of Scripture, the instruction given by Philip was seasonable; the one preached, the other perceived the Lord Jesus, and believed on him; water was at hand, and the apostle having finished the affair was caught away. But Paul, you say, was baptized instantly: true; because Judas, in whose house he was, instantly knew he was a vessel of mercy. The condescension of God may confer his favours as he pleases; but our wishes may mislead ourselves and others." It is therefore most expedient to defer baptism, and to regulate the administration of it according to the condition, the disposition, and the age of the person to be baptized; and especially in the case of little ones. What necessity is there to expose sponsors to danger?[8] Death may incapacitate them for fulfilling their engagements, or bad dispositions may defeat all their endeavours."[9] "Jesus Christ said indeed, *hinder them not*, &c., but that they should come to him as soon as they are advanced in years, as soon as they have learnt their religion, when they may be taught whither they are going, when they are become Christians, when they begin to know Jesus Christ. What

---

[8] This is plainly the opinion of a lawyer on the delicate situation of sponsors under a heathen government. Minors were not of age till 25. The law had taken no cognizance of baptism, and if persecution should commence, minors and sponsors would be involved in sufferings, for encouraging a community not incorporated by law. Rob. Hist. of Bap. p 179.   [9] Id. ch. 21.

is there that should compel this innocent age to receive baptism? and since they are not allowed the disposal of temporal goods, is it reasonable that they should be entrusted with the concerns of heaven?"[10] "They just know how to ask for salvation, that you may seem to give to him that asketh. Such as understand the importance of baptism, are more afraid of presumption than procrastination, and faith alone saves the soul."[1]

8. This is the first recorded reference in history to minor baptism. The mildness of Tertullian's manner evinces the spirit of the Christian, and proves his answer given, *to be an opinion* supported by Scripture and the custom of the church. He is not encountering a rite long established; if it had been so, we should have seen, with his views of baptism, something of that burst of genius against the innovation, as we find so firmly and finely displayed in his defence of Christianity. From the inquiries, we see the New Testament examples alone regulated the female preacher's views. These were illustrated by Tertullian in a way exhibiting a *preparation necessary* in order to receive baptism. The lady observed that the eunuch and Paul received baptism as soon as they asked for the ordinance; He shows these to have been extraordinary cases, and therefore cannot be taken to support the case of children, who understand not what they ask for. He refers to Scripture, and says, *let them come, let them ask, let them be instructed.* Why should *they* attend an ordinance which is expressive of death to sin, who are innocent of known sins?

The children referred to *were not little ones in arms,* but those who could ask, *just ask,* for things without knowing their value; and upon such, men do not con-

---

[10] Dupin's Eccl. Hist. cent. 3. p. 80.   [1] Rob. ubi. sup.

fer temporal good, then why spiritual? Besides, a change in the policy of government would render a sponsor's situation very critical, or an evil disposition in the baptized would rescind his benevolent designs.

9. In the creed bearing Tertullian's name, no reference is made to infant baptism:[2] and though Christians were charged with eating their own offspring,—which calumny they considered the most cruel, and to this slander he refers to in his Apology, chap. 7, and all their books are full of the subject;—yet not one syllable transpires about infant baptism.[3] Tertullian could recommend *expediency* in religion, and was an admirer of those rites and ceremonies adopted in the Alexandrian school. It advocated giving honey and milk to the newly baptized, signing with the cross, trine immersion, and anointing the baptized.[4] A man who could so far lose sight of the beautiful simplicity of the gospel would never have opposed the infant rite, had such practice been known in his days, His eldership in the church at Carthage, his careful examination of candidates, with his rebaptizing those who came over from other churches, prove that this rite was unknown in the Carthaginian church. On the subject of minor baptism we find nothing more for *forty years*. The corruption of the church, with which Tertullian stood connected at Carthage, was more than a match for his reforming zeal, he consequently quitted it, and united himself to the Montanists, about six years after he had given them his views on baptism. In this society Tertullian's principles met encouragement; his austerity was indulged; and the purity of communion sought in the old church, was realized in its wished-for sanctity. A separate

[2] Jortin's Rem. v. ii. b. 2. pt. 2. p. 25.   [3] Robins. Res. p. 49.   [4] Wall's Hist. pt. 2. pp. 281—291.

congregation of these people was formed by him at Carthage, which continued two hundred years. Tertullian's method of admitting members with the Montanists, was by severe examination, and they rebaptized all such as joined them from other communities. He advocated every Christian man's preaching, baptizing, and administering ordinances; and for dispensing with a separate order of men termed clergy.[5]

230 10. ORIGEN was a native of Alexandria, and was born of Christian parents: he received his education under Clemens and Ammonius Saccas. He assisted Clemens as catechist when eighteen years of age. In this school pupils were not baptized at their first admission into the academy, which is clear by the case of six martyrs, two of whom died unbaptized. Origen is said to have accompanied his pupils to the place of execution. When the school was broken up, some were catechumens, and others had been lately baptized. Origen was a man of sober morals: but he was an eccentric genius, and his theological speculations were the most wild and extravagant in the world.[6] It was held as a maxim in this school, and Origen supported it, " that it was not only lawful, but even praiseworthy to deceive, and even to use the expedient of a lie, in order to advance the cause of truth and piety." About the time Origen went to school, the affairs of religion underwent a very considerable change. As the old pastors were removed by death, the new ones, and particularly those from the Alexandrian school, were for introducing the new doctrines and discipline, so that a mixture of Jewish, Gentile, and Christian modes, formed a code of laws for religious affairs. Origen embraced eagerly this new species of doctrines, explain-

[5] Robins. Bap. 183.   [6] Rob. Bap. pp. 223. 224. 227.

ing the Scriptures in the most licentious manner, which proved exceedingly pernicious to the interests of true religion. His symbolic views were auxiliary to his own mutilation. He advocated strongly the new system of education, and though many of the pious opposed it, from their convictions of its pernicious consequences on the minds of ministers, yet Origen's influence prevailed, and Platonism and Christianity triumphed!

Origen's views of believers' baptism we have detailed. The genuine Greek works of this writer contain nothing in favour of infant baptism, but on the contrary, baptism is always spoken of in relation to the adult. The Latin pieces of this Father do speak of infant baptism,[7] but they are proved by Dr. Gale to be spurious parts.[8]

11. CYPRIAN, a high churchman, and a paragon to clergymen of every age, was born at Carthage.

246

In 246 he entered on a Christian profession, and united himself to the dominant church in that city. Robinson says, he was an ignorant fanatic, and as great a tyrant as ever lived. His affluence was considerable, and probably from his largesses, and benevolent distribution of property, he was chosen two years

---

[7] Dr. Wall quotes the following to prove the *uninterrupted* practice of infant baptism. Origen is made to say, " Having occasion given in this place, I will mention a thing, *that causes frequent inquiries among the brethren:* Infants are baptized for the forgiveness of sins. Of what sins? or when have they sinned? None is free from pollution, though his life be the length of one day upon earth: and it is for that *reason,* because by the sacrament of baptism the pollution of this birth is taken away, that infants are baptized." Hist. pt. 1. p. 54. If this quotation was genuine, it would prove from the *frequent inquiries,* pædobaptism to have been a modern thing. But Origen's infants were not babes, but the boys and girls of the church school. See Rob. Res. p. 53, and authorities.   [8] Reflec. on Wall. Let. 13. pp. 417—19.

248 after to the bishopric. In this situation Cyprian described the generality of professors as "worldly minded, and greedy of gain. Luxury and effeminacy were very prevalent; profaneness was unrestrained. The intermarriages of Christians and heathens by no means rare. The most outrageous quarrels and disputes were carried on among them with bitter and malignant acrimony. Even pastors were not only neglectful of their flocks, but entirely deserted them. Covetous, fraudulent, and usurious, they travelled through distant provinces in quest of pleasure and gain." Many of the clergy were unmarried, but, who, however, kept single sisters, or beloveds of singular beauty and in the prime of life, This abuse as well as all others mostly prevailed in Africa, and to the honour of Cyprian, he endeavoured to reform or remove these corrupt practices. But the subject was found too indelicate to unfold, and these *virgins* and *mothers* were too closely married to the religious establishments to be put asunder.[9] These proceeds of sinful practices were evidently the result of forty years' peace. During this time the emperor and governors had been tolerant in their measures, and as before observed, professors were found in almost every station under government. Cyprian's reforming measures were supported by the efforts and labours of Donatus; but from some cause a separation ensued, probably from the former's jealousy of a rival, consequently the beneficial services of Donatus do not appear.

[9] Dupin, Cyprian. Mosh. Hist. C. 3. p. 2. c. 2. § 4-6. Robins. Hist. Bap. 201. Morris' Biog. note. It is very natural to conclude that these *holy* fathers would make provision for their offspring in their respective churches; such no doubt was the case in the infant singers, infant readers, which were found in the churches of Africa at this period. Robins. Hist. Bap. pp. 171, 172, 178.

12. In the year 249, Decius ascended the throne. His edicts required all persons to embrace the pagan worship. The churches were unprepared for measures so severe. Apostacy or death were the only terms proposed; and to see these enforced, officers were especially appointed. The consequences were very serious to professors. Cities and towns were depopulated, hills and mountains swarmed with inhabitants. It is very evident that Africa abounded at this period with persons who professed the gospel. Fox says, Donatus fell a martyr, but Cyprian sequestered himself. This state of things lasted about two years, when Cyprian returned to Carthage. On resuming his charge and station in the church, he assumed considerable self-importance. He pleaded the cause of the clergy with more than ordinary zeal, exhibiting their claims and rights from different sources unknown before. Those who had apostatized during the "fiery and bloody trial" Cyprian considered had, by their conduct, renounced their previous faith and baptism; and that, as expressions of sorrow and re-conversion, they should again profess their repentance and faith, and be again baptized in order to re-enter the communion of the church. This act of re-baptizing separated the Roman and Carthaginian churches, and they in solemn assembly mutually anathematized each other. Cyprian's conduct and proceeding, not meeting the approbation of Novatus, he with others withdrew, and united with Novatian at Rome. How soon after his seceding from the church of Carthage, Novatus returned to that city, we know not; but it is evident the Novatianists, with the Montanists, had a church or churches in Cyprian's diocese.

13. It is stated that a country minister, named

257   Fides, wrote a letter to Cyprian in 257, to ascertain how soon after birth, children might be baptized? The existence of such a letter has been questioned[10]: and Jortin admits that some statements of Cyprian's are not to be credited,[1] and particularly since many of the Fathers of this age contradict themselves and each other.[2] But admitting all the circumstances to be correct, the inquiry proves that the subject was novel and the practice unestablished. Cyprian, not having any such practice in the church at Carthage, could not answer this letter: he consequently called together, in a private way, those brethren in the vicinity;[3] and to them he submitted the business. The characters of those pastors we have already exhibited from Cyprian's own lamentation, which is supported by Mosheim, who asserts, that " many of the sacred order, especially in Africa, consented to satisfy the desires of the people, by abstaining from the pleasures of a conjugal life, and endeavoured to do this in such a manner, as not to offer an entire violence to their own inclinations. For this purpose, they formed connexions with those women who had made vows of perpetual chastity; and it was an ordinary thing to admit one of these fair saints to the participation of his bed, but, still under the most solemn declarations, that nothing passed in this commerce that was contrary to the rules of chastity and virtue."[4] Credat Judæus Apella. Sixty-six bishops, without frocks or state pensions, as thus de-

[10] Rob. Hist. of Bap. 195.   [1] Daille's Use of the Fathers, b. 2. c. 2. reas. 2. p. 11.   [2] Remarks, &c. v. ii. b. 2. pt. 2. p. 77.   [3] These meetings could not be held publicly because of the jealousy and persecution of the emperors. Dupin. c. 3. v. i. p. 172. The council of *Sinuessa* in Africa, A. D. 303, was held in a grotto. Id. C. 4. v. ii. p. 240.   [4] Mosh. Hist. C. 3. pt. 2. c. 2. § 6.

scribed, were brought together, and " Agreed that the grace of God should be withheld from no son of man—that a child might be kissed with the kiss of Christian charity as a brother, *so soon as born*—that Elisha prayed to God, and stretched himself on the infant. That the eighth day was observed in the Jewish circumcision, was a type going before—which type ceased when the substance came. If sinners can have baptism, how much sooner infants, who being newly born, have no sin, save being descended from Adam. This, therefore, dear brother, was our opinion in this assembly that it is not for us to hinder any person from baptism and the grace of God, who is merciful and kind, and affectionate to all. Which rule as it holds for all; so we think it more especially to be observed in reference to infants and persons newly baptized," &c.[5]

14. Here infant baptism is entirely different from that proposed in the time of Tertullian. That was the baptism of little ones, who asked to be baptized; this, of new-born babes. That was supported and rejected by New Testament texts and arguments; this is grounded on, and defended, and regulated by Jewish law. That required the consent of sponsors; this mentions none. That was a joining them to the church; this is a dedicating of them to God.[6] This assembly made no reference to any command; the ministers allude to no example going before; if the custom had prevailed at Carthage, no assembly would have been required to answer the inquiries; and when the ministers decide, they only render an *opinion* which they call *their agreement*, nor do they support their opinion by reference to any of the previous Fathers, nor do their reasons agree with those fostered on Origen a few years before. The views of

---

[5] Wall's Hist. C. 3. pt. 2. c. 2. § 6.   [6] Rob. Hist. of Bap. p. 198.

these ministers imply that, in withholding baptism, the grace of God would not be conferred on the sons of men; a sufficient evidence of their degeneracy. While the churches remained independent of each other, this association of ministers could only give an opinion, and recommend the practice; but any part of the assembly was at perfect liberty, at any time, to depart or abstain from the recommendation. "It does not appear," says Robinson, "that infants were baptized at Carthage, or any where else, except in the country where Fidus lived. An opinion of council, that Fidus ought to baptize infants, is very far from proving that the advisers did so, who were in different circumstances."[7] Mr. R. Baxter acknowledges "that Tertullian, Origen, and Cyprian, do all of them affirm that, in primitive times, none were baptized without an express covenanting, wherein they renounced the world, the flesh, and the devil, and engaged themselves to Christ, and promised to obey him."[8] This concession of Mr. Baxter is supported by history, and proves Cyprian and his colleagues to have been the first supporters of infant baptism. An eye-witness says of these Africans, "in spite of their vain boast of orthodoxy, they were pagans and blasphemers, who worshipped idols in secret, and dedicated their children in their infancy to demons."[9] They were

[7] Rob. Bap. p. 199.   [8] Danver's Hist. p. 63.   [9] It is a fact that infant dedication to God by baptism, was first heard of in Africa. A mistaken charity probably first suggested infant baptism. Fides, the inquirer, lived among barbarians who sacrificed children to their gods. Tertullian complained of this custom, and it was long before the Africans left it off. The bible taught Fides how the Jews dedicated children to God, and it was very desirable to rescue children from the fire and dedicate them to Christ. Reeve's Apologies of the Fathers, v. 2, § 30, p. 148. Rob. Bap. p. 199. In the services of the church, youths were employed in Africa. Now, if the fixed time of their admission

more wicked in morals than the pagan Romans had ever been; there was no crime they did not practise."[10] The rules of discipline adopted in general assemblies of ministers, for restraining the clergy, exhibit an awful picture of lewdness. Yet to these men infant baptism is traced, and the persons among whom the practice afterward flourished were men whose mental characters and pretensions in religion were far below zero in the Christian thermometer.[1]

275 15. Africa, towards the close of this century, presents nothing of a lovely feature. We should have refrained detailing such protuberances of corruption, had not the sources of infant baptism been assiduously and logically kept from inquirers. So far from the practice of pædobaptism prevailing, there is no evidence of its existence, after the opinions of these sixty-six bishops were given. One hundred years after, complaints were common, that the tender mothers could not be prevailed with to put their children into the water at baptism.[2] The fact is allowed, that youths were admitted into the old African churches, on repeating a creed, and these were employed in *singing* and *reading;* but "no one," says Wall, "could hold office, or devote himself to the service of the church, who was not baptized."[3] It is also equally evident that minors' baptism, with infant baptism, was first heard of in Africa.[4] But as to

---

could be the eighth day, instead of the eighth year, Fides hoped to rescue babes from the service of idols. For this early date he sought advice. "This view is supported," says Robinson, "by the writings of Tertullian, Cyprian, Victor, Optatus, Arnobius, Minucius," &c. Bap. pp. 185—195. [10] Rob. Hist. of Bap. c. 22, p. 183. [1] Vossius De Baptismo, Disp. 1, c. 6, 7, 8, and Bap. Mag. v. i. p. 435. Dupin, Council of Elvira. [2] Wall's Hist. pt. 1, c. 10, p. 111. [3] Hist. pt. 1, c. 17, p. 256. [4] Rob. Bap. p. 449.

the practice of pædobaptism at the end of this third century, we shall here subjoin testimonies that cannot be refuted.

16. The Magdeburgh Centuriators say, "Concerning the African churches, great corruption did prevail respecting the ordinance of baptism, at least in opinion, both as to the subject, time, manner, and ceremonies, *though as to practice,* they could not give any particular instance."[5] "None," says Mosheim, "were now admitted to baptism, until by menacing and formidable shouts and declamations of the exorcists, they had been delivered from the dominion of the Prince of darkness, and consecrated to the service of God."[6] Gibbon says, "the severity of ancient bishops exacted from the new converts a novitiate of two or three years."[7] See references above, ch. i. s. 3, § 6, 7.

17. The importance attached to baptism, in this century, led corrupt bishops to consider the case and situation of those who were in prison on account of religion, and who at the same time expressed their anxiety to be perfected in the Christian character by the ordinance. Penitents on their dying couches also desired the waters of salvation, with those catechumens who, viewing the ordinance as conveying purity, had deferred baptism till sickness prevented immersion. Such persons in these circumstances were accommodated, as in the case of Lawrence, who poured a pitcher of water on a soldier in prison. This mode of proceeding in case of necessity, and the trifling importance as to the *quantity of water* under such circumstances, is argued by Cyprian.[8] Pouring as a substitute for baptism, and afterwards its

---

[5] Cent. 3, in Danver's, p. 62.   [6] Hist. of the Ch. cent. 3, p. 2, c. 4, § 4.   [7] Ro. Hist. c. 20.   [8] Wall's Hist. pt. 2, c. 9, § 2, p. 354.

copartner, sprinkling, appear to have been invented in Africa, particularly the latter; though the most depraved catholic owned it to be no baptism, and cases are on record of those who could hold no office in the church until they had been immersed, though they had received baptism by aspersion in sickness.[9]

18. Persons, professing the Christian religion, and who never stood connected with the Carthaginian church, abounded throughout Africa. The sects or denominations were very many, though the African interest over which Cyprian presided, has claimed most of the attention of historians from furnishing the readiest materials. Its assumed authority, its spiritual tyranny, and its excessive corruptions, stand prominent on the records of those times. Among the denominations of that day may be named, the Bardesanes, Basilides, Valentinians, Ophites, Monarchians, Patropassians, Hieracites, Sabellians: these, with others, appear to have originated in Africa. Perhaps the most numerous sect were the Manicheans, who appear to have abounded in this province. There were some churches of the Montanists and the Novatianists in this quarter, but as to their extent or influence we are ignorant. These African dissidents, if we may so call them, present fulness and variety. They were found in every degree of distance from the ruling party, by whom they were all termed heretics, and by whom they were *all* persecuted without regarding their proximity or remoteness of faith; so that it is apparent their hatred arose, not from heresy, but from the quintessence of their dissent, *the love of religious liberty*, the UPAS TREE to all religious hierarchies. See Rob. Hist. of Bap. c. 22, and Mosh. Eccl. Hist. cent. 2, p. 2, c. 5.

[9] Wall, ib.

Section III.

AFRICAN CHURCHES CONTINUED.

" Wherefore come out from among them, and be ye separate, saith the Lord, and I will receive you."—*2 Cor.* vi. 17.

300 1. At the commencement of the fourth century, distinct and separate bodies of professed Christians continued to exist throughout the Roman empire. Each church had an elder to preside, while in every province one bishop was invested with a superiority over others, in point of rank and authority. The ancient method of church government seemed, in general, still to subsist, while at the same time, by imperceptible steps, it varied from the primitive rule, and degenerated towards the form of a religious monarchy. This change in church affairs, which commenced last century, was followed by a train of vices which dishonour the character of those who presided over ecclesiastical affairs.[1] **303** In 303, Diocletian, the emperor, after repeated importunities from the pagan priests and others, who were alarmed at the increase of Christians, and the dangers attending their ancient superstition; issued an edict, requiring the Scriptures to be given up to his officers. A fire breaking out in the palace was charged upon Christians, which excited the emperor to severe measures. All bishops were now imprisoned. The third edict encouraged tortures, and every diabolical means were used in order to bring Christians over to sacrifice to the gods. Afflictions disgracefully sinful were inflicted, which cannot de-

---

[1] Mosh, Ec. Hist. v. i. p. 193. c. 2.

cently be explained. Africa is said by Eusebius[2] to have produced vast numbers of martyrs.

The diligence and zeal of the Roman magistrates, in executing these edicts, had liked to have proved fatal to the Christian interest. In 306 Constantine, born in Britain, was saluted emperor, and in 311, Galerius published an edict, ordering all persecution to cease, which was confirmed by Constantine, who in 313 granted a toleration to all persons professing Christianity.

306 to 311

2. On peace being realized in 311, the members, presbyters, and others, in the Carthaginian church, made choice of a pastor to preside over that interest. This business was managed without calling together the various members of the community, and a serious rupture ensued.[3] One objection raised against Cecilian, the new bishop, was, that during the persecution he had delivered the holy Scriptures to the officers of Diocletian. One Donatus took a prominent station in opposition to the choice of the church, and many persons supported his views. "By his superior abilities and virtues," says Gibbon,[4] " he was the firmest supporter of his party." This controversy, in a short time, spread far and wide, not only throughout Numidia, says Mosheim, but even throughout all the provinces of Africa, which entered so zealously into this ecclesiastical war, that in most cities there were two bishops, one at the head of the catholic party, and the other presiding over the Donatists.[5] The churches of the latter amounted to four hundred.[6]

3. These seceders or dissenters in Africa, were called

---

[2] Ec. Hist. lib. 8. cap. 1—10. [3] Claude's Def. of the Reform, v. ii. p. 3. c. 4. [4] Ro. Hist. c. 21. [5] Ec. Hist. C. 4. c. 5. § 2. [6] Rob. Hist. of Bap. p. 213.

Donatists, from the name of their reformer, though by some they were called *Montenses*. The Donatists did not differ from the catholics in doctrine,[7] but in morals, and they seceded on the grounds of discipline from that community.[8] They held with the doctrines of election and reprobation, says Long.[9] The Donatists maintained that THE CHURCH ought to be made up of just and holy men, or at least of those who are such in appearance; and that although wicked men might lurk in the church, yet it would not harbour those who were known to be such.[10] They were zealous in requiring penitence of all those who united with them, and the narrow and solitary way, observes Gibbon, which their first leaders marked out, continued to deviate from the great society of mankind.[1] They thought the church ought to be kept separate from the world, a religious society voluntarily congregated together for pious purposes. With this view they admitted none to fellowship without a personal profession of faith and holiness; and them they baptized.[2] They baptized converts from paganism, and they re-baptized all those persons who came over to their fellowship from other communities;[3] they were very careful to remove from their places of worship every thing that bore any resemblance to worldly communities.[4] While the catholics, under Constantine, were ornamenting their sanctuaries, so as to resemble heathen temples, the Donatists' zeal prompted them to clear the walls and floors of their places of worship of all vestiges of the ancient superstition. The regard which they paid to

---

[7] Camp. Ec. Lect. p. 240. [8] History of the Donatists, p. 60. [9] Claude, Robinson; Jones' Lect. v. i. p. 472. [10] Dupin's Ch. Hist. C. 4. c. 3. [1] Ro. Hist. c. 21. [2] Rob. Hist. of Bap. p. 215. [3] Mosheim, ib. [4] Gibbon's Ro. Hist. c. 21.

purity of communion, occasioned their being stigmatized with the term *Puritans*.⁵

4. The Donatists and Novatianists very nearly resembled each other in doctrines and discipline;⁶ indeed they are charged by Crispin, a French historian, with holding together in the following things, *First*, For purity of church members, by asserting that none ought to be admitted into the church but such as are visibly true believers and real saints; *Secondly*, For purity of church discipline; *Thirdly*, For the independency of each church; and, *Fourthly*, They baptized again those whose first baptism they had reason to doubt.⁷ They were consequently termed Re-baptizers, and Anabaptists.⁸ Osiander says, our modern anabaptists were the same with the Donatists of old.⁹ Fuller, the English church historian, asserts, that the Baptists in England, in his days, were the Donatists new dipped:¹⁰ and Robinson declares, they were Trinitarian Anabaptists.¹

5. The disputes between the Donatists and Catholics were at their height, when Constantine became fully invested with imperial power: A. D. 314.² The catholic party solicited the services of the emperor, who, in answer, appointed commissions to hear both sides, but this measure not giving satisfaction, he even condescended to hear the parties himself; but his best exertions could not effect a reconciliation. The interested part that Constantine took in the dispute, led the Donatists to inquire, *What has the empe-*

314

---

⁵ Jones, ubi sup.   ⁶ Id. v. i. 472.   ⁷ Danver's Treat. p. 272.   ⁸ Baronius' Ann. see above ch. 2. sect. 1st. § 5. note 9. references.   ⁹ Danvers, ib.   ¹⁰ Idem.   ¹ Hist. of Bap. p. 216.   ² About this period Arius arose in Africa; the star called Wormwood fell and embittered the waters of the sanctuary to a great extent, nor are they fully sweetened yet.

ror to do with the church? *What have Christians to do with kings?* or *What have bishops to do at court?* Constantine, finding his authority questioned and even set at nought by the dissidents, listened to the advice of his bishops and court, and deprived the Donatists of their

320 churches. This persecution was the first which realized the support of a Christian emperor, and Constantine went so far as to put some of the Donatists to death. The Circumcellians, men of no religion, saw these dissidents oppressed, and from sympathy, and a love to native freedom, actually took up arms in their defence.[3] Every thing now combined to disturb the peace of the province, to prevent which the emperor found it necessary to abrogate those laws he had previously made against the Donatists. His superstitious regard to the rites of the church, and the Catholic clergy, increased as he declined in life, and consequently through their influence he issued, in 330, his edict against all Dissidents and Seceders from

337 the orthodox cause. These views and measures he supported till 337, when death terminated his career. The ensuing emperors were influ-

348 enced generally by the stipendiary bishops, consequently chequered circumstances attended dissenters. In 362 Julian permitted the exiled Donatists

362 to return and enjoy the sweets of liberty, which revived the denomination, and by their zealous and unceasing efforts, brought over, in a short time, the greatest part of the African provinces to espouse their interest. From various sources of information, it is most evident that the Donatists were a most powerful

---

[3] This conduct of these men is always represented to the disparagement of the Donatists, but later records of Protestants leave the Donatists with credit in this defensive war.

and numerous body of dissenters,⁴ almost as numerous as the catholics, which, considering the strictness of their discipline, and their close adherence to the laws of Zion, is a subject of pleasing reflection. Their influence must have been considerable, since as Mr. Jones remarks, " There was scarce a city or town in Africa in which there was not a Donatist church."⁵

370   6. OPTATUS, Bishop of Mela, or Milevi, a city of Numidia, wrote a book against the Donatist separation, addressed principally to Parmenianus, a minister of that persuasion. In this book he charges the Donatists with removing sacred things out of those places of worship, which came into their possession from other denominations; with washing the walls of such sanctuaries; and thinking themselves more holy than others. He charges them with re-baptizing catholics as if they were heathens; and asserts, in opposition to the views held by the Donatists, that " all men that come into the world, though they be born of Christian parents, are filled with an unclean spirit, *which must be driven away by baptism.* This is done *by the exorcism*, which drives away the spirit, and makes it fly into remote places. After this the heart of man becomes a most pure habitation, God enters and dwells there; when therefore you re-baptize men, you drive out God from his habitation, and the devil re-enters." He does not charge them with unsoundness in the faith, but declares, " All Christians have one faith and one creed." Speaking of the persecution they experienced, he considered the justice of God sent it upon the Donatists to revenge the dishonour they had done to the waters of baptism. Their success in proselyting catholics oc-

⁴ Mosheim's Ec. Hist. ubi supra.   ⁵ Ecc. Lect. v. i. p. 474.

casioned Optatus to call them thieves and heretics.⁶ To make baptism valid, he says, three things are necessary, The Trinity, the faith of him that receives it, the faithfulness of the minister; and then there is no occasion of re-baptizing. He argues, that the faith of him who receives baptism, is necessary to the validity of the sacrament. This view of exorcising the candidate proves Optatus to have been ignorant of modern pædobaptism.⁷

377 7. In 377, the emperor Gratian, influenced probably by the catholic party, who envied the growing prosperity of the Donatists, deprived them of their churches, and prohibited all their assemblies, public and private; but their number and influence prevented the edict being fully executed. At some period during this century, and very probably while under suppressing edicts in Africa, the doctrines and discipline of the Donatists were established in Spain and Italy; but their influence in other kingdoms bore no comparison to their numbers, importance, and operations in their native province. These people maintained their popularity through the century, and continued formidable to their enemies through the ensuing age, but afterwards we shall trace them declining in credit and numbers. Two circumstances combining about the end of this century, operated prejudicially to their interests; the one was a division among themselves, about a man named Maximin, which discord was very considerably adjuvated by the catholics, in order to weaken their energies and importance; the other was,

387 the rise, credit, efforts, and influence of Augustin, bishop of Hippo, with the court of Rome.⁸

⁶ Rob. Hist. of Bap. p. 189. ⁷ Dupin's Ch. Hist. C. 4. v. ii. pp. 87—96. Optatus. ⁸ Mosh. Hist. C. 4, p. 2. c. 5. § 6.

8. AUGUSTIN was born at Thagaste in Numidia (Algiers) A. D. 354, of Christian parents. He was not baptized in infancy. His early life was dissolute, from which conduct he had been unfavourably represented by various writers.[9] His change of views on religion took place while he was under Ambrose's ministry at Milan, by whom he was first baptized. It is probable that Augustin imbibed from the Milanese bishop, the spirit of usurpation and tyranny so prominent in his proceedings. Some parts of this Father's works are excellent, the reading of which will convince any Christian, that he was well acquainted with the innate depravity of the heart. Soon after his baptism he gave up his profession, and returned to Africa, where he was again baptized by Valerius, bishop of Hippo. Here he rose to eminence in the church, and contended with four classes of dissidents from various motives. The Arians he disputed with on the doctrine of the Trinity: the Pelagians, on the points of original sin, and the ingenite state and power of *the human will* to spiritual duties:[10] the Manicheans, on the origin of virtue and vice, with the Donatists on the ceremonies of the

---

[9] There is an obscurity about Augustin's motives and conduct, which is at variance with Christianity; virtues and vices to the extreme have been attached to him. See Dupin's and Mosheim's Histories, with Bayle's Dictionary, and Robins. Hist. of Bap. ch. 23.   [10] The advocates of Pelagianism, say, that Augustin first discovered and propagated those sentiments since termed Calvinistic, but this is an error. The early writers expressed themselves equally decisive on election, predestination, &c. with Austin, though not so frequently; and it is equally evident, that the early churches held his views. The ministers of religion had, for about two centuries, been more engaged in adjusting the new philosophy and arranging ceremonies, than in discussing the doctrines of grace: but the views of Pelagius, when made known, awakened all the native energies of Austin's mind. Pelagius, in con-

church and the expediency of infant baptism. It is probable that Augustin, in the heat of controversy expressed himself on different subjects more energetically than he would have done in the absence of exciting causes. Innocent of Rome, Ambrose of Milan, Augustin of Hippo, with others, had united their influence in supporting the catholic church, and these bishops in 390 received the sanction of the emperor Honorius, in establishing superstitious rites against the zeal and efforts of many pious and judicious Christians.[1] This union of secular and spiritual power operated alike on all dissidents. In 398 a council of bishops at Carthage petitioned the emperor for the removal of all heathen temples, and the destruction of all images, which was granted. In 399 the temples were razed, and Christianity was said to be much extended.[2] This combination was prejudicial to the Donatists, whose churches were numerous in this province " and which were served by no less than four hundred bishops."[3]

9. The Donatists had hitherto maintained themselves in reputation, and their affairs were in a good state. The catholics having Augustin as their head, with other zealous adjutors, exerted every means for their suppression; but finding their preaching and writing effect very little alteration; they, in 404, sent a deputation to the emperor Honorius, requesting him to enforce those edicts, made in previous reigns, against the Donatists. The emperor first imposed a fine on all those who refused to return into the bosom

---

ference, found all the valuable learning and authority of previous ages against him, which no doubt regulated him in abjuring his error. See Dupin's Lives and Works of the Fathers. Cave's ditto. Daille's Use of the Fathers. Toplady's Hist. Proof. Gill's Cause of God and Truth.   [1] Mosh. Hist. C. 4. § 22.   [2] Baronius Ann. C. 4. c. 9. A.D. 399.   [3] Mosh. Hist. C. 4. § 7.

405 of the church, banishing the pastors of the refractory. The year following, severe measures were adopted, but the magistrates were remiss in their execution. This occasioned a council at Carthage, which sent a deputation to the emperor, soliciting the appointment of special officers to execute his edicts with vigour. Though weakened by these severe measures, the dissidents were yet considerable.

408 In 408, after Stilicho, the general, had been put to death, they increased in strength, and in the ensuing year, they had accessions to their interests, **409** when from their rising importance the emperor granted a law in favour of religious liberty; but the united exertions of catholics occasioned the abrogation of this law the following year. Tired with the **410** appeals of these contending parties, the emperor sent a tribune with full power to conclude the unhappy contest. Consequently a public meeting was called, and as Lardner says, "a famous conference **411** was held at Carthage in 411."[4] In this celebrated synod, the number of ministers from the different churches, in both denominations, was found to be nearly equal; though some ministers of the dissenting party were unavoidably absent.[5] The catholics numbered two hundred and eighty-six, and the Donatists, two hundred and seventy-nine. The defeat of the dissidents is not attributed to the Catholics' majority, but principally to Augustin's influence at court and his writings. The defeated Donatists appealed to the emperor, but without attaining any beneficial result.[6]

412 10. In 412 Cyril was ordained bishop of Alexandria. One of his first acts was to shut

---

[4] Lardner's Cred. of the Gospel Hist., vol. iv. pt. 2. c. 67. p. 96.   [5] Ibidem.   [6] Mosheim's Ec. Hist. C. 5. p 2. ch. 5.

up all the churches of the Novatianists, and strip them of every thing of value. Augustin, supported by a kindred spirit in Cyril, exercised all his influence, and consequently the edicts procured against the Donatists, were now of a more sanguinary character. The Catholics found by experience, that the means hitherto used had been ineffectual against the Donatists; they now prevailed on Honorius, and Theodosius, emperors of the east and west to issue an edict, decreeing, *That the person re-baptizing, and the person re-baptized, should be punished with death.* In consequence of this cruel measure martyrdoms ensued. Gibbon remarks on these edicts, that " three hundred bishops, with many thousands of the inferior clergy, were torn from their churches, stripped of their ecclesiastical possessions, banished to the islands, proscribed by laws, if they presumed to conceal themselves in the provinces of Africa. Their numerous congregations, both in cities and the country, were deprived of the rights of citizens, and the exercise of religious worship. A regular scale of fines, from ten to two hundred pounds of silver, was curiously ascertained according to the distinctions of rank and fortune, to punish the crime of assisting at a schismatic conventicle; and if the fine had been levied five times, without subduing the obstinacy of the offender, his future punishment was referred to the discretion of the imperial court. By these severities, which obtained the warmest approbation of Augustin, great numbers were reconciled to the catholic church : but the fanatics (or faithful) who still persevered in their opposition, were provoked to madness and despair."7 Augustin owned, the city of Hippo had been full of conventicles, till he procured penal laws for their suppression. When

---

7 Ro. Hist. Ch. 33.

the Donatists reproached him with making martyrs of their bishop and elders, and told him God would require an account of their blood at the day of judgment; he replied, "I know nothing about your martyrs, martyrs! martyrs to the devil. There are no martyrs out of the church, beside, it was their obstinacy, they killed themselves."[8]

11. The Donatists rebaptized all persons coming from other professing communities; this conduct Augustin disapproved, and observes, "You (Donatists) say they are baptized in an impure church, by heretics; but the validity of the baptism depends upon God's authority, not on the goodness or sanctity of the person who officiates." Their objections to his infant baptism, he endeavours to answer, remarking, "Do you (Donatists) ask for divine authority in this matter?[9] though that which the whole church practises,[10] is very reasonably

---

[8] Robins. Hist. of Bap. c. 23. p. 215. [9] This question shows, that the Donatists required scriptural authority for their faith and practice in all the affairs of God's house. [10] Innocent fell in with this practice and infant communion, and after Zosimus, Boniface, in 418, was bishop of Rome. This Boniface inquires of Augustin, "Suppose I set before you an infant, and ask you whether, when he grows up, he will be a chaste man or a thief? Your answer, doubtless, will be, *I cannot tell.* And whether he, in that infant age, have any good or evil thoughts? you will say, *I know not.* Since you therefore dare not say any thing, either concerning his future behaviour, or his present thoughts; what is the meaning, that when they are brought to baptism, their parents, as sponsors for them, make answer and say, to the inquiry, Does he believe in God? they answer, *he does believe.* I entreat you to give me a short answer to these questions, in such a manner, as that you do not urge to me the prescription of the customariness of the thing, but give me the reason of the thing." Augustin felt the difficulty of giving a reason for his own custom, and subjoined a silly reply, gets angry, and concludes by saying, " I have given such an answer to your questions

believed to be no other than a thing delivered by the apostles,[1] yet we may take a true estimate, how much the sacrament of baptism does profit infants, by the circumcision which God's former people received."[2]

Augustin was requested by the Donatists to state "what good the sacrament of Christ's baptism does to infants?" He says in reply, "As to which matter it is piously and truly believed, that the faith of those by whom the child is presented, or offered to be consecrated, profits the child." But Austin does not say what advantage attends the child where the sponsors have no faith, as is so common in the present day. These inquiries from the dissidents of Africa, are similar to those often made by the Baptists of the present day, satisfactorily proving their denominational character. This assertion is further established by Mr. Long, who says, "though there were great feuds between the Donatists

---

as I suppose is to ignorant or contentious persons not enough, and to understanding and quiet people, perhaps more than enough." Again, "He that does not believe it [infant baptism], and thinks it cannot be done, is indeed an infidel." Wall's Hist. pt. 1. c. 15. p. 196. Note.—The questions and answers were the relics of believers' baptism, which when used about an infant, was a lie before God! If the church had always practised infant baptism, why so many inquiries from Donatists and Catholics in the *fifth century*? Augustin being required to answer so many questions, and explain its utility, proves how great a share he had in introducing the rite, and in his reply, he considers scripture and tradition on an equal footing in the church, while the catholic community is the only church.   [1] The first recorded inquiry respecting minor baptism was, "May youths be baptized so soon as they ask for the ordinance?" the second period of this rite stated, "Our opinion is that the grace of God should be withheld from no son of man;" Augustin insinuates apostolic authority, though the bishop of Rome requested information on the propriety and utility of the infant rite!!!   [2] Wall's Hist. pt. 1. p. 182—7.

and others, yet they were professed Anabaptists."³ " They did not only re-baptize the adults, that came over to them, but refused to baptize children, contrary to the practice of the catholic church."⁴ Though Austin confines the church to the catholic body, yet it must not be forgotten, that there were churches more or less extensive throughout Africa, besides the Donatists, and known as Manicheans, Montanists, Novatianists, and others, whose morals were far more excellent than even Saint Augustin's,⁵ but all these were heretics in his view, and objects of his most virulent animosity.

12. The difficulty of establishing infant baptism, even among the licentious clergy and people of Africa,⁶ suggested to Austin the expediency of calling together a number of his brethren, which he effected at Mela, in Numidia. Amidst *ninety-two* ministers, Augustin presided; he, with them in this assembly, since called a council, issued the following manifesto of their charity to dissidents, " *That it is* OUR WILL *that all that affirm that young children receive everlasting life, albeit they be not by the sacrament of grace or baptism* RENEWED; *and that will not that young children, which are newly born from their mother's womb, shall be baptized to the taking away original sin,* THAT THEY BE ANATHEMATIZED.⁷" Having attained eminency in the church, and the support of his brethren to enforce the doctrine of infant salvation from water baptism, another assembly of divines was convened the same year at

---

³ History of the Donatists, p. 60. ⁴ Id. p. 103. Ecbertus and Emericus, two catholic writers, assert the same, Danver's Hist. Bap. p. 272, &c. ⁵ Bayle and some French historians say he was a hard drinker. ⁶ Rules were made in every council at this period, to restrain the licentious clergy. ⁷ Mag. Cent., in Danver's Hist. pp. 118—9.

Carthage, to enforce the rite, and occasion its universality if possible. The council solemnly declared, "WE WILL *that whoever denies that little children by baptism are freed from perdition and eternally saved*, THAT THEY BE ACCURSED."[8] So little regarded were the proceedings of this first assembly, that disputes have existed as to its date; but Innocent, Bishop of Rome, havinge͞xpressed his concurrence to Augustin, a little before his dissolution, which took place in 417, we place the Milevitan council in the preceding year.[9] Believers' baptism has never borrowed a foreign aid for its support; it originated from heaven, John i. 33, and has been maintained to this day among the followers of the Lamb, by the same divine teaching and sustaining power; while every cruel and oppressive measure has been engaged to suppress the practice, and to substitute infant baptism and rhantism in its room. The establishment of this rite by these severe censures, in time, raised the catholic community into numerical importance, and by patronizing the infant cause, the bishop of Rome became a father (papa) to the church. His authority was allowed or disallowed by the adoption or rejection of this rite,[10]

---

[8] Danvers, ubi sup. This practice commenced as here, with a mistaken view as to children's condition. "Jesus himself did not baptize children, nor did he order his disciples to do it; nor would they have forbidden infants to be brought unto him, if they had known anything about infant baptism; *if while he declared infants to be of his kingdom*, if while he had such a fair opportunity of being explicit as to their baptism, and of setting an example of it, &c., we may learn, that infants may be acknowledged of Christ's kingdom, brought unto him, and obtain his blessing without being baptized."—M'Lean on Christ's Commission, p. 123.
[9] Ivimey's Hist. of the Bap. v. 1. p. 23. *note.* "The necessity of pædobaptism was never asserted in any council, till about the year 418." Episcopius and Limborch, in Gibbs on Bap. p. 129.
[10] Consequently the extension of the pure church and kingdom of

as in England, in 596, and among the Albigenses in 1178, which shall be fully shown. His advice was sought by Spanish bishops, respecting the mode of baptizing children, and he has devised or sanctioned means for sanctifying by water the fœtus and embryo in every stage. Every class of servants under his holiness, in the church and out, who received this *his mark*, from the crowned head to the lowest menial, has felt the pope's honour involved in the infant rite. Sequently they all have advocated, and enforced by fire and sword, the sanctifying ceremony in opposition to the Baptists in every age. Every national establishment, as a daughter or division of the Romish community, adopts the measure as the best palladium to its constitution. But to return from this digression; the instruction sought by many ministers from Augustin and Innocent, on church affairs, respecting this rite and other discipline,[1] the former's controversy with Petilianus, a pastor among the Donatists on infant baptism, with his calling together and presiding in those assemblies which issued such decided measures—show Augustin to have been the active innovator, at the same time the difficulty he realized in imposing the ceremony on the Africans, proves the novelty of the thing. These features " point Augustin out as the first who ventured to attack at law, believers' baptism. The innovators went, therefore, on the forlorn hope, and a plain tale puts them down. They did not pretend to ground infant baptism on Scripture, but tradition; and as they could not cite a law, human or divine, they ventured to place it on universal custom."[2] Yet strange as it may appear, that which

Jesus Christ, can be traced *only* where this rite and all human ceremonies are repudiated, and where the law of Zion alone regulates.   [1] Dupin's Ecc. Hist. C. 5, v. iii. pp. 195—8.   [2] Rob. Hist. of Bap. p. 281.

was said to be a universal custom, required the penalty of damnation to enforce!!! How sadly does the Carthaginian curse descend on the heads of Austin's successors in practice, who hold his rite, but who deny his doctrine!³

13. The laws, edicts, and canons were more or less oppressive to the dissidents for twenty-eight years. The invasion of the Vandals in 428 relieved the oppressed from the scourge of licentious bishops and a cruel court. These invaders entered Africa from Spain; many who followed the army were protected by them in full liberty, under the ancient name of Goths, Gothmen, or Goodmen. The Vandals, like other German tribes, had no king, no priest, and consequently were the avowed friends of liberty.⁴ The Donatists' situation and circumstances became ameliorated under this new dynasty, though they never regained their former extent, nor recovered their early popularity and vigour. For one hundred years, Africa was governed by people called barbarians, yet their conduct was milder towards the followers of the Lamb and the Christian interest, than the Catholics had ever been. During this period, the

---

³ We have suggested that *pouring and sprinkling* originated in Africa. Augustin says, a complete harmony of sentiment existed between him and a young man, his companion; the young man was taken ill, and became insensible; Augustin, fearing his death, baptized him (by pouring) while in an *insensible state*; on the young man's partial restoration, he was told what had been done during his stupor; he listened with horror, and treated Augustin as his greatest enemy, Facts, &c., p. 32. Had no undue importance been attached to the rite, or had the custom been familiar in such cases, no such excitement of horror would have been realized; but the novel view of its sanctity regulated the saint in giving, and the sinner as to the consequence of sinning after, the administration.   ⁴ Robinson's Ecc. Research. ch. 7, p. 106.

Vandals allowed the Donatists to enjoy the sweets of civil and religious freedom, which, probably, did not really conduce to their spiritual prosperity; but when **534** the empire of the Vandals was overturned, in 534, the privileges of religious freedom ceased to the Donatists, with the government of these barbarians.

The Donatists still, however, remained a separate body, possessed their churches, and defended themselves from the reproach of their enemies. They industriously tried every means to resuscitate their interests; **591** but the hostility of the rising pope, Gregory, operated considerably on society, to their prejudice. This pope wrote to two African bishops, requiring them to exert themselves in every possible way, to suppress the Donatists. Marked out for vengeance, and realizing opposition and persecution in every form, they disappeared. It is presumed these people, "of whom **604** the world was not worthy," emigrated to Spain and Italy, or mingled with the pagans in the interior, and worshipped the Redeemer as opportunities offered. From their conduct in assembling in caves and dens of mountains to worship, they obtained the name of Montenses, i. e., mountaineers.[5] In the seventh century, the Donatists dwindled away almost into ob- **750** scurity, but about the middle of the eighth century, the gospel light was quite extinguished in Africa; and, as Gibbon observes, it never after enlightened any territory, nor can it be considered as having any extensive existence in the present day.[6]

---

[5] Idem, p. 112. In Abyssinia and Africa, immersion is now practised.—Millar's Geo., v. i. pp. 356 and 367.   [6] Ro. Hist. ch. 51. See Dupin, *Donatus and Optatus*. Mosh. Ecc. Hist. Hist. of the Donatists, by Mr. T. Long, Prebendary of St. Peter's,

14. To review the history of such a people, so correct in morals, simple in spiritual worship, scriptural in faith and practice, for the period of above four centuries, is a pleasing employment. The continued preservation which the Donatists realized amidst trials the most formidable from crowned and mitred heads, is a satisfactory proof of their character, as forming part of that church against which the gates of hell shall never successfully prevail. We cannot help realizing a sacred respect for the memories of this body of people, whose religious profession and views were so nearly allied to our own; and some feelings of pleasure may be lawfully indulged at the remembrance of being their legitimate successors.

Section IV.

Oriental Churches.

"Beware lest any man spoil you through philosophy and vain deceit, after the tradition of men, after the rudiments of the world," &c.—*Col.* ii. 8.

1. By the oriental churches are intended those communities of Christians formed by the apostles and their successors, in those parts of Asia situated in the Levant, or east of Italy. It appears probable that the gospel was preached in Idumea, Syria, and Mesopotamia, by Jude; in Pontus, Galatia, and the neighbouring parts of Asia,

---

Exon. Claude's Defence of the Reform. v. i. part 8, ch. 4. Lardner's Works, v. iv. p. 2, c. 67, pp. 91—103. Mr. W. Jones's Lect. on Ecc. Hist. lect. 25.

by Peter; in the territories of the seven Asiatic churches, by John; in Parthia, by Matthew; in Scythia, by Philip and Andrew; in the northern and western parts of Asia, by Bartholomew; in Persia, by Simon and Jude; in Media, Carmania, and several eastern parts, by Thomas; from Jerusalem to Illyricum, by Paul, as also in Italy. In most of which places Christian churches were planted in less than thirty years after Christ, and ten before the destruction of Jerusalem.[1]

34 2. These worthy men, scattered as they were on Stephen's death, went everywhere preaching the word. They disseminated the celestial seed in all the provinces and cities through which they passed. Many Christian societies were gathered and formed by them, all bearing a striking resemblance to the parent institution,[2] which original society was composed of those only " who gladly received the word and were baptized," Acts ii. 41.[3] The doctrines and discipline of these communities very soon awakened the enmity of Jews and Gentiles to the followers of the Lamb. Nero, who

64 it is said was, at the commencement of his reign, favourable to Christianity, changed his line of policy, and was the first emperor to enact laws against the disciples of Jesus. Among the martyrs at

---

[1] A. Young on Idolatry, v. ii. pp. 215—34. [2] Mosh. Hist. Cent. 1, pt. 1, c. 4, § 5. [3] The word BAPTIZE is purely Greek, and the orientals are supposed to understand its meaning. Its import can be decided by the practice of the Greeks, which practice ever has been *to dip.* Dr. King's Rites of the Gr. Ch. Office, Bap., Rob. Res. p. 91. Immersion in the East could be easily performed, since each house has a bagnio, which consists generally of two or three rooms, leading to the top room or bath, paved with marble, &c., and possessing every conveniency for bathing, Rob. Res. c. 9. Adam's Antiq. p. 378. Potter's Greece, b. 1, c. 8. Horne's Crit. Intro. to the Scrip, v. iii. pt. 4, c. 6, § 3. See above, ch. 1, s. 1, § 17, and references there.

this period, are enumerated Peter and Paul. His cruel example was followed by Domitian in this century, and others at after periods, who, without examining the claims of Christianity, indulged their prejudices against the followers of its dictates. The number of martyrs in the first ages was very great, which is allowed by all impartial historians.[4]

3. Errors more or less pernicious to the welfare of souls, crept into the churches during the apostles' ministry. It was in the oriental churches where almost all the disputes on doctrine arose.[5] A disposition prevailed in this quarter, to accommodate the two dispensations, and, by blending baptism with circumcision, to secure a more extensive community, while the honour of each dispensation should remain unabated. The question being important, the elders and brethren at Jerusalem, on hearing the circumstance, decided very solemnly, that if any were circumcised, Christ would profit them nothing, and thus a glorious liberty was secured to the Christian converts.[6] The same class of disputants ob-

---

[4] Mosh. Hist. C. 1, pt. 1, c. 5. [5] Camp. Lect. 14, p. 240.
[6] See Acts xv. It is very remarkable in this discussion, that no allusion was made to baptism as succeeding the place of circumcision; this proves the two economies to be distinct in their subjects, the one from the other: and so must the first adopters have viewed them, or they would not have continued for years to practise *both* circumcision and baptism, *if one was understood as superseding the other.* Those who ground their practice of infant baptism, on circumcision *prefiguring* baptism, should act consistently; and as circumcision was administered universally throughout the land of Canaan, baptism should be administered universally (i. e., to children, servants, and slaves) in England or any country where the gospel is preached. Only males were circumcised—only males should be baptized. Faith, neither personal nor relative, was a condition of circumcision; faith, as a pre-requisite to baptism, should not be required either in the child or in the parent. All

scured the way of a sinner's acceptance before God, which called forth the epistles to Galatia and Rome, wherein a sinner's justification without the deeds of the law, is admirably argued. But

51 and 57

children who were circumcised, partook of the passover; all children who are baptized, should receive the Lord's Supper. All children who were circumcised were thenceforth considered members of the Jewish church, and without any subsequent conversion or profession of faith, were entitled to all its privileges; all children who are baptized should be received as members of the visible church of Christ, and have a right to *its* privileges, independent of any work of grace or profession of faith, in their future lives; but in this consistency the pædobaptists fail. See Gibbs on Bap.

The covenant of grace and circumcision is said, by early and late pædobaptists, to be *the same*, and upon this identity they ground their strong reasons for infant baptism; if this ground can be proved untenable, by showing a distinction in these covenants, their last refuge is destroyed. Now it is very evident these two covenants were distinct economies, for the following reasons:—

1. The covenant of grace is God's eternal purpose to save from wrath, Eph. iii. 11, and many saints were saved by it, Heb. xi. 1—7; before the covenant of circumcision was revealed, which covenant rite was not known till A. M. 2106, and when Abraham was 99 years old, Gen. xvii. 24.

2. The covenant of grace was preached to Abram, Gal. iii. 8, when he was 75 years old, Gen. xii. 1, so that he was in the enjoyment of its promises twenty-four years before he heard of circumcision, Gen. xvii. 10.

3. The covenant of grace includes all believers, and these, of all nations through time; while the other covenant excluded all pious Gentiles, with females of every age, yet comprehended all those of Abraham's household, though those were, like Esau, reprobate as concerning the election of grace, Isa. i. 9.

4. The covenant of grace is God's free mercy, revealed and promised through Christ, to the worthless, Rom. iii. 24; but circumcision made the whole law obligatory on the receiver, Rom. ii. 25, and was opposed to the blessings promised in the covenant of grace, Gal. v. 2, 3, 4.

the great evil to the Christian cause was its coalition with the science styled by its advocates, *gnonis*, or *the way to the true knowledge of the Deity.* " The Greeks," says Campbell, "were always keen disputants, and it was by them that most of the first heresies were broached. Their condition, early habits, natural character, with their copious and ductile language, conspired to inure them to disputations. Hence, sprang those numerous sects into which the Christian community was so early divided."[7] So that it becomes exceedingly evident that the Grecian atmosphere was congenial to native freedom and nonconformity, and when spiritual claims were made by one party, dissensions ensued — nonconformists, who had *always* been dispersed all over the empire, maintained their original claim in religion to think and act for themselves. Here we trace the rising class, who adhered to THE TRUTH through ages of ignorance, superstition, and vice ; " as it seems clear," observes Robinson, " that Greece was the *parent*, Spain and Navarre the *nurses*, France the *step-*

---

5. The covenant of grace embraced *not* the children of the flesh, Rom. ix. 6—8 ; but the other covenant included all Abraham's *fleshly* offspring, Gen. xvii. 12, &c.

6. The ordinance of the covenant of grace was refused by John to those persons who were in possession of the privileges of Abraham's covenant, Matt. iii. 9.

7. The covenant of circumcision was to have an end, Zech. xi. 10, Heb. viii. 8. But the covenant of grace was eternal, Jer. xxxii. 40, Heb. viii. 13.

8. If these covenants be the same, Christ and Abraham are heads of it ; two beginnings are shown to one compact. Different terms of admission or introduction are pointed out, Gal. v. 3, and Heb. viii. 10. Different periods of duration are shown, Heb. viii. 8, and Isa. lv. 3. Consequently, these covenants cannot be one ; and, therefore, infant baptism receives no support from this source.— See M'Lean on Abra. Cov.   [7] Camp. ubi sup.

mother, and Savoy the *jailer* of this class of Christians known afterwards by the name of WALDENSES." But, amidst all the diversity of speculative opinions, they all agreed in administering baptism by immersion.[8]

₉₈ 4. When Trajan ascended the throne, the third general persecution was set on foot. The severity of his edicts was felt in Pontus and Bithynia, over which provinces the younger Pliny was governor. The profession of Christianity was so general in Asia, that the governor, in enforcing Trajan's measures against Christians, perceived that their extinction would nearly annihilate the inhabitants of his province. He acknowledged, in writing to the emperor, that the heathen temples were forsaken, yet he apprehended it inexpedient to search for Christians.[9] Trajan replied, by say-

₁₀₀ ing, they should not be sought for as heretofore, and those accused, and who felt disposed to accommodate themselves to the religion of the empire, or pagan customs, should be spared, but those who remained inflexible to their profession should be put to death.[10] Under this reign, females were tortured, to make them criminate each other, but while on the rack, they said, "We are Christians, and no evil is done among us." It was a regular custom, at this period, for Christians to meet together for divine worship, to sing hymns to Christ, who was worshipped as God almost throughout the East; to exhort one another to abstain from all evil, and to commemorate Christ's death; to observe the first day of the week, which was regarded by all Christians.[1] Yet Pliny calls these heavenly engagements, " a depraved superstition." Such views the most polished heathens

---

[8] Researches, pp. 73, 93, 320. [9] Epis. b. 10, let. 97 and 98. [10] Jones's Ecc. Lect. v. i. pp. 194—8. [1] Mosh. Hist. v. i. 91 and 109.

encouraged, respecting the doctrines of the cross and spiritual worship.

5. We have already mentioned Justin Martyr, for the sake of exhibiting his views on the ordinance. This early and learned writer of the eastern churches was born at Neapolis, the ancient Shechem of Palestine.

132

On his embracing Christianity, he quitted neither the profession nor the habit of a philosopher. He selected various and natural circumstances to impress the mind with the doctrine of the cross, which in a few ages aided in perverting the gospel altogether. In his dialogue he says, "the roasted lamb was made into the figure of a cross, by impaling or spitting it, from head to tail, and then from one shoulder to the other, with a skewer, on which last was extended the fore feet, and thus it was roasted." He wrote two apologies for his persecuted brethren, and fell a martyr to the cause he espoused, in A.D. 167.

167

What influence Justin's philosophic notions had at this period in aiding Plato's views, about a middle state after death, we know not, but it is certain such views were partially embraced by some persons in the Christian interest.[2] These views once embraced, led to decide on the subject *who* occupied this middle state, while others were

---

[2] Mosh. Ecc. Hist. c. 2, ch. 3, § 2, 3. The *sprinkling of water* is spoken of by several of the Fathers as purely heathenish. "Justin Martyr says, that it was an invention of demons, in imitation of the true baptism signified by the prophets, that their votaries might also have their pretended purifications by water." See Middleton's Letters from Rome on this subject, p. 139. Tertullian, in his book on baptism, says, "The heathens did adopt a religious rite, particularly in the mysteries of Apollo and Ceres, where persons were *baptized* for their *regeneration* and pardon of their perjuries." "Here we see," he says, "the aim of the devil, imitating the things of God." Wall's Hist. v. i. c. 4, p. 50.

anxious to know, " what became of those persons who died unbaptized?" This middle state and the answer to the inquiry were made to quadrate, and in the following centuries, Plato's intermediate state was by several able Fathers assigned to the unbaptized.[3]

6. In most of those Christian congregations planted by the apostles, a plurality of pastors was settled. To conduct their affairs with harmony and prudence, it was necessary they should often meet and consult together. These meetings, made up of pastors, deacons, and members, were properly a council of the congregation. Everything regarding worship and discipline was settled among themselves. When points were difficult or disputed, a more general company of ministers and disciples met, as the apostles had done at Jerusalem, to consult and promote love, truth, and unity. This course probably suggested to churches the propriety of a regular intercourse with one another. A stated meeting ensued of all the churches in the same canton or province, wherein they fully discussed church affairs.

170 From the confidence the church had in their ministers, when the distance was great, the affairs of the churches were intrusted to a deputation of elders and deacons with others. From these friendly meetings arose a sort of republic association of the churches in a particular province. The metropolis being the most centric, was usually the place of meeting. At first, the office of president seems generally to have been elective, and to have continued no longer than the sessions of the synod. The bishop of the place where the association was held, from a sort of natural title to preside in the convention, came, by the gradual but

---

[3] Thus the neglect of baptism led in two centuries to the adoption of a purgatory of which we shall hereafter speak.

sure operation of custom, to be regarded as the head of the body. This in time, aided by other auxiliary causes, established a metropolitan bishop,[4] which, when fully matured, gave a seat and conferred authority on the papistical monster.

175 7. During the greater part of this century, Christian churches were independent of each other; nor were they joined together by association, confederacy, or any other bonds but those of charity. Each Christian assembly was a little state, governed by its own laws, which were either enacted, or at least approved, by the society; but in process of time, as above noticed, all the churches of a province were brought into one ecclesiastical body.[5] With this accumulating corporation, a desire prevailed among ministers to increase the numbers of adherents to their respective interests. But instead of increasing their ministerial exertions, and giving a simple exhibition of divine truths as in the first planting of Christianity, the pastors increased the numbers of rites and ceremonies in the Christian worship; thus an acommodation was afforded to Jews and Pagans, and their conversion facilitated to the sophisticated doctrines of the cross.[6] As the boundaries of the church were enlarged by an easier ingress, the number of vicious and irregular persons who entered into it, proportionably increased. Most of the churches at the **195** end of this century assumed a new form. As the old disciples retired to their graves, their children, along with new converts, both Jews and Gentiles, under new ministers from the Alexandrian school, came forward and new-modelled the cause.[7]

---

[4] Camp. Lect. lec. 9, and Mosh. Hist, C. 2, p. 2, ch. 2, § 2.
[5] Mosh. ut ante. [6] Id. c. 2, p. 2, c. 4, § 2. [7] Mosh. Hist. C. 2, pt. 1, ch. 1, § 12. Rob. Res. c. 6, p. 51.

When the evil of the new system had developed itself, a new course of discipline was adopted; but the character of the community was changed, and purity with primitive simplicity took leave of such mixtion.[8] The ceremonies introduced occasioned strife and discord. Victor, Bishop of Rome, insisted upon Easter being observed by the Asiatic churches, at the same time it was kept by the western. His authority and request being disregarded, he thundered out his excommunications against the orientals. This conduct in Victor broke the friendly communion which had before subsisted between the churches in the east and west.[9] Having now traced the features of the churches generally, and finding their assumption of power, with their aspect and composition, of an antichristian character, we must dissent from these, and leave them; directing our investigation to other claimants, until we can trace some honourable and scriptural distinction.

200 8. The innumerable Christians of the East, who were not in communion with either the Greek or Roman churches, may be divided into two classes. The *first* consists of such as in ages past dissented from the Greek church, and formed similar hierarchies, which yet subsist independent of one another, as well as of the Grecian and Romish communities. The *second* consists of those who never were of any hierarchy, and who have always retained their original freedom. The number of such orientals is very great, for they lived dispersed all over Syria, Arabia, Egypt, Persia, Nubia, Ethiopia, India, Tartary, and other eastern countries. " It is remarkable," says Robinson, "that although they differ, as Europeans do, on specu-

---

[8] Mosb. Hist. C. 2, pt. 2, ch. 3, § 16, and pt. 2, c. 1, § 4—12.
[9] Id. ch. 4, § 11.

lative points of divinity, yet they all administer baptism by immersion, and there is no instance to the contrary."[10]

9. The Messalians or Euchites (the one a Hebrew term, the other Greek, and signifying *a praying people*) had in Greece a very early existence. These terms had also a very extensive application among the Greeks and orientals, who gave it to all those who endeavoured to raise the soul to God, by recalling and withdrawing it from all terrestrial and sensible objects.[1] These people, like all other nonconformists, are reproached and branded with heresy by the old orthodox writers; but, whatever errors may have been mixed up with their creed, it would appear *devotion and piety* formed the ground of the stigma, so that a puritanical character is fully implied. These Messalians were evidently the *parent stock* of Nonconformists in Greece. They attributed to two opposite causes, the sources of good and evil, much as we do in the present day; but their enemies, recording their views, have made them a people to be wondered at, and to be avoided. This way of misrepresentation was the only means the dominant party had to suppress " the men more righteous than themselves," before the church was endowed with a sword. The morality of this people was severe and captivating to the simple, but their discipline and worship are both reproached.[2] This parent stock of nonconformists was divided and subdivided by the clergy into various classes of heretics. They were often named from the country they inhabited, as Armenians, Phrygians, Bulgarians, and Philippopolitans, or as it was corruptly sounded in the west, Popolicans, Poblicans, Publicans. Some were called after the

---

[10] Rob. Hist. Bap. p. 484. [1] Mosh. Hist. C. 4, pt. 2, ch. 5, § 24. [2] Rob. Hist. Bap. p. 208.

names of their teachers, as Pauleanists, Novatianists, Donatists, Paulicians, and many more names were found in this class.[3] The term Euchites among Greeks was a general name for Dissenters, as the Waldenses was in the Latin church, and Nonconformists in England.[4] This large body of Dissenters were resident in the empire from the first establishment of Christianity, till its destruction in the thirteenth century.[5]

10. In Greece, says Dr. Mosheim, (who whenever he alludes to dissidents always evinces " the spider of the mind,") and in all eastern provinces, this sort of men were distinguished by the general and invidious name of Euchites or Messalians, as the Latins comprehended all the adversaries of the Roman pontiff under the general terms of Albigenses and Waldenses. It is, however, necessary to observe, that the names above mentioned were vague and ambiguous in the way they were applied by the Greeks and orientals, who made use of them to characterize, without distinction, all such as complained of the multitude of useless ceremonies, and of the vices of the clergy, without any regard to the difference that there was between such persons, in point of principles and morals. There are several circumstances which render it extremely probable that many persons of eminent piety and zeal for genuine Christianity, were confounded by the Greeks with these enthusiasts. In short, the righteous and the profligate, the wise and the foolish, were equally comprehended under the name Messalians, whenever they opposed the raging superstition of the times, or looked upon true and genuine piety as the essence of the Christian character.[6] In regard to baptism, these dissidents in the East were so

---

[3] Rob. Res. p. 58.   [4] Id. p. 56.   [6] Mosh. Hist. C. 12, pt. 2, ch. 5, § 1.

far from rejecting it, that if they erred, it was in baptizing *too much*, if the expression may be allowed. "They rebaptize," said one of their opponents, "but instead of being immersed in water, they ought to be plunged in hell."[7]

11. Towards the conclusion of the second century, one Montanus, who lived in a Phrygian village called Pepuza, undertook a mission to restore Christianity to its native simplicity. One class of professors being at the period carried away with Egyptian symbols, while others made up a system of religion from philosophic notions, oriental customs, and a portion of the gospel; apparently prompted this humble individual to attempt a reformation, or rather a restoration, of the primitive order of things. Being destitute of classical lore himself, he required it not in others who were willing to further his designs. He was decidedly hostile to those ministers, who with the new system, emanated from Alexandria. He was very successful in his labour of love, since his views and doctrines spread abroad, and were received through Asia, Africa, and in part of Europe. His doctrine and discipline, though severe, gained him the esteem of many who were not of the lowest order. Some ladies of opulence aided Montanus with their services and their fortunes.[8] We noticed the inquiries made of Tertullian, by females in this Christian community, respecting minor baptism,[9] and of Tertullian seceding from the Catholic church in Carthage, and his uniting with the Montanists, on the grounds of purity of communion. From Tertullian's works, his views and arguments in support of their doctrines, with the nature of their discipline, can

---

[7] Rob. Hist. p. 208.   [8] Mosh. Hist. C. 2, pt. 2, ch. 5, § 23.
[9] See ch. 2, s. 2, § 7, and note 18.

be ascertained. He formed in his own city a separate congregation, which continued for two hundred years.

220 Agrippinus its first pastor, with Tertullian, admitted members by examination and baptism, but all such as joined the Montanists from other communities were re-baptized.[10]

12. A name often appears in church history, which it will be necessary for us to mention and illustrate. A

227 physician, named MANES, embraced Christianity, and taught others the views he adopted. It is plain he had many followers in this, and in the following centuries. An endless variety of tales are told of this man, and his adherents, who were called after him, *Manicheans*, which name became a kind of warning *Merino* to all the orthodox. Their enemies being the recorders of their creed and discipline, deserve little credit, as in this case, with others already mentioned, their interested accusers confounded all Dissenters with the profligates and the enthusiasts, and most state clergy have pursued the same path and spirit. This class of orientals was unconnected with all hierarchies, and consisted of innumerable churches in different countries.[1] Though errors were probably mixed up with this new system, one circumstance is favourable to these people, that of their enumeration by early catholic writers, with the Messalians, Novatianists, Donatists, and Paulicians, whose memories and creeds have been rescued from undeserved reproach. We do not expect perfection in any body of Christians, but taking dissidents in every age, they have been found preferable in their knowledge of doctrines, and their practice of morals, to any community in national forms; while it is easy to discover these only have maintained civil and religious freedom, 1 Cor.

---

[10] Rob. Hist. Bap. p. 183. [1] Id. p. 496.

vii. 23, in their native dignity. These people accounted for the origin of evil as many had done before them, supposing it to arise out of physical or natural imperfections. They rejected the Old Testament, (as a rule to Christians, of which more hereafter.)

The leading errors in the African churches arose from their adopting the old Testament rites, which probably occasioned these Christians with others to reject its precepts.

Their morals were rigidly severe, their worship simple but mixed with oriental visions. Their doctrines were a mixture of national superstitions with the tenets of Christianity. Their exact views are probably not ascertained, and the reproaches heaped upon all nonconformists, leave us room to exercise charity in their case and creed. Their congregations, like those of the English dissenters, were divided into hearers and members, whom they called *auditors* and *elect*. They refused oaths, remonstrated against penal sanctions, and denied the authority of magistrates over conscience. Dr. Mosheim has demonstrated that they did administer baptism to those who desired it, but not without the candidates' consent, and that they did not baptize infants :[3] which is further evident by those books published against dissidents; wherein are shown that all parties administered baptism, single or trine, and all re-baptized.[4] The Manichean reproach has been charged on the Paulicians and Albigenses, since these people have been rescued from the stigma of palpable and damnable errors, we doubt not had similar investigation been pursued by unprejudiced men; a similar result would have ensued to a considerable extent, respecting the Manicheans.

[3] Comment. on the Affairs of the Christians before Constantine, &c., in Rob. Bap., p. 496. [4] Rob. Res., p. 212.

299 13. In reference to the orientals, we observed, "during the first three centuries Christian congregations all over the East subsisted in separate independent bodies, unsupported by government, and consequently without any secular power over one another. "*All this time they were baptist churches*, says Robinson, and though all the Fathers of the first four ages down to Jerome (A.D. 370.) were of Greece, Syria, and Africa, and though they give great numbers of histories of the baptism of adults, yet there is not one record of the baptism of a child till the year 370." The Grecian conventicles, as their practice proves beyond all contradiction, held that the decrees and constitutions of prelates were not binding on conscience; that river water was preferable to consecrated water for baptism.[5] It has been affirmed by modern writers that Greeks are Anabaptists, but they do not repeat baptism. The reason is plain; dipping includes sprinkling, but sprinkling does not include dipping. There is an officer in the Grecian church called *the baptist or dipper*, who administers baptism, in the present day, to all who have not been immersed. This will explain many anecdotes, says Robinson, in the Russian church. The Greek church admitted none into her communion, of the reformed church, but who must be baptized anew.[6] No church, says Wall, ever gave the communion to any person before they were baptized :[7] though the ancients reckoned that Christians might and ought to hold communion, notwithstanding difference of opinion in lesser matters.[8]

300 14. On the commencement of the fourth century the Christian church enjoyed peace, but

---

[5] Id. pp. 55, 56.   [6] Rob. Hist. Bap. p. 511.   [7] Hist. of Inf. Bap. pt. 2. c. 9. § 15. p. 440.   [8] Id. pt. 1. c. 11. § 11.

303 in 303 this halcyon period was disturbed by the edicts of Diocletian, this persecution threatened
306 the extirpation of the Christian interest. In 306 Constantine was saluted emperor, and a change was soon effected in the policy of the government by
310 Constantine declaring himself a Christian, and
311 ordering by edict in the ensuing year all persecution to cease.[9] The emperor having obtained the sole guardianship of the empire, and to strengthen his interest with a vast number of his subjects, pays particular attention to the bishops and clergy, who previous to this period were obscure men, and little more
313 is known of them than their names.[10] In 313 he issued his edict granting religious liberty to
316 all Christians. In 316 he gave liberty to those slaves who would receive baptism. In
320 320 he issued his edict against the Donatists, and some suffered death. The year before he
326 relieved the catholic clergy from taxes, and in 326 evinces moderation towards the Novatianists because of their soundness in that faith he had the year before established in the council of Nice.[1] He now incorporated the church with the state, and transferred the seat of government from Rome to Byzantium, and called it Constantinople from his own name. Here his imperial majesty erected the spacious and splendid church of St. Sophia. As an appendage to this elegant building, Constantine built the baptistery of St. John, in the style of a convocation-room in a cathedral. It was very large and was called the great Illuminary. In the middle was the bath, in which baptism was administered: it was supplied with water by pipes,[2] and there

---

[9] Mosh. Hist. C. 4. pt. 1. c. 1. § 4—6.   [10] Rob. Res. p. 120.   [1] Dupin. Cent. 4. v. ii. p. 11—16. Constantine. Gib. Ro. Hist. c. 20. Jones' Lect. v. i. 354.   [2] T. D. Fosbroke's

were outer rooms for all concerned in baptism of immersion, the only baptism of the place.[3] Every thing in this church goes to prove that baptism was administered by trine immersion, and only to instructed persons. The

Ency. of Antiq. v. i. pp. 46 & 103, and Pilkington's Sacred Elucidations, v. 2. pt. 4. of Baptism.   [3] Baptisteries are of different forms and of very high antiquity, as that of St. John's connected with the church of Constantinople. In Italy, although the churches were numerous, in some of the most considerable cities there was only one general baptistery, to which all resorted. Of the baptisteries of Rome the Lateran is the most ancient. This baptistery was made out of an old mansion-house given by Constantine to Bishop Sylvester, and was endowed with a handsome income, the dimensions have been preserved. Rob. Hist. of Bap. c. 14. One was prepared for the baptism of Clovis, king of France, and his majesty, with three thousand of his subjects, *were plunged*, says Mezeray, on Christmas day, 496. The baptistery of Pisa, both externally and internally, presents a fine display of the most exquisite workmanship. See Penny Cyclop. Art. Bap., Ency. Britan. & Antiquarian Repository, v. ii. p. 423. The baptistery of Florence is remarkable for the beauty of its gates. The Italian baptistery in appearance is not dissimilar to the octagon in Ely Cathedral. Lon. Ency. Art. Bap., Rob. Hist. of Bap. ch. 16. p. 89.

1670 Dr. Wall says, "the Greek church, in all its branches, does still use immersion; and so do all Christians who have not submitted to the pope's authority." Hist. Inf. Bap. p. 1. c. 2. § 2.

1815 "This day, (says Dr. Pinkerton, Russia,) "was excessively cold, being upwards of ten degrees of frost, and the water in the font almost freezing. I expressed my surprise to the priest that they did not use tepid water, seeing the infant had to be three times dipped over head and ears in the icy bath," &c. Again, he remarks, "The Duchobortzi make the sacraments to consist only in a spiritual reception of them, and therefore reject infant baptism. Their origin is to be sought for among the Anabaptists. This people have excited great attention" (in Russia).

1824 The Syrians baptize their children, says Missionary Wolf, by placing the child in the fountain, so that part of the body is in the water, then the priest three times takes water in his hands and pours it on the child's head, repeating at each time the name

canon laws, the officers, the established rituals, the Lent sermons of the prelates, and the baptism of the archbishops themselves.[4]

15. The change effected in the affairs of the church by Constantine, was attended with serious consequences to the well-being of the community. After he had adjusted the Nicene creed, he issued a law and sent it to all the presidents of provinces, requiring all persons to conform to his creed. The emperor condemned his past forbearance, as an occasion of men's being seduced by these erroneous people. By this edict, says Eusebius, the dens of heretics were laid open, and the wild beasts, the ringleaders of their impiety, were scattered. "This edict," observes Lardner, "was principally directed against the Novatianists, &c. and all others, who by private meetings endeavoured to support heresies."[5] His choice of clergy soon led him to erect splendid churches, and to richly adorn them with pictures and images, which bore a striking resemblance to the pagan temples.[6] The clergy of these churches became vicious, and they contended with each other in the most scandalous manner; they trampled on the rights of the people, as by endowments they were raised above them. They imitated the luxury of princes, and consequently ignorance and superstition soon prevailed among the people. Reverence now began to be paid to the memory of departed saints. The people, being left by those state paid clergy, soon had their minds diverted from the simple worship of the New Testament to the scene of the Re-

---

of one person in the Trinity. After this the body is immersed. Jewish Expositor, for September, 1824.

The rubric of the present Greek church requires dipping in baptism. Gale's Reflect. p. 158.   [4] Rob. Bap. p. 63.   [5] Cred. of the Gospel, v. iv. ch. 70. p. 169.   [6] Lon. Ency. Art. Rom. Cathol. p. 647.

deemer's labours. The Holy Land had peculiar charms, pilgrimages were made, discoveries of relics, belonging once to a sacred name, and an enviable treasure, which awakened ambition, and opened a door to a system of pious frauds.[7] After having opened the way into the church for every evil, and provided a chair for the man of sin, Constantine took leave of all his earthly grandeur, May 22, 337, aged 66.[8]

Section V.

ORIENTAL CHURCHES CONTINUED.

It was needful for me to write unto you, and exhort you that you should earnestly contend for the faith which was once delivered unto the saints.—*Jude* 3.

1. The council of Nice, already referred to, took notice of two sorts of Dissenters, who held separate assemblies. These were the Cathari and Paulianists, the

---

[7] Mosh. Hist. C. 2, pt. 2, c. 2, § 8.   [8] The dangers attending the church of God at this period, are shown in God's sealing his own people, Rev. vii. 3. The sealing in the forehead suggests an open profession, and a visible piety in the Lord's servants. This mark is not baptism, as Bishop Newton fancies, since that is not God's work, and is given alike to friends and foes, nor is that rite ever called in the New Testament a seal, but is plainly the work of the Holy Spirit, by which they were sealed to the day of redemption, Eph. i. 13, and without which Spirit, they would not be God's servants, nor would the Novatianists in Italy, the Euchites in Asia, the Donatists in Africa, the Paterines in Italy, the Paulicians in Armenia, the Albigenses and Waldenses, have been *preserved* from the surrounding contagion for a day, but they were *sealed* or *secured*.

latter were a kind of semi-Arians; the former were Trinitarians (Novatianists,) who viewed the Catholic church as a worldly community. These Puritans or Novatianists were exceedingly numerous in Phrygia.[1] These Dissenters baptized all that joined their assemblies by immersion in the name of the Trinity, on a personal profession of faith; and if they had been baptized before, they re-baptized them. Canons now were enacted by aspiring prelates,[2] yet the Greek Christians paid very little regard to any ecclesiastical rule, and though successive assemblies were called, the more the bishops tried to enforce uniformity, the faster what they called heresy spread; so that, in

350

---

[1] Lardner, Cred. of the Gos. v. iii. p. 2, c. 47, p. 310. [2] During the last century, baptism was viewed as preparing the soul for glory, and sequently, it was delayed for years, or till death approached. This delay and neglect, these prelates were anxious to recover the people from, and in their expressions and zeal for the ordinance, they brought the people to the other extreme, and pernicious consequences ensued.

360 *Basil* expressed to his people the bitter complaints those would make, who died unbaptized.

360 *Gregory Nazianzen* speaks of different punishments for different persons, in another world, which is to be regulated by their treatment of baptism.

374 *Ambrose* says, " For no one comes to the kingdom of heaven but by baptism. Those not baptized may have a freedom from punishment, which is not clear."

380 *Chrysostum* declares, there is no receiving the bequeathed inheritance before one is baptized.

388 *Augustin* asserts, " Salvation of a person is completed by baptism and conversion."

These assertions awakened each person under these prelates' charge, to receive baptism; the penitent, the prisoner, sickly persons and children, the dying, and dead bodies, received the purifying rite, in order to avoid *the purgatory* of the unbaptized. This

the twelfth century, the world was full of (dissidents,) heretics.³

2. It appears highly probable, from many circumstances, that both the greater and lesser Armenia were enlightened with the knowledge of the truth, not long after the first rise of Christianity. The interests in communion with Rome and Constantinople were, in this fourth century, incorporated with the parent society.⁴ The character of the Armenians was, that they were a frugal, laborious, stern, and peaceable people, if let alone, but formidable and warlike, if oppressed; which accounts for the policy of the government at early periods, and the evils resulting in its change of measures towards Dissenters in these and other provinces.⁵ While the catholics were engaged

350

---

was the strong limb to pædobaptism!!!   ³ Rob. Res. pp. 71—3.   ⁴ Mosh. Hist. C. 4, pt. 1, ch. 1, § 19. *note.* No one circumstance ever gave such footing, or ever strengthened national establishments so much, as infant baptism. Minor baptism was confined to no age; it might have been at fourteen years, as in the Georgian nation, which embraced Christianity under Constantine, Wall, pt. 2, p. 260, or at seven or six, as recorded, Rob. Hist. Bap. pp. 144, 299. But the general delay of baptism was a distress to the clergy, Id. 249. Gregory at Constantinople, A.D., 381, and Austin, at Hippo, introduced new views and rites. The first considered children might be dipped at three years of age, Id. 349, and also babes, if in danger of death, Id. 249, as dying unbaptized, left their future state uncertain, ut sup.; the latter asserts, infants are baptized for the pardon of sin, Wall, i. 303. The anxiety on the part of the orthodox, to rescue children from the errors of the Arians, was in this age manifest. No way promised so much success as the obligations to keep the creed into which each was solemnly baptized. This charity in both parties, Arians and Trinitarians, furthered the infant cause, and gave additional importance to those interests which aspired to orthodoxy or eminency in numbers. See Eight causes furthering Pædobaptism, Rob. Bap. c. 27.   ⁵ Rob. ut sup.

381

about the relics of Palestine, and professors in hierarchies were subsiding into an awful and secure slumber, a reformer appeared, in the person of one AERIUS, a presbyter monk. "He excited divisions," says Mosheim,[6] throughout ARMENIA,[7] Pontus, and Cappadocia, by propagating opinions different from those that were commonly received. He condemned prayers for the dead, stated fasts, the celebration of Easter, and other rites of that nature, in which the multitudes erroneously imagine that the life and soul of religion consist. One of his principal tenets was, that the bishops were not distinguished from presbyters by any divine right; but, that according to the institution of the New Testament, their offices and authority were absolutely the same. His great purpose seems to have been that of reducing Christianity to its primitive simplicity.[8] He erected a *new society*, and we know, with the ut-

375

---

[6] Mosh. Hist. c. 4, p. 2, ch. 3, § 21. [7] Wolf, the Missionary, says, "The priest (of Armenia) puts the child into the water, and washes the head with three handfuls of water, and prays, and saith, 'I baptize thee in the name,' &c., and then dips the child," &c. Bap. Mag. 1826, v. xviii. p. 29. This is confirmed by Missionaries Smith and Dwight, who say, according to the rules of the Armenian church, baptism consists in plunging the whole body in water three times, as the sacred formula is repeated. Miss. Resear. in Armenia, p. 312, &c. See Simon's Critical History of the Relig. and Customs of Eastern Nations, chap. 12 and 13, p. 134, &c. [8] We are unacquainted with this reformer's views and success. The mode of baptizing in the East. is farther stated by Millar, who asserts, "In all the *oriental* provinces with the *northern* nations, immersion is the only mode of baptism, the child is dipped three times in Russia, as in the Greek church." Geog. v. ii. p. 480, col. 1.

1825

1832

Each house in the East has its bagnio, where there is every convenience for bathing in hot or cold water, Lady Montague's Letters, let. 43, v. ii. Rob. Bap. c. 9.

"The Russians baptize adults in the river, by trine immersion,"

most certainty, that it was highly agreeable to many good Christians, who were no longer able to bear the tyranny and arrogance of the bishops of this century."

3. We have now no interesting matters to give, nor can we detail any information, to break the monotony of the aspect of the interests generally, for nearly two centuries. The Nonconformists continued to be dispersed all over the empire, and had trusted to Providence for liberty to worship. Their history is large, and has proved difficult to many. The clergy were always troublesome, but never attempted their conversion. Some emperors had been indifferent to them, others had cherished them, others had persecuted them. We shall leave the general history, and endeavour to identify one class of consistent Puritans. Few of the clergy of the establishments could compose a discourse in the seventh century, when Mahomet arose to scourge the nations.9

612

Millar's Geog. ib. and see Authorities quoted in Robinson's Letter to Dr. Turner, Works, v. iv. p. 235.

Bathing was a practice of great antiquity; the Greeks, as well as the heroic age, are said to have constantly bathed. Immersion would to such be very agreeable, Floyer's Hist. of Bathing. Dr. G. S. Howard's New Royal Encyclo. v. i. Art. Bathing. Sir R. Ker Porter's Travels, v. i. p. 231. On Baths. 9 Mahomet has rendered *baptizo* in the Koran, *divine dying*. Immersion is only one part, the tinging of the soul with faith and grace, is the other; or tincturing the mind with the doctrines of the gospel, we should say. In this way all through the Koran, he has fully translated the word, Rob. Bap. p. 7, and 493. But dying is not done by sprinkling or pouring, but the subject dyed is dipped. Gale's Ref. Let. 3, p. 83. The Mahometans are totally immersed, or bathed in water. Sale's Koran, v. i. s. 4, pp. 138—40. This mode of baptizing is further evident from the most respectable historians. The mosque of Damascus, says Dr. Pocock, has an octagon baptistery, View of the East, v. ii. b. 2, c. 8, p. 120. On each side of the mosque, are fountains for the purpose of washing before wor-

Mosheim speaks of a *drooping* faction, in this century, with whom the Greek church was engaged in the most bitter and violent controversy. This drooping faction in Armenia, he calls Manicheans, and says they were revived by Paul and John, two brothers, who revived the doctrine, and modified it, from which sprang a new sect. But as Dr. Mosheim's account is at variance with others, we shall select our materials of this new sect from other sources.

650

4. It was about the year 653, that a new sect arose in the East,[10] under the name of Paulicians, which deserves our attention. There resided in the city of *Mananalis*, in *Armenia*, an obscure person of the name of CONSTANTINE, with whom this sect appears to have originated. One day, a stranger called upon him, who had been a prisoner among the Saracens, in Syria, and having obtained his release, was returning home through this city; he was kindly received by Constantine, and entertained some days at his house. To requite the hospitality of his generous host, he gave Constantine two manuscripts, which he had brought out of Syria;

653

ship, Id. v. ii. b. 3, ch. 1, p. 128. No unbaptized person may enter a Mahometan church, Lon. Ency. v. i. p. 59, col. 2. Pitt's Relig. and Customs of the Mahom. pp. 80—2. Robins. Hist. Bap. c. 35. Gale's Ref. Let. 4, p. 122.

The Syrians, the Armenians, the Persians, and all the oriental nations, who must have understood the Greek word *baptizo*, have practised dipping, and it is so rendered in their versions of the Scriptures, Rob. Hist. Bap. p. 7. Ryland's Cand. Reasons.

Baptizo is rendered *to dip*, by the Peshito, Syriac, Arabic, Ethiopic, Coptic, Gothic, German of Luther, Dutch, Danish, and Swedish versions. See Greenfield's Def. of the Mahratta version, pp. 40—44. [10] In Vaughan's Life of Wickliff, v. i. c. 2, s. 1, p. 115, the denominational aspect of this sect is suppressed, *though Gibbon has spoken out*; this course is pursued through that work. Those who neglect part of the commission, are afraid to mention its performance to other denominations.

and these were the four gospels, and the epistles of the apostle Paul. From the nature of the gift, it is not unreasonable to conclude that the stranger set a value upon these manuscripts, that he was acquainted with their contents, and was one who knew *the truth*, all which receives corroboration from the fact, that he had been an office-bearer, a deacon in a Christian church. It is equally probable that the conversation of Constantine and his guest would occasionally turn upon the contents of these manuscripts. That his conversation and present had some effects on the mind of Constantine, is evident, for, from the time he got acquainted with the contents of these writings, it is said he would touch no other books. He threw away his Manichean library, exploded and rejected many of the absurd notions of his countrymen. He became a teacher of the doctrines of Christ and his apostles.[1] "He formed to himself," says Milner, "a plan of divinity from the New Testament; and as Paul is the most systematic of all the apostles, Constantine very properly attached himself to his writings with peculiar attention. From the attention (this sect paid) to this apostle's epistles and doctrine, they obtained the name of *Paulicians*." "In the present instance," continues Milner, "I see reason to suppose the Paulicians to have been perfect originals. The little that has been mentioned concerning them, carries entirely this appearance; and I hope it may be shortly evident that they originated from a heavenly influence, teaching and converting them; and that, in them we have one of those extraordinary effusions of the divine Spirit (on his word), by which the knowledge of Christ and the practice of godliness is kept alive in the world."[2]

These originals, or rather, *restorers of the New Tes-*

---

[1] Jones's Lect. on Ec. Hist. v. ii. pp. 179.   [2] History of Church, Cent. 9, ch. 2.

tament order of things, being allowed by all historians to have been the encouragers, if not the main strength of the Albigensian churches in France, at after periods; we shall be the more particular in our attention to their character and practice.[3]

5. The Paulicians sincerely condemned the memory and opinions of the Manichean sect, and complained of the injustice which impressed that invidious name on the simple followers of Paul and Christ. The objects which had been transformed by the magic of superstition, appeared to the eyes of the Paulicians in their genuine and naked colours. Of the ecclesiastical chain, many links were broken by these reformers; and against the gradual innovations of discipline and doctrine, they were strongly guarded by habit and aversion, as by the silence of Paul and the Evangelists. They attached themselves with peculiar devotion to the writings and character of Paul, and in whom they gloried. In the gospels, and epistles of Paul, Constantine investigated the creed of the primitive Christians; and whatever might be the success, a Protestant reader will applaud the spirit of the inquiry. In practice, or at least in theory, of the sacraments, the Paulicians were inclined to abolish all visible objects of worship, and the words of the gospel were, in their judgments, *the baptism and communion of the faithful.* A creed thus simple and spiritual, was not adapted to the genius of the times, and the rational Christian was offended at the violation offered to his religion by the Paulicians.[4]

6. In confirmation of the above historian, as to their views of the ordinance of Baptism, we subjoin the authorities of a few respectable writers.

In these churches of the Paulicians, the sacraments

---

[3] Gibbon's Ro. Hist. ch. 54.   [4] Gibbon, ut sup.

of baptism and the Lord's Supper, they held to be peculiar to the communion of the faithful; i. e., to be restricted to believers.[5]

The Paulicians or Bogomilians baptized and re-baptized adults by immersion, as the Manicheans and all other denominations did in the East, upon which mode there was no dispute in the Grecian church.[6]

"It is evident," says Mosheim, "they rejected the baptism of infants. They were not charged with any error concerning baptism."[7]

"They with the Manicheans were Anabaptists, or rejecters of infant baptism," says Dr. Allix, "and were consequently often reproached with that term.[8]

They were simply scriptural in the use of the sacraments," says Milner, "they were orthodox in the doctrine of the Trinity, they knew of no other Mediator than the Lord Jesus Christ.[9]

7. These people were called Acephali or headless (from having no distinct order of clergy, or presiding person in their assemblies) and were hooted in councils for re-baptizing in private houses, says Robinson, and holding conventicles; and for calling the established church a worldly community, and re-baptizing such as joined their churches.[10] The religious principles and practices of these people are purposely mangled and misrepresented, but it is possible to obtain some evidences of what they were. They are charged with neglecting the Old Testament; but they knew *that* economy was abolished, they therefore rejected it as a rule of faith, not as history. The expounders of Genesis filled the church with vain disputes about matter and spirit,

---

[5] Jones's Lect. v. ii. p. 181. [6] Rob. Bapt. p. 211; and Res. pp. 90—93. [7] Mosh. Hist., Cent. 2, pt. 2, ch. 5, § 4 and note. [8] Rem. Ch. Pied. ch. 15, p. 138, and Rob. Bap., p. 497. [9] Ch. Hist. Cent. 9. ch. 2. [10] Res. p. 92.

the origin and duration of the world. They saw the priests set up Exodus, Numbers, Leviticus, and Deuteronomy, as rules for an hierarchy. The books of Joshua, Judges, Samuel, Kings, and Chronicles, gave kings authority to slay and kill in the cause of Jesus. And the infant cause not complied with, required the *cutting off*, which has been but too successfully prosecuted by the advocates of the rite. The Paulicians, with other dissenters, rejected the Pentateuch and the historical books down to Job, as a rule of faith and practice in a Christian community, and received the devotional and prophetical parts with the New Testament, as a law for the Lord's house.[1] The writings and the lives of their eminent ministers are totally lost; so that we know nothing of these men but from the pens of their enemies, yet even these confess their excellency.[2]

8. But we now return to their efforts. Constantine gave himself the scriptural name of Sylvanus. He preached with great success in Pontus and Cappadocia, regions once enlightened and renowned for Christianity and suffering piety (1 Pet. i.) were again blessed with the gospel through his exertions.[3] Great numbers of disciples were made and gathered into societies. *The body of Christians in Armenia came over to the Paulicians, and embraced their views.* In a little time, congregations were gathered in the provinces of Asia Minor, to the westward of the river Euphrates. *Their opinions were also silently propagated in Rome, Milan, and in the kingdom beyond the Alps* (France).

Churches were formed as much upon the plan and model of the apostolic churches as it was in their power to bring them. Six of their principal churches took

---

[1] Res. p. 90, and Hist. of Bap. p. 450.   [2] Milner's Ch. Hist. Cent. 9. ch. 2.   [3] Ibid.

the names of those to which Paul addressed his epistles, Rome, Corinth, Ephesus, Philippi, Colosse, Thessalonica; while the names of Sylvanus's fellow-teachers were, Titus, Timothy, Tychicus, "This innocent allegory," says Gibbon,[4] "revived the memory and example of the first ages." The Paulician teachers were thus distinguished, only by their scriptural names. They were known by the modest title of fellow-pilgrims, by the austerity of their lives, their zeal or knowledge, and the credit of some extraordinary gifts of the Holy Spirit. They were incapable of desiring the wealth and honours of the Catholic prelacy; such antichristian pride they bitterly censured; and even the rank of elders or presbyters was condemned as an institution of the Jewish synagogue.[5] There is no mention in all the account of this people of any clergy among them.[6] Though charged with the Manichean errors, they have been honourably freed from this reproach by respectable writers.[7] They called themselves Christians, but the Catholics they named Romans, as if they had been heathens.[8]

9. We have here exhibited a confession of simple worship, a scriptural constitution to their churches and its officers, with a blameless feature in the manners of these Christians, which has been conceded by their enemies. Their standard of perfection was so high in Christian morals that their increasing congregations were divided into *two classes* of disciples.[9] They had not any

---

[4] Ro. Hist., ch. 54. [5] Id. *note*, "The candour of Gibbon is remarkable in this part of his history."—Milner. [6] Rob. Res., p. 80. [7] Jortin's Rem. on Hist. v. iii., p. 498, and Lardner's Cred. of the Gosp. History, pt. 2, ch. 63, v. iii., p. 546. [8] Lardner, Id. p. 407. [9] These *two classes* can be traced through the Albigensian, Waldensian, German, and Dutch Baptist Churches, from this parent stock.

ecclesiastical government, administered by bishops, priests, or deacons: they had no sacred order of men distinguished by their manner of life, their habit, or any other circumstance from the rest of the assembly. They had certain teachers whom they called companions in the journey of life; among these there reigned a perfect equality, and they had no peculiar rights, privileges, nor any external mark of dignity to distinguish them from the people. They recommended to the people without exception, and that with the most affecting and ardent zeal, the constant and assiduous perusal of the Scriptures, and expressed the utmost indignation against the Greeks who allowed to the priests alone an access to those sacred fountains of divine knowledge.[10]

No object can be more laudable than the attempt to bring back the Christian profession to its original simplicity, which evidently appears to have been the aim of the Paulicians, though for this commendable conduct, terms of reproach and epithets of disgrace have been heaped on their memories by interested historians and dictionary writers. In this good work of preaching and evangelizing provinces, Sylvanus

680

spent twenty-seven years of his life, taking up his residence at COBOSSA, and disseminating his opinions all around. The united exertions of these people, their scriptural views, doctrine, discipline, and itinerating system, were attended with evident displays of divine approbation, and multitudes embraced a gospel simply and fully preached.

10. Alarmed at the progress these novel opinions were making, and discovering the growing importance of the Paulicians, the church party "engaged in the most bitter and virulent controversy with them." In-

---

[10] Mosh. Hist. C. 9, p. 2, ch. 5, § 5.

effectual in their efforts the Greek emperors began to persecute them with the most sanguinary severity. The Paulicians were sentenced to be capitally punished, and their books, wherever found, to be committed to the flames; and further, that if any person was found to have secreted them, he was to be put to death, and his goods confiscated.

A Greek officer, named *Simeon*, armed with legal and military authority, appeared at CORONIA to strike the shepherd, Sylvanus, and to reclaim, if possible, the lost sheep. By a refinement of cruelty, this minister of justice placed the unfortunate Sylvanus before a line of his disciples, who were commanded, as the price of their pardon, and as proof of their penitence, *to stone to death their spiritual Father*. The affectionate flock turned aside from the impious office; the stones dropped from their filial hands; and of the whole number, only one executioner could be found. This apostate, Justus, after putting Sylvanus to death, gained by some means admittance into communion, and again deceived and betrayed his unsuspecting brethren; and as many as were treacherously ascertained, and could be collected, were massed together into an immense pile, and by order of the emperor, consumed to ashes. Simeon, the officer, struck with astonishment at the readiness with which the Paulicians could die for their religion, examined their arguments, and became himself a convert, renounced his honours and fortune, and three years afterwards went to Cobossa, and became the successor of Constantine Sylvanus, a zealous preacher among the Paulicians, and at last sealed his testimony with his blood.[1] To free the East from those troubles and commotions said to arise from the Pauli-

---

[1] Milner and Jones, ut sup.

cian doctrines, a great number of them were transported into THRACE during this century; but still a greater number were left in Syria and the adjoining countries. From Thrace these people passed into Bulgaria and Sclavonia, where they took root, and settled in their own church order.

From these churches, at after periods colonies were sent out, and they are said to have inundated Europe,[2] though some relics of these ancient communities were to be traced till the fifteenth century.

700 11. From the blood and ashes of the first Paulician victims, a succession of teachers and congregations repeatedly arose. The Greeks, to subdue them, made use both of arguments and arms, with all the terror of penal laws, without effecting their object. The great instrument of this people's multiplication was, *the alone* use of the New Testament, of which some pleasing anecdotes are related. One Sergius was recommended by a Paulician woman to read Paul's writings, and his attention to the sacred records brought him to embrace their views. For thirty-four years he devoted himself to the ministry of the gospel. Through every city and province that Sergius could reach, he spread abroad the savour of the knowledge of Christ, and with *such* success, that the clergy in the hierarchies considered him to be the forerunner of Antichrist; and declared he was producing the great apostacy foretold by Paul. The emperors, in conjunction with the clergy, exerted their zeal with a peculiar degree of bitterness and fury against this people. Though every kind of oppressive measure and means was used, yet all efforts for their suppression proved fruitless, "nor could all their power and all their barbarity, ex-

703

---

[2] Mosh. Hist., c. 11, p. 2, ch. 5, § 2, 3.

haust the patience nor conquer the obstinacy of that inflexible people, who possessed," says Mosheim, "a fortitude worthy of a better cause"!!!

741

12. The face of things changed towards the end of the eighth century, and the prospects of this harassed people brightened under the emperor Nicephorus, who restored to them their civil and religious privileges. During this auspicious season, the Paulicians widely disseminated their opinions, and it is recorded that they became formidable to the East.³ Those persecuting laws which had been suspended for some years, were renewed and enforced with redoubled fury, under the reigns of Michael and Leo, who made strict inquisition throughout every province in the Grecian empire, and inflicted capital punishment upon such of them as refused to return to the bosom of the church. These decrees drove the Paulicians into desperate measures. "Oppression maketh a wise man mad."⁴ The Paulicians are now charged with having put to death some of their clerical oppressors, and also of taking refuge in those provinces governed by Saracens, and that in union with those barbarians, they infested the Grecian states.

795

802

811

The power and influence of these dissidents were found to be so great as to suggest the policy of allowing them to return to their own habitations, and dwelling there in tranquillity. The severest persecution experienced by them was encouraged by the empress Theodora, A. D. 845. Her decrees were severe, but the cruelty with which they were put in execution by her officers was horrible beyond ex-

845

---

³ Chambers' Cyclop. Art. Paulicians. ⁴ Gibbon renders an indirect apology for the conduct of these people at this period. Hist. ch. 54.

pression. Mountains and hills were covered with inhabitants. Her sanguinary inquisitors explored cities and mountains in lesser Asia. After confiscating the goods and property of *one hundred thousand of these people*, the owners *to that number* were put to death in the most barbarous manner, and made to expire slowly under a variety of the most exquisite tortures. The flatterers of the empress boast of having extirpated in nine years that number of Paulicians. Many of them were scattered abroad, particularly in Bulgaria. Some fortified the city of Tephrice and Philippopolis, from which last city they were called Philippopolitans; and though they were driven hence, yet the spirit of independence was not subdued. A portion of this people emigrated from Thrace, and their doctrines soon struck deep root in European soil. Such as escaped from the inquisitors fled to the Saracens, who received them with compassion; and in conjunction with whom, under experienced officers, they maintained a war with the Grecian nation for the period of one hundred and fifty years. During the reign of John Zimicus, they gained considerable strength, and during the tenth century, they spread themselves abroad throughout different provinces. From Bulgaria they removed into Italy, and spreading themselves from thence through the other provinces of Europe, " they became extremely troublesome to the Roman pontiffs upon many occasions." Here the history of this interesting people rests, so far as it respects the Levant; but we shall give a slight statement of their migratory movements in order to make our future sections illustrative of these people, though under different names.

13. " From Italy," says Mosheim, " the Paulicians sent colonies into almost all the other provinces of Europe, and formed gradually a considerable number

of religious assemblies, *who adhered to their doctrine*, and who realized every opposition and indignity from the popes. It is undoubtedly certain, from the most authentic records, that a considerable number of them were, about the middle of the eleventh century, settled in Lombardy, Insubria, but principally at Milan; and that many of them led a wandering life in France, Germany, and other countries, where they captivated the esteem and admiration of the multitude by their sanctity. In Italy, they were called *Paterini* and Cathari. In France, they were denominated *Bulgarians*, from the kingdom of their emigration, also *Publicans*, instead of *Paulicians*, and *boni homines*, good men; but were chiefly known by the term Albigenses, from the town of Alby, in the Upper Languedoc. The first religious assembly which the Paulicians formed in Europe is said to have been at Orleans, in the year 1017, on which we shall enlarge under the churches in France, to which we shall repair after we have traced their existence and labours in the kingdom of Italy.

14. Here we may be permitted to review the apostolic character and exertions of this extensive body of people, while we may express our surprise at the virulent opposition, the cruel measures used, and the extensive sacrifice of human life, for successive ages, on the alone ground of religious views. A special instance of divine grace was displayed in this people's rise and early success; and we must attribute their preservation and enlargement to the exercise of the same compassion. An evident mark of apostolic spirit possessed by this people must be admitted by all: without any funds or public societies to countenance or support the arduous undertaking, otherwise than their respective churches, the Paulicians fearlessly penetrated the most barbarous

parts of Europe, and went single-banded, and single-eyed, to the conflict with every grade of character. In several instances they suffered death or martyrdom, not counting their lives dear, so that they could promote the cause of their Redeemer. See Mosheim's History. Gibbon's Ro. Hist. ch. 54. Robinson's Eccl. Res. ch. 6, pp. 74—79. Jones's Lectures on Eccl. Hist. v. II., pp. 179—184.

Section VI.

CHURCHES IN ITALY RESUMED.[1]

"I know thy works, and where thou dwellest, even where Satan's seat is: and thou holdest fast my name, and hast not denied my faith," &c.—*Rev.* ii. 13.

1. THIS passage given by John is so graphic of the situation and circumstances of the Novatian and Paterine churches, that we are constrained to allow it as expressive of the people of whom God took special cognizance. If the man of sin is constituted by a succession of popes,[2] why might not ANTIPAS be represented by a succession of reforming men, as opposers of the *sinful system?* Αντί-πας, *against the whole*, antipa or antipapacy. The error in explaining the revelations has been in making one part of John's vision speak a present history of some churches, and a future history of others;[3] though John declares of the whole, the

---

[1] See above, ch. 2, s. 1, § 9, 10, and connect the Novatian churches with this section. [2] Newton on the Prophecies, v. ii., pp. 88, 106. [3] These seven churches were in prophetic accordance with the other parts of the Apocalypse, and John gives no room for other conclusions; for,

things were shortly "to come to pass." Antipas, in the church of Pergamos, has confused every literal exposition of the passage. In confirmation of this view of this part, placed as a motto over the history of the Paterines, it is obvious, that the two-edged sword was the only weapon these people used: and this approved instrument of their Lord, ver. 12, enabled *Antipas* to overcome.

2. Socrates states that, when the church was taken under the fostering care of Constantine, and on his party using severe measures against dissenters, the dominant party called themselves *the catholic church;* but the oppressed and suffering party

330

---

1. No proof exists that the actual state of those seven churches was described at the time of writing these addresses, and a forced construction is evidently given by *literal* writers.

2. No one can support, from historic details, a reasonable and literal accomplishment of the things contained in the addresses to *those* churches: the candlestick is removed, not from one, but from all.

3. The addresses close with an application to ALL the churches; that is, of the age to which the prophecy alludes, and not to the *one church only*, bearing the inscription of the address.

4. The state of things at Pergamos does not accord with that church being *the seat of Satan*, which must be at Babylon, or Rome, agreeably to other plain passages, and which is allowed by M'Crie and others.

5. "It does not appear that any Christian church existed at Thyatira, till 200 years after Christ."—*Maddock*.

6. The other emblems in the Apocalypse are divided into prophetic periods; and there is not the least indication from the writer of a change in the mode of address.

7. It is a "*a revelation of things to come;*" but if the things in those churches actually existed, John could have forwarded an epistle to each church as other apostles did, and so have rectified abuses without calling it "*a revelation of things which must shortly come to pass:*" the character *the whole* book sustains.

was known by the name, *the church of martyrs*.⁴ In a previous section, we have given the outlines of these suffering people, under the denomination of Novatianists, and endeavoured to trace their history till penal laws compelled them to retire into " caves and dens," to worship God. While oppressed by the catholic party, they obtained the name of *Paterines ;* which means *sufferers*, or what is nearly synonymous with our modern acceptation of the word *martyrs*,⁵ and which indicated an afflicted and poor people, trusting in the name of the Lord; and which name was, in a great measure, restricted to the dissenters of Italy, where it was as common as the Albigenses in the south of France, or Waldenses in Piedmont.

575 We left off our narrative of the Novatianists at the end of the sixth century; yet it is very evident Dissenters continued in Italy, as is proved by the complaints of the clergy;⁶ which point is ceded to us by Dr. Mosheim.⁷ " It was by means of the Paterines," says Dr. Allix, " that *the truth* was preserved in the dioceses of Milan and Turin."⁸ These churches, it **660** would appear, were aided and resuscitated in the seventh century, since Gibbon asserts that the sentiments and doctrines of the Paulicians were propagated at Rome and Milan.⁹ And we are informed by Bonizo, bishop of Sutrium, that the Paterines arose, or **750** became more conspicuous, during Stephen II.'s pontificate.¹⁰

---

⁴ Lib. 1, cap. 3, 6.   ⁵ Allix's Rem. on the Anc. Ch. of Pied., ch. 3, p. 25; and Jones's Hist. of the Christ. Ch., v. ii., p. 107.   ⁶ Rob. Res , p. 408.   ⁷ Mosh. Hist., Cent. 12, pt. 2, ch. 5, § 4, note.   ⁸ Allix's Rem. Pied., Ch., ch. 19, p. 175.   ⁹ Ro. Hist., ch. 54.   ¹⁰ Allix's Id., ch. 14, p. 124.

3. "The public religion of the Paterines consisted of nothing but social prayer, reading and expounding the gospels, baptism once, and the Lord's supper as often as convenient. Italy was full of such Christians, which bore various names, from various causes. They said a Christian church ought to consist of only good people: a church had no power to frame any constitutions; it was not right to take oaths; it was not lawful to kill mankind, nor should he be delivered up to the officers of justice to be converted; faith alone could save a man; the benefit of society belonged to all its members; the church ought not to persecute; the law of Moses was no rule for Christians." The Catholics of those times baptized by immersion:[1] the Paterines, therefore, in all their branches, made no complaint of the mode of baptizing; but when they were examined, they objected vehemently against the baptism of infants, and condemned it as an error.[2]

They are also freed from the baneful charge of Manicheism;[3] and are not taxed with any immorality, but were condemned for virtuous rules of action, which all in power accounted heresy. At different periods, and from various causes, these Baptists considerably increased. Those of their churches where baptism was administered, were known by the name of baptismal churches: and to such churches all the Christians in the vicinage flocked for baptism. When Christianity

800

---

[1] *Note.* In 754, Stephen, bishop of Rome, was requested, by some monks who privately consulted him, to say, whether in case of illness baptism by pouring could be lawful. He was the first who gave the opinion of its validity, which consequently became authentic law for administering the baptism by pouring. Rob. Bap., pp. 428-9.   [2] Rob. Bap. p. 211, where authorities are quoted largely.   [3] Dr. Allix's Pied., ch. 18, and Dr. Jortin's Rem. on Ecc. Hist., vol. v., p. 53.

spread into the country, the people met for worship where they could, but all candidates came up to the baptismal church to receive the ordinance. In time baptisteries were built in the country, and, like the old ones, were resorted to by the neighbouring inhabitants. There was a shadow of this among the reformed churches of Piedmont.[4]

946 4. Atto, bishop of Vercilli, complained of these people in 946, as other clergy had done before; but from this period, until the thirteenth century, dissidents continued to increase and multiply. The wickedness of the clergy[5] considerably aided the cause of dissent. There was no legal power in Italy, in those times, to put dissenters to death. This kingdom, therefore, would very naturally become a retreat to those who suffered in other provinces on account of religion. Its contiguity to France and Spain, which kingdoms abounded with Christians of this sort, would naturally aid and strengthen their interests; besides the preaching of Claude,[6] with other reformers, added to the number of dissenters. All these were incorporated into the churches of Italy, and were now known by the term Paterines; "a name which came," says Mezeray, "from the glory they took in suffering patiently for *the truth.*"[7]

---

[4] Rob. Hist. of Bap., p. 357. [5] The clergy were not only ignorant, but they were adulterers and Sodomites (Dr. Allix's Rem. Ch. Pied., p. 88); and so avaricious as to sell any sacred thing for money. Their illegitimate children were provided for out of the revenues of the church; but they could not be so supported without proving their connexion and membership, which was established only *by baptism.* This urgency pushed forward baptism from minors to infants. Rob. Bap., pp. 805, &c., 514. [6] Claude, bishop of Turin, was a Spaniard, Arian, and Catholic, yet he loudly proclaimed his view of truth, in opposition to the errors of the times. [7] French Hist., p. 287.

5. Among these people, a reformer or principal minister appeared, who attained some eminency. One *Gundulphus* appears to have had many admirers.[8] Having given some persons in his connexion a portion of spiritual instruction, he sent them forth as itinerants, to preach the gospel. Some of his followers were arrested in FLANDERS; and on their examination, they acknowledged they were followers of Gundulphus. "They are charged," says Dr. Allix, "with abhorring baptism: i. e., the Catholic baptism." These disciples said in reply, "The law and discipline we have received of our master, will not appear contrary either to the gospel decrees or apostolical institutions, if carefully looked into. This discipline consists in leaving the world, in bridling carnal concupiscence, in providing a livelihood by the labour of our hands, in hurting nobody, and affording charity to all, &c. This is the sum of our justification, to which the use of baptism can superadd nothing. But if any say that some sacrament lies hid in baptism, the force of it is taken off by three causes. 1st. Because the reprobate life of ministers can afford no saving remedy to the persons baptized. 2ndly. Because whatever sins are renounced at the font, are afterwards taken up again in life and practice. 3rdly. Because a strange will, a strange faith, and strange confession, do not seem to belong to a little child, who neither wills nor runs, who knoweth nothing of faith, and is altogether ignorant of his own good and salvation, in whom there can be no desire of regeneration, and from whom no confession of faith can be expected."[9] That these people held views on the ordinances similar to the Baptists of modern

---

[8] Allix's Rem. on Ch. of Pied., ch. 11, p. 94.   [9] Pied. Ch., ch. 11, pp. 94-5.

times, is allowed by all respectable writers. "They were well-meaning and honest, though ignorant and illiterate men," says Dr. Jortin.[10]

1040   6. The Paterines were, in 1040, become very numerous and conspicuous at Milan, which was their principal residence: and here they flourished at least two hundred years. They had no connexion with the church, nor with the Fathers, considering them as corrupters of Christianity. They called the cross the abomination of desolation standing in the holy place; and they said *it was the mark of the beast.* Nor had they any share in the state, for they took no oaths, and bore no arms. The state did not trouble them, but the clergy preached, prayed, and published books against them, with unabated zeal;[1] while there was no legal use of the sword, *a let* was realized, which proved favourable to their sentiments and prosperity. The Paterines were decent in their deportment, modest in their dress and discourse, and their morals were irreproachable. In their conversation, there was no levity, no scurrility, no detraction, no falsehood, no swearing. Their dress was neither fine nor mean. They were chaste and temperate, never frequenting taverns or places of public amusement. They were not given to anger or violent passions. They were not eager to accumulate wealth, but were content with a plain plenty of the necessaries of life. They avoided commerce, because they thought it would expose them to the temptations of collusion, falsehood, and oaths; and they chose to live by labour or handicraft. They were always employed in spare hours, either in giving or receiving instruction.

7. Their churches were divided into sixteen com-

---

[10] Rem. on Ecc. Hist., vol. v., p. 27, and Milner's Ch. Hist., c. 11, ch. 2.   [1] Rob. Res., p. 405.

partments, such as the English Baptists would call associations. Each of these was subdivided into parts, which would here be called churches or congregations. In Milan, there was a street called Pararia, where it is supposed they met for worship. Their bishops and officers were mechanics, weavers, shoemakers, who maintained themselves by their industry. They had houses at Ferrara, Brescia, and in many other cities and towns. One of their principal churches was that of Concorezzo, in the Milanese; and the members of churches, in this association, were more than 1500. During the kingdom of the Goths and Lombards, the Anabaptists, as the Catholics called them, had their share of churches and baptisteries, during which time they hold no communion with any hierarchy. After the ruin of these kingdoms, laws were issued by the emperors, to deprive dissenters of baptismal churches, and to secure them to the Catholic clergy. Consequently the brethren worshipped in private houses, under different names. Each of the houses where they met seemed to be occupied by one of the brethren: they were marked so as to be known only among themselves, and they never met in large companies in persecuting times; and though they differed in some things, yet there was a perfect agreement in all those points mentioned above.[2]

945 to 1059

8. There were many Greeks from Bulgaria and Philippopolis, who came to settle in Italy, about the time that the emperor Alezias Comnenas disturbed the Philippopolitans, and burnt *Basil*, the Bogomilan or Paulician.[3] "It is difficult," says Moshem, "to fix the pre-

[2] Rob. Res., ch. 11. The language of the Paterines is very strongly expressed against Inf. Bap. See Gregory and Muratori, with others, quoted in Robinson's Res., 408, note 9; and Hist. Bap., p. 211, note 4. [3] Id. Research., p. 409. *Note*, the

cise period of time when the Paulicians began to take refuge in Europe."

About the middle of the eleventh century, a considerable number of them settled in Lombardy, Insubria, and principally at Milan; they were in Italy called Paterini or Cathari. In process of time, they sent colonies into almost all the other provinces of Europe, and formed gradually a considerable number of religious assemblies, who adhered to their doctrine. A set of men like to the Paulicians or Paterines proceeded in vast numbers out of Italy, in the following ages, and spread like an inundation through all the European provinces. Thus Italy, who gave *a seat* to the beast, sent forth those moral streams, to prevent the world from becoming stagnant with pollution.[4]

---

word *Bogomilus* means in the Russian language, "Calling out for mercy from above." A Bogomilan was a praying man.

[4] These Dissenting Baptists were the only class in this kingdom not given up to the corruption of the times. Luxury, covetousness, and adultery universally prevailed among the catholic clergy. Prelates, habited in purple robes and gold, converted nunneries into stews, and parks and mansions were had for seraglios. They were awfully wicked in Italy; cures and sinecures were provided for their children. Presbyters were common at 12 years of age, and boys were bishops. We have seen that solicitude on the part of parents for the welfare of their offspring, with the Alexandrian school, first led to youths' baptism. Infant pollution was understood to be removed by water baptism, and the ordinance was the only means of saving the soul from purgatory. The importance *now* attached to baptism required the priest to attend every woman in labour, but the plan was farther matured, by inventing various instruments and different distilled waters for the *fœtus in utero!* Abortives and dead bodies received the sanctified liquid; all which evils have the same authority for their existence as Pædobaptism, and shame from the scattered rays of truth will abolish the one as it has the other. To detail faithfully *the conduct* of clergymen, and *the progress* of infant baptism, would present the filthiest account

9. A reformer now appeared in Italy, and one
1137 who proved himself a powerful opponent to the church of Rome, and who in fortitude and zeal was inferior to no one bearing that name, while in learning and talents he excelled most. This was ARNOLD of BRESCIA; a man allowed to have been possessed of extensive erudition, and remarkable for his austerity of manners; he travelled into France in early life, and became a pupil of the renowned Peter Abelard. On leaving this school, he returned into Italy, and assumed the habit of a monk, began to propagate his opinions in the streets of Brescia, where he soon gained attention. He pointed his zeal at the wealth[5] and luxury of the Roman clergy. The eloquence of Arnold aroused the inhabitants of Brescia. They revered him as the apostle of religious liberty, and rose in rebellion against the bishops. The church took an alarm at his bold attacks;
1139 and in a council, (1139) he was condemned to perpetual silence.[6] Arnold left Italy, and found

ever issued from the press. Yet these men, daring to reform the abuses of the church, are by Pædobaptists reproached to this day, Mezeray, p. 115, Mosh. v. ii. p. 167, Rob. Bap. p. 305, &c., Dr. M'Crie, p. 16, Dr. Allix's Ch. Pied. c. 10, p. 88. See Bap. Mag. v. ii. p. 435. Dr. Wall's Hist. pt. 2, p. 379. [5] Not only were great fees required by the clergy for every duty to the living and the dead, but when any malady prevailed in a nation, as in France, A.D. 996, the afflicted were taught to propitiate heaven, by giving their property to the clergy (Mezeray, p. 204), and as the tenth century drew to a close (999), a general panic prevailed throughout the catholic world, from Rev. xx. 2—4, that the last judgment was approaching. The rich endowed churches, while the wily clergy in the writings excluded any future claimant of the gift under the pain of Judas's punishment!!! From the view of their own edifices and mansions being useless, the nobility and gentry permitted their homes to go to decay. See Mosh. Hist. v. ii. p. 108. Jones's Lect. on Ec. Hist. v. ii. p. 196, &c. Lon. Ency. v. xi. p. 290. [6] M'Crie's History of the Reform. in Italy, p. 3, &c.

an asylum in the Swiss canton of Zurich. Here he began his system of reform,[7] and succeeded for a time, but the influence of Bernard made it necessary for him to leave the canton. This bold man now hazarded the desperate experiment of visiting Rome, and fixing the standard of rebellion in the very heart of the capitol. In this measure, he succeeded so far as to occasion a change of the government, and the clergy experienced for ten years a reverse of fortune, and a succession of insults from the people.[8] The pontiff struggled hard, but in vain, to maintain his ascendency. He at length sunk under the pressure of the calamity. Successive pontiffs were unable to check his popularity. Eugenius III. withdrew from Rome, and Arnold, taking advantage of his absence, impressed on the minds of the people the necessity of setting bounds to clerical authority; but the people, not being prepared for such liberty, carried their measures to the extreme, abused the clergy, burnt their property, and required all ecclesiastics to

[7] Who can question the necessity of a reform? From the immense wealth of the church, idleness and every evil was found among the clergy. Religion was a jest!!! A dispute existed as to which liturgy, the Gothic or Roman, should be used in the church, this was decided by *single combat*, Mosh. v. ii. p. 220. The festivals of fools and asses were established in most churches. On days of solemnity, they created a bishop of fools; and an ass was led into the body of the church, dressed in a cape, and four-cornered cap. When the people were dismissed, it was by the priests braying three times like an ass, and the people responded in an asinine tone, Jones's Lect. v. i. p. 534. At stated times, the more remarkable events in the Christian history were represented in a kind of mimic show. But such scenic representations, though they amused the gazing populace, were injurious to religion, Mosh. C. 13, p. 2, c. 4, § 1. Yet, for his efforts, Arnold, in the eyes of clergymen and state writers, was a sad heretic. [8] Mosh. Hist. v. ii. p. 318.

swear to the new constitution. "Arnold," says Gibbon, "presumed to quote the declaration of Christ, that *his kingdom was not of this world.* The abbots, the bishops, and the pope himself, must renounce their *state*, or their salvation." The people were brave, but ignorant of the nature, extent, and advantages of a reformation. The people imbibed, and long retained the colour of his opinions. His sentiments also were influential on some of the clergy in the Catholic church. He was not devoid of discretion, he was protected by the nobles and the people, and his services to the cause of freedom; his eloquence thundered over the seven hills. He showed how strangely the clergy in vice had degenerated from the primitive times of the church. He confined the shepherd to the spiritual government of his flock.

1144 It is from the year 1144, that the establishment of the senate is dated, *as a glorious era*, in the acts of the city. Arnold maintained his station *above ten years*, while two popes, either trembled in the Vatican, or wandered as exiles in the adjacent cities.[9] "The wound appeared unto death," but the pope having mustered his troops, and placing himself at their head, soon became possessed of his official dignity.[10] Arnold's friends were numerous, but a sword was no weapon in the articles of his faith.

1155 In 1155, this noble champion was seized, crucified, and burnt. His ashes were thrown

---

[9] Ro. Hist. ch. 69. [10] This reverse of things re-established all the old characters and corruptions. These corruptions were seen in the discovery of 6000 heads of infants in a warren, near a religious nunnery, Danv. p. 128, and until this *exposing period*, the Catholics had baptized men, women, and children in the fonts *quite naked*, Wall's Hist. pt. 2, p. 379. While others had their children disinterred, and baptized in the Father's name. See Bap. Mag. v. i. p. 435, from Vossius.

into the river. "The clergy triumphed in his death; with his ashes, his sect was dispersed; his memory still lives in the minds of the Romans." Thus, the deadly wound was healed. Though no corporeal relic could be preserved to animate his followers, the efforts of Arnold in civil and religious liberty were cherished in the breasts of future reforming spirits, and inspired those mighty attempts, in WICKLIFFE, HUSS, and others.[1]

10. His memory was long and fondly cherished by his countrymen, and his tragical end occasioned deep and loud murmurs; it was regarded as an act of injustice and cruelty, the guilt of which lay upon the pope and his clergy, who had been the occasion of it. The disciples of Arnold, who were numerous, obtained the name of ARNOLDISTS; these separated from the communion of the church of Rome, and long continued to bear their testimony against its numerous abuses.[2] "This unhappy man," says Mosheim, "seems not to have adopted any doctrines inconsistent with the spirit of true religion. He considered the clergy should be divested of all their worldly possessions, and live on the contributions of the people. This reformer, in whose character and manners there were several things worthy of esteem, drew after him a great number of disciples, who derived from him the denomination of Arnoldists; and, in succeeding ages, discovered the spirit and intrepidity of their leader, as often as any favourable opportunities of reforming the church were offered to their zeal.[3]

11. The sentiments of Arnold on the ordinances is thus established. *Bernard,* whose influence occasioned Arnold's leaving Zurich, accuses his followers of mocking at infant baptism. He also received a like accusation

---

[1] Jones's Lect. v. ii. p. 211.   [2] Allix's Re. Ch. Pied. C. 18, p. 170, &c.   [3] Hist. v. ii. p. 318.

from *Evervimus,* in Germany, who said the Arnoldists condemn the (catholic) sacraments, particularly baptism, which they administer only to the adult. They do not believe infant baptism, alleging that place of the gospel,[4] whoever shall believe and be baptized shall be saved.

Arnold was condemned by the Lateran council of 1139 for rejecting infant baptism.[5]

Arnold had laid to his charge, that he was unsound in his judgment about the sacrament of the altar and infant baptism.[6] He is said to have held the opinion of Berengarius,[7] and that from him the Waldenses were called Arnoldists.[8]

Arnold denied that baptism should be administered to infants.[9]

---

[4] Wall's Hist., p. 2, ch. 7, § 5, p. 234. Dr. Allix's Rem. on Ch. Pied. c. 16, p. 140. [5] Wall's Hist. p. 2, c. 7, § 5, p. 242. [6] Allix on Ch. Pied., c. 18, p. 171. [7] Id., p. 174. [8] Id. Facts oppos. to Fict., p. 46. [9] Jones's Lect., v. ii., p. 215. The method of enlarging the church catholic was singularly adapted through ages to acquire the object. Albert, a canon, was commissioned to dragoon the Livonians into the profession of Christianity, and to oblige them, by force of arms, to receive the benefits of baptism. Mosh. 2, 234. In ordinary cases baptism in the church was thus regulated. The candidate, having passed through a course of preparatory instruction, all of human invention, was at length pronounced fit. Salt was then applied to his mouth as a sign of the excited desire of baptismal water. He was exorcised, or purified, from all demoniacal and magical influence. The priest then breathed on him, in token of his receiving the Holy Spirit, the principle of spiritual and eternal life. His nose and ears were anointed with spittle, his breast and shoulders were anointed with oil, and after many more ceremonies, he was dipped three times, and on coming out of the water he was anointed with chrism, and crowned with other rites, all of the same nature. Jones's Lect., v. ii., p. 199, &c.

1160   12. It is acknowledged that the Latin church[10] was, during this century, troubled with the PURITANS, a term, according to Mosheim, expressive of the successors of the Novatianists; but the pontiffs were particularly annoyed by the Paulicians who emigrated in numbers from Bulgaria, who leaving their native land spread themselves throughout various provinces. Many of them, while doing good to others, and propagating the gospel, were put to death with the most unrelenting cruelty.[1] Their accessions from different sources made the Puritan or Paterine churches very considerable, and to their enemies very formidable, even before the name of Waldo of Lyons was known. Besides these foreign accessions, some books had been written and circulated by the Puritans, while several reformers appeared in different kingdoms, all advocating the same doctrines and practice; so that the clergy and pontiff were aroused to vigorous opposition. In 1180,

1180   the Puritans had established themselves in Lombardy and Puglia, where they received frequent visits from their brethren who resided in other countries; in this and the next century they were to

---

[10] The members of this church were principally engaged in erecting places of worship during this age. The rich gave their property, and the poor did the work of beasts, Mosh. 2, p. 290. Inscriptions on such buildings, baptisteries, and fonts are often found, viz.—

> "Our wealthy Lady Theudolind founded and built this baptistery in the life-time of our Lord Agiluf."

Or a more modern one is,

NIΨON ANOMHMATA MH MONAN OΨIN.

(Wash thy sins, not thy face only.)

[1] Mosh. Hist., C. 12, pt. 2, c. 5, § 4.

be found in the capital of Christendom.[2] Effective measures were matured about this time, when Waldo and his followers were driven from France.

13. In 1210, the Paterines had become so numerous and so odious to the state clergy, that the old bishop of Ferrara obtained an edict of the emperor Otho IV. for the suppression of them; but this measure extended only to that city.

1210

In five years after, Pope Innocent III. of bloody celebrity, held a council at the Lateran, and denounced anathemas against heretics of every description. Dr. Wall declares that this council did enforce infant baptism on the dissidents, as heretics taught it was to no purpose to baptize children.[3]

1215

In this council, the Milanese were censured for sheltering the Paterines. After a variety of efforts to suppress them, the cruel policy of the court of Rome extended its sanguinary measures over Italy. In 1220, Honorius III. procured an edict of Frederick II. which extended over all the imperial cities, as had been the case for some years over the south of France, and the effects of the pontiff's anger was soon felt by the deniers of the infant rite. These edicts were every way proper to excite horror, and which rendered the most illustrious piety and virtue incapable of saving from the most cruel death such as had the misfortune, says Mosheim, to be disagreeable to the inquisitors.[4] No alternative of escaping those human monsters presented itself but that of flight, which was embraced by many; "indeed," Mosheim observes, "they passed out of Italy, and spread like an inundation throughout the European provinces,

1220

---

[2] M'Crie's Reform. in Italy, p. 4. [3] Hist. of Inf. Bap., pt. 2, p. 242. [4] Ecc. Hist., v. ii., p. 426, 430.

but Germany in particular afforded an asylum where they were called Gazari instead of Cathari (Puritans). One Ivo, of Narbonne, was summoned by the inquisitor of heretical pravity. Ivo fled into Italy.

1243 At Como he became acquainted with the Paterines, and accommodated himself to their views for a time. They informed him, after he was a member of their society, that they had churches in almost all the towns of Lombardy, and in some parts of Tuscany; that their merchants, in frequenting fairs and markets, made it their business to instil their tenets in the minds of the rich laymen with whom they traded, and the landlords in whose houses they lodged. On leaving Como, he was furnished with letters of recommendation to professors of the same faith in Milan; and in this manner, he passed through all the towns situated on the Po, through Cremona and the Venetian states, being liberally entertained by the Paterines, who received him as a brother, on producing his letters, and giving the signs which were known by all that belonged to the sect.[5]

1245 14. The thirteenth century exhibited in Italy two objects that struck devout observers; the one was the simple manners of the Paterines, which appeared to great advantage in contrast with the lives of their neighbours; the other was the predictions of Joachim, abbot of a monastery, foretelling a reformation of the whole catholic church. This simplicity was seen in its native form in their separate communities. The Paterines knew their discipline could not possibly be practised in the church; they therefore withdrew, constantly avowing the sufficiency of Scripture, the competency of each to reform himself, the right of all,

---

[5] M'Crie's Ref. in Italy, p. 4, &c.

even of women, to teach; and openly disclaiming all manner of coercion in matters of religion. The wisdom of the Paterines in separating wholly from the Roman church, appears in a striking light, when contrasted with the weakness of those who continued in that communion, and endeavoured to incorporate the morality of the Paterines into the established church, in order to reform the community.[6] In conformity with their declaration of the sufficiency of the Scriptures to regulate a Christian church, they had houses in many cities, in which they assembled for religious worship, with their barbs[7] or religious teachers.

15. The publication of the above books, with others by some monks, awakened the pontiff to adopt measures for the destruction of all opponents; consequently under one term, that of heretic, all were proscribed; and though the Paterines complained of being mixed up with fanatics, their complaints were disregarded. The bishops and clergy were glad to have a reasonable pretext for the extirpation of those people who checked their ambitious projects, and who by their example and instruction kept the community awake to their defects and impiety. Means of a vigorous and corresponding character to those so successfully employed against the Albigenses had been used for ridding Italy of dissenters. While the Dominican friars had been carrying on their inquiries, and preaching down heresy in France; a corresponding order of men had pursued a similar course in Italy against the Paterines, who no doubt consider-

---

[6] Rob. Res., p. 414.   [7] The exact etymology of this word is not shown; the dissenters were called Barbarus by the literati, and it might be a contraction of that word; or Barbe, a beard, from their venerable elders wearing long beards; or barbet, a shagged dog, might be used by their enemies to convey, like method-ist, ana-baptist, contempt or reproach.

ably increased in this kingdom from the refugees who escaped the crusaders in Languedoc.

The effects of the above inquisition, though severe, were not so great on the Paterines as the pope desired, and therefore he obtained in the beginning of Frederick's reign, as before mentioned (1224), a cruel decree denouncing all Puritans, Paterines, Arnoldists, &c., &c. expressed in these terms, "*We shall not suffer these wretches to live.*" A second, third, and fourth followed, all of the same cruel and virulent character. The edicts declared that all these Paterines to whom the bishops were disposed to show favour, *were to have their tongues pulled out*, that they might not corrupt others by justifying themselves,[8] others were to be committed to the flames. These measures were cordially approved by the pope, who to give the imperial edicts the desired effect, accompanied them with his bull.

16. The above measure, though severe and continued in force for years, did not extirpate the Paterines, as we find in the middle of this century, " they had," says Reiner, four thousand members in the perfect class, but those called disciples were *an innumerable multitude.*"[9] And notwithstanding the persecutions to which they were exposed, they maintained themselves in Italy, and kept up a regular correspondence with their brethren in other countries. They had public schools where their sons were educated, and these were supported by contributions, from churches of the same faith in Bohemia and Poland.[10] Their prosperity irritated the pontiff, who on Frederick's death, 1250, and during an interregnum, resolved on extirpating heresy. The usual methods were attempted, preaching

1250

---

[8] Allix's Pied., p. 297. Jones's Lect., v. ii. p. 397. [9] Wall's Hist., pt. 2, p. 246.   [10] Perrin in M' Crie.

and mustering crusaders; but after every effort devised for their instruction, they appeared no less in number, and still formidable to their adversaries. Indeed, it was found in the middle of this century that the Paterines had *exceedingly increased*, so that his Holiness found it necessary to give full powers to his inquisitors, and to erect a standing tribunal, if possible, in every country where Puritans were known to infest. These inquisitors were armed with all imaginable power, to punish all those persons who dared *to think* differently to the pope and his successors. Unity of views, sentiments, and practices, was to be effected by these cruel measures; but instead of accomplishing this object, we conclude the Paterines were dispersed abroad into other provinces, or else they retired into obscurity, from either of which circumstance their local names would become extinct. The terror of the inquisitors awed the Italians into silence; but it is highly creditable, indeed, there are some reasons to believe the Paterines did continue dispersed in Italy till the reformation in Germany. It is very probable that many of these people became incorporated with the Waldensian churches in the valleys of Piedmont, which at this period enjoyed, under the dukes of Savoy, the sweets of religious liberty: this incorporation could be easily effected, since it is proved by Allix and others, that the most part of the Paterines held the same opinions as the churches in the valleys, and therefore were taken for one and the same class of people.[1]

1260

17. The straitened circumstances of the Vaudois in Pragela, suggested the propriety of seeking for a new territory; this they obtained on their own terms of liberty in Calabria, a district in the north-east of Italy.

---

[1] Rem. on Pied. p. 112. Mosh. Hist. v. ii., p. 225, note.

This new settlement prospered, and their religious peculiarities awakened displeasure in the old inhabitants; but the landlords, well pleased with their industry, afforded them protection. This colony received fresh accessions from time to time of those who fled from the persecutions raised against them in Piedmont; and continued to flourish when the reformation dawned on Italy, after which they were barbarously murdered.[2]

18. These plain facts allow us to conclude, that Italy must have, in parts, enjoyed the lamp of truth from apostolic days. That the cathari or Puritan churches continued for ages is acknowledged, of the views of which we have spoken. Such churches were strengthened by the Baptists from Bulgaria, whose sameness of views admitted their incorporation. When these congregations became too large to assemble in one place, they parted and held separate assemblies, in perfect unity with each other.[3] They owned the Scriptures as a rule of conduct, and administered the ordinance of baptism to believers by one immersion.[4] They maintained church discipline even on their ministers, as examples are recorded.[5] They were always found on the side of religious liberty, and considered the oppressing clergy *the locust* which darkened and tormented the world. They were persecuted, awed, dispersed, or destroyed, yet their spirit and conduct will be again exhibited in future sections of our history.

[2] Jones's Lect. 2, p. 420.　Mc. Crie's Ref. in Italy, p. 7.
[3] Rob. Hist. Bap., p. 356.　[4] Id. Research., p. 384.　[5] Jones' Lect. v. ii., p. 273.　Rob. Ecc. Res., ch. 11, passim.

Section VII.

CHURCHES IN GAUL.

"I will give power unto my two witnesses,[1] and they shall prophesy," &c.—*Rev.* ii. 3, 4.

1. Taking the general features of this prophecy, it appears to have had a more exact accomplishment in the Albigensian and Waldensian churches, than in any other statement of religious communities on record. This application to them of the terms, the two candlesticks and two witnesses, appears more reasonable than any other exposition given. It is rather remarkable, that these two churches took for their emblem a candlestick and seven stars, surrounded with a motto of "the light shining in darkness."

2. It has been asserted, with considerable grounds of probability, that the gospel was preached in Gaul, France, by the great apostle of the Gentiles: but we have no records that mention, with certainty, the establishment of Christianity in Transalpine Gaul, before the second century. Pothinus, or Photinus, a man of exemplary piety and zeal, set out from Asia, and laboured in the Christian cause with success among the Gauls; that from his efforts churches were established at Lyons and Vienne, of

60

110

---

[1] These witnesses were to prophesy 1260 days. In 533, the church and empire were both regulated by the Justinian code; and in 1260 years after, the Republican French government, in 1792-3, abrogated *this* union, when the establishment of priesthood and church by law was abolished. Here Justin's acts appear in reference to a state-church entirely rescinded, and the consequence was serious to the pope and his hierarchy.

158 which Photinus himself was the first pastor.

Irenæus is supposed to have visited Lyons about A.D. 158, and succeeded to the pastorate of that church after Photinus's death. While Irenæus held this situation, the churches experienced a severe persecution, **177** under the emperor Marcus Aurelius, of which Irenæus gave some particulars to the churches of Asia. He asserts, that the heathens were very bitter against the followers of the Redeemer. The vilest calumnies were propagated against them, consequently they were prohibited appearing in any house, except their own; they were forbidden to appear in the baths, in the markets, or in any public places. The first attack came from the populace by means of shouts, blows, dragging their bodies, plundering their goods, with all the indignities and indecencies that might be expected from a fierce and outrageous multitude. Many were hurried to the magistrates—others were led to martyrdom. Some professors, at the beginning of the trial, lapsed into idolatry, which occasioned the brethren the keenest sorrow, they knowing the serious consequences of apostacy under such circumstances. Most of those who fainted under the commencement of this fiery trial, were brought to repent, and were restored. A woman named *Biblis*, under torture, said, in answer to her accusers, "How could they (Christians) devour infants, which were not suffered to eat the blood of brutes."[2] Their sufferings are detailed in most histories.[3] This state of things lasted eighteen years; during which period, apologies were written for the suffering churches and presented to the emperor, which in some instances were found to moderate the prejudices of their enemies.

---

[2] See above Sect. 2, § 2, 4.   [3] Euseb. Ecc. Hist. Lib. 5, cap. 1. Milner and Jones.

—While other nations were adoring trees, fountains, and other ridiculous objects, the inhabitants of Gaul were most of them Christians, and diverse churches existed in the second century in Narbonne, Gaul.[4] Simondi says, that "Toulouse had scarcely ever been free of this heresy from its first foundation, which the fathers transmitted to their children from generation to generation, almost from the origin of Christianity."[5]

3. The city of Lyons was again visited with the vengeance of the emperor. Severus, in 202, treated the Christians of this city with the greatest cruelty. Such was the excess of his barbarity, that the rivers were coloured with human blood, and the public places of the city were filled with the dead bodies of professors. It is recorded of this church, that since its formation it has been watered with the blood of twenty thousand martyrs.[6] These severities led Christians to reside on the borders of kingdoms, and in the recesses of mountains; and it is probable the Pyrenèes and Alps afforded some of those persecuted people an asylum from local irritation. It is more than probable, that Piedmont afforded shelter to some of these Lyonese, since it is recorded that Christians in the valleys during the second century, did profess and practise the baptizing of believers which accords with the views of Irenæus and others recorded during the early ages.[7]

202

4. Novatian, whose labours were attended with so much success in Italy and in the East, is said to have influenced some churches in France. "About the year 250," says Mezeray, "divers holy men came from Rome as preachers, who planted churches in

250

---

[4] Mezeray's Fr. Hist., p. 4, fol.   [5] History of the Crusades, p. 6.   [6] Collier's Gr. Hist. Dict. Art. Lyons.   [7] See above, Sect. 2, § 4.

several parts, as at Thoulouse, Tours, and other places."⁸ Faustus, bishop of Lyons, with several other French bishops, says Milner, wrote to Stephen, bishop of Rome (254), concerning the views and practice advocated by these Novatianists; who again wrote to Cyprian, of Carthage. This bishop replied to Stephen, supporting strongly the cause of *the church* against Schismatics. *Marcian*, pastor of *Arelate*, united himself to the Novatianists.⁹ Though the gospel had an early footing in Gaul, it appears to have partaken of the early corruptions, which were evidently checked by Novatian and his adherents, which becomes clear from the anger and reproach apparent among Cyprian, and his ambitious brethren.

254

In 430, the Burgundians, a people of Germany, who had received the Christian faith, came into, and obtained a settlement at, Vienne and Lyons:¹⁰ but their influence on these interests is not recorded, though their views of baptism will be given in the German section. The soundness of the Novatian creed was allowed at Rome, and the same was seen in the council of Arles, and at Lyons, where, from their views on predestination, they appear to have been distinguished.¹

430

455

5. The south of France is separated from the north of Spain by the Pyrenean mountains, which extend from the Mediterranean Sea to the Atlantic: that is above two hundred miles, and in breadth, in several places, more than a hundred. The surface is, as may be supposed, most wonderfully diversified. Hills rise upon hills, mountains over mountains, some bare of verdure, others covered with forests of huge cork-trees,

---

⁸ French Hist., p. 4.   ⁹ Hist. of the Ch. C. 3, ch. 13.
¹⁰ Mezeray's Hist. Fr., p. 8.   ¹ Id., p. 19.

oak, beech, chesnut, and evergreens. Nature, in all her original wildness and beauty, is here seen undisturbed, and giving forth in profusion all those productions which can gratify the eye, regale the sense, and satisfy alike the peasant and the prince. Numerous flocks of sheep and goats enliven the hills, while the herdsmen and manufacturers of wool inhabit the valleys; and corn and wine, flax and oil, hang on the slopes. When travellers of taste pass over some parts of the Pyrenèes, they are in raptures, and are at a loss for words to express what they behold. To these mountains, in all periods, the sons of freedom fled. Here the Celts found shelter. Here the Goths realized a refuge, when the Saracens overran Spain. On the south side of these mountains was Spain, and particularly the province of Catelonia, which was inhabited by those persons who originated the Waldenses. Persons holding sentiments in accordance with the true Waldenses, were very numerous in Spain;[2] they were thousands, and tens of

---

[2] The early state of the Spanish churches is unknown; nor do we know whether Paul paid his promised visit to the Christians in this kingdom. In the third century, several denominations of Christians prevailed in Spain. In the fourth century, the Donatists visited it; and the Hieracites, with the Manicheans, were there. There is no regular history of Spain till 324, at which time the Roman church had no influence over others: the primitive discipline was maintained, and the independency of the churches not greatly interrupted. These churches were united by the tie of charity to the churches in Gascony, in France. Their mode of administering baptism, in A.D. 409, was by dipping; nor does it appear that they baptized any but believers. Rob. Res. 197. In the sixth century, the subject of *single* and *trine* immersion was agitated, which, in 617, was adjusted among the Catholics, by Pope Gregory declaring *trine* immersion not essential to salvation. During this century, besides Jews and Catholics, there were abounding in Spain, Manicheans, Priscillianists, Acephali

thousands.³ On the north of these mountains was France, particularly Gascony and Languedoc, which two provinces became inhabited by persons of a corresponding character with those of Spain. "At an early period," Dr. Allix says,⁴ "the churches of the north of Spain were always united with those of the south of France." The religious views of these people are now known by the term Albigenses, from their residing at or near Albi, a city about forty-two miles north-east of Toulouse. These people were considered a rough, uncultivated, and unpolite people by the historians and writers of their day.⁵

500 6. In the language of councils at this period, Christians are denominated, either from their opinions, heretics, or with a view to their discipline, (Paulicians), Sebellians, with others, all termed heretics by Catholics. All these Christians administered baptism by immersion, single or trine; and all baptized those who offered themselves for their respective communions. Id. p. 213. There is no trace of minor nor infant baptism till 517, and in 572, the charges for baptizing infants were so excessive, that many infants *were lost*, which frighted timorous mothers into compliance: and thus the rite and the trade of infant salvation went still together. While these practices were found in the church, persons holding believers' baptism were spread all over Spain; but *one class*, from inhabiting Catalonia, at the foot of the mountains, was called *Navarri*—i. e., inhabitants of valleys; these, at after periods, left Spain for France and other provinces, and were called Vaudois in France and Piedmont. Rob. Res., ch. 9, 10. M'Crie's Reform. in Spain.
³ Rob. Res., p. 299. ⁴ Albig. Ch., ch. 11, p. 109. ⁵ A.D. 496. On the eve of Christmas-day, Clovis, founder of the French monarchy, and his sister, Audofledis, "were plunged in the sacred lavatory." More than 3000 of his subjects followed his example. The Baptistery was erected for the occasion, while the monarch was being instructed. Mezeray's Fr. Hist., p. 15. A sermon preached to Clovis and those baptized with him, on our Saviour's crucifixion, led the monarch to cry out, "If I and my Franks had been there, THAT should not have happened."

schismatics; but there was one article of discipline in which they all agreed, and from which they were frequently named, that was BAPTISM. They held the Catholic community, not to be a church of Christ; they therefore re-baptized such as had been baptized in that community, before they admitted them to their fellowship. For this conduct they were called Ana-baptists. These Baptists in France and Spain called themselves Christians; and censured the fraud of those who imposed on the world, by being called Catholics. They quoted abundance of Scripture to prove a New Testament church consisted only of virtuous persons, born of water and the Holy Spirit; they separated from the Catholics, on account of the impurity of their church; they took the New Testament for the rule of their faith and practice. "The Albigenses admitted the catechumi," says Dr. Allix, "after an exact instruction, and prepared them for receiving baptism by long-continued fasts, which the church observed with them.[6] Thus these Christians baptized Pagans and Jews, they re-immersed all Catholics; and they baptized none without a personal profession of faith.[7] In a council held

524 at Lerida, 524, it was decreed, that such as had fallen into the prevarication of Ana-baptism, as the Novatianists, with others, if they should return to the Catholic church, should be received, provided they had been baptized in the name of the Trinity. Dissidents made no such distinctions; they immersed converts, and re-baptized others. We have here stated the views and practices of the early Baptists, and are compelled to consider the inhabitants of the foot of the

[6] Rem. on Ch. Pied., ch. 2, p. 7. [7] Robinson's Eccles. Res., p. 246.

Pyrenèes, whether living on the Spanish side or in the French provinces, as one and the same class of people, Vaudois, who could shift to either kingdom, as circumstances of oppression or liberty occurred in the respective kingdoms.

7. At how early a period the opinions of the Bulgarians, Paulicians, or Bogomilans, were propagated beyond the Alps, is uncertain to us, though the period of awful ignorance in the Catholic church, during the seventh century, would suggest the time.[8] Neither have we any means of ascertaining, whether the old Puritan churches originated the name of Albigenses, or that a church of dissidents was formed at Albi, by emigrants from Bulgaria or Italy. Mosheim says, they received their teachers, or the conformation of their officers to eldership, from the churches in Italy.[9] In 714, the Moors entered Spain, and conquered that kingdom.[10] Their conquest is said to have been rather favourable to liberty, and even religious freedom could be procured for a small sum,

---

[8] The state of the Catholic clergy in France at this period was awful; Mezeray says, most of them pursued a military life;—clergy kept concubines, and deacons, four or five at a time. Ignorance alarmingly prevailed. Bishops were enjoined to learn and understand the Lord's prayer. The bishops could not be prevailed on to exhort the people. Women gave blessings to the people with the sign of the cross; and conferred on virgins sacerdotal authority. Even a woman, named Joan, filled the office of pontiff. Fr. Hist., p. 112, 115, 138. "The genuine religion of Jesus was unknown in this century to clergy and laity, excepting a few of its doctrines contained in the creed." The offices of religion devolved on boys. Mezeray's Ib. Mosh. Hist., v. ii., p. 167, 421, and v. iii., p. 132, and v. i., p. 503. Rob. Res., p. 258. Dr. Wall. Hist., pt. 1, p. 256. [9] Mosh. Hist., v. ii., p. 224, note. [10] Ockley's Hist. and Conq. of the Saracens.

yet these Baptists disdained to purchase *a native right*, consequently they fled to the mountains which separate Catalonia from Narbonensian Gaul.¹

732 France was alike subject to those marauders from 721 to 732, with the rest of the western empire. At the latter date, Charles Martel was successful in recovering his kingdom from the usurpers: and this military chieftain took the treasuries of the church, with which he rewarded his soldiers.² To what extent the Puritan churches realized injury from the barbarians, we do not know; though it is evident the mountains afforded an asylum to many Christians while they governed those kingdoms: and when tranquillity was restored, the Spanish refugees emigrated, and settled in the French provinces, near the foot of the Pyrenèes. Near the middle of the eighth century, many thousands of these people, with their wives, children, and servants, of whose views and practice in religion we have spoken, emigrated over the Pyrenèes, from the Spanish to the French foot of the mountains.³

8. During the sovereignty of Charles the Great, the several kingdoms and provinces contiguous to France, were kept in agitation from his military enterprises. In his religious career, he brought into France from Rome, the Georgian liturgy, which was appointed to supersede the Gallican, this bold innovation caused some confusion in the kingdom. He resolved on subduing the Saxons, who were pagans, and inhabited a great part of Germany, but this he found impracticable. In the end, his imperial majesty proposed to the whole nation the dreadful alternative, either of being assassinated by the troops, or of accepting life on condition of professing

---

¹ Jones's Eccl. Lect. v. ii. p. 409.   ² Mezeray's Fr. Hist. p. 82.   ³ Gibbon's Ro. Hist. c. 52, and Rob. Res. p. 242.

themselves Christians, by being baptized, and the severe laws, yet stand in the capitularies of this monarch, by which they were obliged, on pain of death, to be baptized themselves, and of heavy fines, to baptize their children within the year of their birth. These people, with Frisians and Huns, were constrained to embrace the Christian religion. This was *the first law in Europe* for infant baptism, and it was consigned to the clergy to enforce, which they did, by converting all the irritional part of kingdoms, to the profession of Christianity. The clergy dwelt largely on the ceremonies of baptism, particularly the necessity of trine immersion.[4] and the church was fully engaged in adjusting the internal divisions and appointing officers for this newly-acquired territory. Probably, the devotion of Charlemagne and the clergy to Germany, allowed the unassuming Vaudois to realize some tranquillity; we are unacquainted with the influence of this human injunction on the Dissenters in the south of France.

789

9. It is recorded of Hinchmar, Bishop of Laudan, in France, that he renounced infant baptism, and that his diocese were accused in the synod of Accinicus of not baptizing children.[5] This minister

850

---

[4] Rob. Hist. of Bap. p. 282, ch. 26.   [5] Baptism remained in the Catholic church," says Mezeray, (Fr. Hist. p. 117, xxiii. king,) "the same, and was performed by dipping or plunging, not by throwing or sprinkling." Stephen, the pontiff, 754, gave his opinion, that if children *were sickly*, pouring should in such cases of necessity be valid baptism; but ordinarily, it was administered by three dippings." "Immersion was first left off in France," says Dr. Wall, (Hist. Inf. Bap. pt. 2, p. 220,) "and there, the Antipædobaptists are traced." Pouring, aspersion, lustrations, and sprinklings, were customs among the heathen, before Christ or Moses, Potter's Antiq. of Gr. v. ii. p. 248, &c. Dr. Wall's Hist. Inf. Bap. pt. 1, p. 501. These lustrations, holy water, and sprinklings, were by the Catholics borrowed from the heathens, as is fully

comes in for his share of reproach from Catholics and Protestants, which is no obscure proof of his reforming measures disturbing the hirelings in office. The ensuing age has been fitly termed, by Baronius, a Catholic annalist, the *iron, leaden, and obscure age;* he says, "Christ was then, as it appears, in a very deep sleep, there were wanting disciples who, by their cries, might awaken him, being themselves all fast asleep." This is perfectly true of the Catholic community; but while this long night of silence and deep sleep, with awful darkness, brooded over every branch of that establishment, the BAPTISTS were not inactive. It was in the tenth century that the Paulicians emigrated from Bulgaria, and spread themselves abroad through every province of Europe.[6]

900

When we consider their object in diffusing truths and holding up the lamp for other's guidance, their self-denials and trials, we cannot withhold from them the praise due to their names. The boon such a people proved, to the nations sitting in darkness and death, will be made evident in the day of decision. They rest from their labours, and their works will follow them. Many of the Bulgarian Baptists lived single, and adopted an itinerant life, purposely to serve the cause of their Redeemer. "It was in the country of the Albigeois, in the southern provinces of France," remarks Gibbon,[7] "where the Paulicians mostly took root." These people were known by different names in various provinces.[8]

10. The French Paulicians or Albigenses, were plainly of the same order in church affairs, as the Bulgarians.

shown in Dr. Middleton's letter from Rome, pref. xv. and pp. 136—143, and Rob. Hist. of Bap. pp. 421, 458. [6] Mosh. Hist. C. 10, pt. 2, ch. 5, § 2.   [7] Ro. Hist. ch. 54.   [8] Mosh. Hist. v. ii. p. 224, Chamb. Dict. Art. Paul. and Albig.

They had no bishops;[9] the candidates were prepared for baptism by instruction and stated fasts.[10] They viewed baptism as adding nothing to justification, and affording no benefit to children.[1] They received members into their churches after baptism, by prayer, with imposition of hands and the kiss of charity.[2]

They did not allow of the catholic baptism of infants, but baptized those again who went over from that church to their community.[3]

They were divided into two classes, *the perfect and imperfect*, the latter class lived in the enjoyment of things like other men.[4] They were agreed in regarding the church of Rome as an apostate church. They rejected her sacraments as frivolous. While her clergy were ornamented and arrayed in rich vestments, the Albigensian teachers were satisfied with a black coat.

990 11. While the catholic community was in an awful slumber, or under those feelings of consternation, as this century drew to a close, and the clergy immured in luxury and vice, the Paulicians or Albigenses were endeavouring to reform men by a simple exhibition of divine benevolence. "Many efforts were made," says Mosheim, "by Protestants, *the witnesses of the truth*, by whom are meant, such pious and judicious Christians as adhered to the pure religion of the gospel, and remained uncorrupted amidst superstitions. It was principally in *Italy* and *France* that this heroic piety was exhibited."[5] This is an honourable concession to these reforming Baptists. The Paterines were the zealous ad-

---

[9] See above, ch. 5, sec. 5, § 7.   [10] Dr. Allix's Rem. Ch. Pied. ch. 2, p. 7, and ch. 12, pp. 103-4.   [1] Id. ch. 11, p. 95. Dr. Jortin's Rem. on Ecc. Hist. vol. v. p. 226.' Ency. Brit. Art. Albig.   [2] Jones's Lect. v. ii. p. 275.   [3] Rob. Res. p. 463.   [4] Ency. Brit. art. Albig.   [5] Hist. v. ii. p. 198.

vocates of reformin Italy, while the same class of Christians, under the name of Bulgarians, Publicans, *boni homines*, Albigenses, with several other titles,[6] openly avowed in France the same doctrines and discipline of the Redeemer. Their united efforts were directed to restore Christianity to her original purity, and to her legitimate and exalted claims. We have now imperfectly detailed, to the end of the tenth century, an account of the only religious body of people who were not immured in the corruptions of the times, and who unceasingly proclaimed the word of truth, in the face of every class of superstitions, and every degree of vice both in clergy and laity.

12. Having stated the views of the early Dissenters, Euchites, Novatinaists, Manicheans, Bogomilans, Bulgarians or Paulicians; and proved their denominational character, it will be necessary to conclude this section by reference to modern writers. "No point," asserts Mosheim, "is more strongly maintained than this, that the term Albigenses in its more confined sense, was used to denote those heretics who inclined toward the Manichean system, and who were originally and otherwise known by the denominations of Catharists, Publicans, or Paulicians, or Bulgarians. This appears evidently, from many incontestable authorities."[7] This slur of heterodoxy is asserted by Robinson; but what import he intended to convey by the term, we know not. The same writer asserts, "Greece was the parent of these Dissenters; Spain and Navarre, the nurses; and that France was the step-mother."[8] Dr. Allix allows the Albigenses to be looked upon as a colony of the Vaudois.[9] Being satisfied of their genealogy, we observe the reproach of

---

[6] Hist. p. 225. [7] Ch. Hist. C. 11, pt. 2, ch. 5, § 2, note, and Cent. 13, pt. 2, ch. 5, § 7, note. [8] Ec. Res. p. 320.
[9] Rem. on the Albig. Ch., C. 11, p. 114.

Manicheism has been improperly applied. We have no means of ascertaining what this offensive doctrine was, as enemies cannot be safely credited where their interest is involved.

It is said, the Manicheans held that good and evil proceeded from opposite causes: if this is all their heresy, if fully investigated, probably many of our modern churches would be involved in the same crime; but since the Paulicians sincerely condemned the memory and opinions of the Manicheans, and complained of the injustice of giving them that term,[10] whatever those errors were, they ought not to be united with their name. The reproach is allowed by Dr. Allix *as not* belonging to the Albigenses;[1] which is conceded by Dr. Jortin, who asserts they had very little of the Manichean system attached to them.[2] It is very probable the Albigenses held some opinions in common with the Manicheans, as they did in the discipline of believers' baptism,[3] but these Vaudois were not heretical in their views. Baronius says, "they were confuted at a conference before the Bishop of Albi, from the New Testament, which alone they admitted; *they professed the catholic faith*, but would not swear, and were therefore condemned."[4]

The centuriatories of Magdeburgh clear them of heresy.[5] Bishops Usher and Newton, with Dr. Cave, have declared their soundness in the faith of the gospel.

13. Dr. Mosheim says, "The Waldenses were less pernicious than the Albigenses,"[6] but this view is com-

---

[10] Gibbon's Ro. Hist. ch. 54, vol. x. p. 156.   [1] Rem. Albig. Ch. pref. xi. and ch. 11, p. 95.   [2] Rem. on Ec. Hist. vol. v. p. 53.   [3] Mosh. Com. on the affairs of the Christians before Constant. s. 111.   [4] Annals, Cent. 12.   [5] Vol. iii. Cent. 12, cap. 8, pp. 548-9. Lord Lyttleton's Life of Henry II. vol. iv. p. 395, oct.   [6] Ch. Hist. v. ii. p. 432, note.

bated by modern writers, without giving any satisfactory elucidation.[7] Now, it must appear plain that the Albigensian churches, in their original constitution, did partake of the early puritan discipline, since those societies were, to some extent, made up of those who retained the stern views of Novatian. There is no impropriety in our supposing the "pernicious" difference to consist in some, if not all, of those churches, like the Novatian societies, refusing communion to those who apostatized or fell into flagrant sins, while this severe exclusion might not have been enforced in the churches of Piedmont. That the Albigensian churches partook of this excluding discipline, is acknowledged by Dr. Allix.[8]

Section VIII.

CHURCHES IN FRANCE CONTINUED.

And when they shall have finished their testimony, the beast shall kill them.—*Rev.* xi. 7.

1000 1. On entering upon the details of the eleventh century, we are called to realise emotions of joy and sorrow: joy, because a succession of pious men are raised up to advocate the cause of truth and virtue; sorrow, because their labour of love every where is attended with opposition and suffering; though the prospect of death itself does not appear to

---

[7] Dr. Maclean in Mosheim, and Jones's History of the Christian Church, vol. ii. p. 36. 5th ed. [8] Rem. on Albig. Ch. c. 16. p. 145, and Pied. Ch. c. 17. p. 156.

have checked their work of faith and patience of hope. One of the earliest names, as a reformer, in France, is LEUTARD, who arose (1000), and preached to the people in the bishopric of Chaalous. This man gained many followers.[1] The labours of the Paulician Albigenses, or Vaudois, with Leutard, are noticed by GERBERTUS,

1003 who became a disciple, and died 1003.[2] The zealous and commendable exertions of these puritans were the means of collecting religious societies, one of the earliest on record was brought thus prominent by the sufferings they experienced from their enemies. "The first religious assembly which the Paulicians had formed in Europe, is said to have been discovered at

1017 Orleans, in the year 1017, under the reign of Robert. A certain Italian lady is said to have been at the head of this sect.[3] Its principal members were twelve canons of the cathedral of Orleans, men eminently distinguished by their piety and learning, among whom Lisosius and Stephen held the first rank; and it was composed, in general, of a considerable number of citizens, who were far from being of the lowest condition. A council, held at Orleans, employed the most effectual methods that could be devised, " to bring these people to a better mind;" but all endeavours were to no purpose: they adhered tenaciously to their principles, and therefore were condemned to be burnt alive;[4] which sentence thirteen actually realised.

2. These puritans, that came into France from Bulgaria, were murdered without mercy. They held that baptism and the Lord's supper possessed no virtue to

---

[1] Mezeray's Fr. Hist. p. 228.   [2] Allix's Rem. Albig. Ch., C. 10, p. 94.   [3] Female teachers were allowed in these churches. The advantages and benefits to religion, from their devoted efforts, are shown by several writers. M'Crie's Reform. in Italy, p. 187, &c.   [4] Mosh. Ch. Hist. v. ii. p. 225.

justify.⁵ "These worthy clergymen," observes Archbishop Usher, "affirmed that there was no virtue capable of sanctifying the soul, in the Eucharist or in baptism." They are charged with denying baptism and the sacraments: they denied baptism to confer grace, and denied the ordinance to children. All those who practised the baptism of infants at this period considered the ordinance as conferring grace, which is allowed by Dr. Wall.⁶ Their denial of the infant rite was enough, in those times, to occasion their enemies to say they denied the ordinance.⁷ These people's characters were blackened with shocking crimes; but Mosheim allows, that even their enemies acknowledged their sanctity, and that the accusations were evidently false.⁸

1019 3. A synod was held at Toulouse, to consider the most effectual method to rid the province of the Albigenses;⁹ and though the whole sect was in **1022** 1022 said to have been burnt, yet the emigrants from Bulgaria, coming in colonies into France, kept the seed sown, the churches recruited, and soon after, the same class of people was found inhabiting Languedoc and Gascony.¹⁰ It is recorded that LEUTHERICUS, Archbishop of Sens, and who was a disciple of Gerbertus, advocated those views which afterwards were charged on Berenger. Leuthericus died in 1032.¹ **1032** Three years after, we become possessed of two names which resounded through Europe, and whose labours were accompanied with those beneficial effects and permanent results, as to be well worthy of the name of Reformers. BRUNO and BERENGER, or BEREN-

---

⁵ Jortin's Remarks, &c. vol. v. p. 226.   ⁶ Wall's Hist. pt. 2, c. 6, p. 105, and pt. 2, c. 10, § 2, p. 451.   ⁷ Danver's Hist. p. 295.   ⁸ Hist. of the Ch. v. ii. pp. 225-6.   ⁹ Allix's Rem. Ch. Albig. c. 11. p. 95.   ¹⁰ Mezeray's Fr. Hist. p. 229.   ¹ Allix's Rem. Ch. Albig. c. 10. p. 93.

1035 GARIUS, were reformers in France, A. D. 1035; almost as early as Gundulphus appeared in Italy, with whom probably they were in correspondence. Berenger, by his discourses, charmed the people, and drew after him vast numbers of disciples. Some men of learning united themselves with him, and spread his doctrines and views through France, Italy, Germany, and other kingdoms.[2] The effect of these Reformers' preaching was not only enlightening the ignorant, but it gave encouragement to the dissenters to come more prominently into society. The alarm was great to the Catholics: one of their prelates, Deodwin, Bishop of Leige, states that "there is a report come out of France, and gone through Germany, that Bruno, Bishop of Angiers, and Berengarius, archdeacon of the same church, maintain that the host is not the Lord's body; and as far as in them lies, overthrow the baptism of infants." Matthew of Westminster speaks of Berenger as having corrupted all Italy. "It means," says Dr. Allix,[3] "that his followers, who were of the same stamp with the Paterines, kept to the primitive faith of the church, which it was the object of the popes to remove them from; and in their opposing the church of Rome, they were called heretics and corrupters, though this name and practice belonged rightly to the popish party." His followers were so numerous, that old historians relate, that France, Italy, Germany, England, the Belgic countries, &c., were infected with his principles.[4] This proves that persons existed in these provinces in the profession of his sentiments, and who readily gave him support so soon as he appeared in the character of a reformer. Berenger, in his zeal against the corruptions

---

[2] Mezeray's Fr. Hist. p. 229.   [3] Allix's Pied. c. 14. pp. 122-3.   [4] Usher in Bp. Newton's Diss. on the Proph. v. ii. p. 245. Facts opposed, &c. p. 42. Usher in Danver's, p. 288.

of the church, calls the Roman community " a church of malignants, the council of vanity, and the seat of Satan." He was required by the pope to abjure his errors, and burn his writings, which he actually did; and yet, while he lived, he wrote and spoke in the same severe strain.

4. One VALDO was a chief counsellor of Berenger's, and was remarkable for *purity* of doctrine. He was an eminent man, and had many followers;[5] but, from unknown causes, no further reference is made to Bruno or Valdo. Berenger is said to have followed the views of Leuthericus, Archbishop of Sens, who, as before stated, was a disciple of Gerbertus. Berenger began the work of reformation when young, and continued to preach for fifty years. He died 1091, aged 80.[6] Notwithstanding his versatility of mind, he left behind him, in the minds of the people, a deep impression of his extraordinary sanctity; and his followers were as numerous as his fame was illustrious.[7] His views of religion appear to have been scriptural. His followers were called Gospellers for one hundred years, and many of them suffered death for their opinions. On his followers being examined, they said " baptism did not profit children."[8] Many Berengarians suffered death for their opinions, and for opposing infant baptism.[9] Bellarmine says, " the Berengarians admitted *only adults* to baptism, which error the anabaptists embraced ";[10] and Mezeray declares Berenger to have been

---

[5] Mosh. Ch. Hist. v. ii. p. 320, note. Rob. Res. p. 303.
[6] Wall's Hist. pt. 2, p. 216. Mezeray, p. 229. Pædobaptists of late days confine Berenger's views to transubstantiation; but were not baptizing in a state of nudity, and conveying sanctified water to the unborn, with giving the abluent waters to the dying and dead, equally as offensive as eating the body and drinking the blood of Christ? [7] Mosh. v. ii. p. 216. [8] Usher in Danv. p. 288. [9] Montanus, p. 83. Baronius' An. 1223. [10] Facts

head of the Sacramentarians, or Anabaptists.¹ The Berengarians were of the same stamp with the Paterines.² The Berengarians, from the identity of doctrines, were called Albigenses; Berengarians and Vaudois were equivalent terms.³ Morell declares, it was computed in 1160, that *above eight hundred thousand persons* professed the Berengarian faith.⁴ "Thus it cannot be supposed," says Dr. Allix, " that the Albigenses were the disciples of Peter Waldo; and consequently they are to be considered originally as a colony of the Vaudois."⁵

1110 5. About the year 1110, in the south of France, in the provinces of Languedoc and Provence, appeared PETER DE BRUYS, preaching the gospel of the kingdom of heaven, and exerting the most laudable efforts to reform abuses, and remove the superstitions which so awfully disfigured the beautiful simplicity of gospel worship.⁶ His labours in the good cause, we are told, were crowned with abundant success. He was made the honoured instrument of awakening the attention of many to the great concerns of eternity, and pointing them to "the Lamb of God who taketh away the sin of the world." He was under the protection and favour of a nobleman, named Hildephonsus.⁷ He is said to have been a priest of Toulouse; but after his conversion and union with the Albigenses, he became one of their chief ministers. During his ministry the Catholics were busy in erecting temples for worship. The opulent contributed their wealth, while the poor cheerfully performed the services allotted to beasts of burden. Each expected, from his labours and gifts, a

opposed, &c. p. 42.   ¹ Fr. His. p. 229.   ² Dr. Allix's Ch. Pied. c. 14. p. 123.   ³ Facts ubi sup.   ⁴ Mem. p. 54 in Bap. Mag. v. i. p. 435.   ⁵ Ch. of Albig. c. 11. p. 114.
⁶ Mosh. Ch. Hist. v. ii. p. 198.   Allix's Albig. Ch. c. 14, p. 121.
⁷ Clark's Martyrol. p. 79.

reward of Paradise;[8] but the Albigenses preached that gold was not the means of building, but rather of destroying the church.[9]

6. The religious sentiments of Peter de Bruys are not fully known; but the following particulars are handed down to us by historians:—that the ordinance of baptism was to be administered only to adults;[10] that it was a piece of idle superstition to build and dedicate churches to the service of God, who, in worship, has a peculiar respect to the state of the heart, and who cannot be worshipped with temples made with hands; that crucifixes are objects of superstition, and ought to be destroyed; that, in the Lord's supper, the real body and blood of Christ were not partaken of by the communicants, but only represented in the way of symbol or figure; and lastly, that the oblations, prayers, and good works of the living, can in no way be beneficial to the dead.[1] Prateolus, Mezeray, and Bellarmine record that Peter de Bruys held baptism to be useless to children who wanted the exercise of reason.[2] The Petrobrussians, those who withdrew from the church of Rome, did reckon infant baptism as one of the corruptions, and accordingly renounced it and practised only adult baptism. "All those baptized (immersed) in their infancy were re-baptized," says Dr. Wall,[3] "before they could enter their churches." Peter de Bruys held, that persons baptized in infancy are to be baptized after they believe; which is not to be esteemed *re-baptization*, but right baptism.[4] His followers were called Petrobrus-

---

[8] Mosh. Hist. c. 12, p. 2, c. 3, § 2.　　[9] Allix's Albig. Ch. p. 39.　　[10] Mezeray's Hist. p. 276.　　[1] Mosh. Hist. v. ii. p. 315.　　[2] Facts op. p. 45. Allix's Albig. c. 14, p. 124. [3] Hist. Inf. Bapt. pt. 2, c. 7, § 8, p. 250.　　[4] Danver on Bap. p. 290, from Osiander. In this century they plunged the subject in baptism three times in the sacred font. Mezeray's Fr. Hist.

sians, and were very numerous in France and the Netherlands.[5] From him the Albigenses were called Petrobrussians.[6]

7. The place where Peter de Bruys first raised his voice against corrupt practices is now called Dauphine. The clergy were aroused, and by their influence he and his companions were expelled that province. Other provinces and kingdoms shared in his itinerant labours.[7] His doctrines were readily received among the mountaineers (Vaudois)—the villagers, and they found numerous advocates among the country people and in populous towns, particularly about Toulouse. His crime was, in influencing the people to leave the Romish church. The people were re-baptized; the churches were profaned; the altars dug up; of their sacred wooden crosses the Petrobrussians made a fire, and roasted their meat on Good Friday, in defiance of the fast; priests were scourged, monks imprisoned, &c. &c.;[8] while it is allowed that the purity of their morals found friends among the clergy and laity.[9]

8. The Petrobrussians, to justify themselves from the calumnies of Peter of Clugny and others, sent forth a work in answer to the question, "WHAT IS ANTICHRIST?" It is generally supposed to have been the production of Peter de Bruys, and is said to have been written so early as 1120. It bears internal evidence of having been composed for the purpose of vindicating the writer and his friends in their separation from the church of Rome. In reference to the ordinance, it declares, "A third work of Antichrist consists in this, that he attributes the regeneration of the Holy Spirit

1120

---

12 cent. p. 288.   [5] Lon. Ency. Art. Petrobruss.   [6] Facts opposed to Fiction, p. 45.   [7] Mezeray's Fr. Hist. p. 276.
[8] Wall's Hist. pt. 2, p. 251.   [9] Dr. Allix's Albig. Ch. c. 20. p. 188.

unto the mere external rite, baptizing infants in that faith, teaching that thereby baptism and regeneration must be had; on which principle he confers and bestows orders, and indeed grounds all his Christianity; which is contrary to the mind of the Holy Spirit."[10] This view was supported by a confession of their faith, in fourteen articles, published about the same time. In this confession they acknowledge the apostles' creed; believe in the Trinity; own the Canonical books of the Old and New Testament; scriptural character of God, of Adam, and his fall; work of Christ as Mediator; abhorrence of human inventions in worship; that the sacraments were signs of holy things, and that believers should use the symbols or forms when it can be done; though they may be saved without those signs; they own baptism and the Lord's supper; and express their obedience to secular powers.[1] Peter de Bruys continued his labours during a period of twenty years, when he was called to seal his testimony with his blood. He was committed to the flames at St. Giles, a city of Languedoc, in France, by an enraged populace, instigated by the clergy of the catholic church, who very justly apprehended their traffic to be in danger from this new and intrepid reformer.[2]

9. Within five years of Bruys's martyrdom, HENRY, of Toulouse, who had been a disciple of his, appeared as a reformer. He travelled through different provinces, and exercised his ministerial functions in all places, with the utmost applause from the people. He declaimed with great vehemence and fervour against the vices of the

---

[10] Jones's Lect. v. ii. p. 262.   [1] Hist. of the Ch. Church, by W. Jones, v. ii. p. 53. Gilly's Narrative, Appendix 12.
[2] Allix's Albig. Ch. c. 14, p. 124, and Jones's Lect. v. ii. p. 207.

clergy, and the superstitions they had introduced into the church.[3] Contemporary with Bruys, Henry, and Arnold, was that extraordinary man, BERNARD, abbot of Clairval in France, whose learning and sanctity rendered him an object of general admiration, whose word appears to have regulated almost every court in Europe, and whose counsels decided the policy of the Catholic community, from the pope to the peasant. Though Bernard fully concedes the points of corruption in the hierarchy, and of children being promoted to dignities in the church,[4] yet his influence was fully given to uphold the man of sin, by all the severe measures of the times. We do not wish to detract from his excellencies; but all those features of sanctity about him, were placed in direct opposition to those good men who strove to reform abuses in the Catholic community, as we now exhibit. Writing to the Count of St. Giles, Bernard thus describes the state of affairs: "How great are the evils which we have heard and known to be done by Henry, the heretic, and what he is still every day doing in the churches of God! He wanders up and down in your country in sheep-clothing, being a ravenous wolf! but according to the hint given by our Lord, we know him by his fruits. The churches are without people—the people without priests—priests without reverence—and lastly Christians without Christ. The life of Christ is denied to infants, by refusing them the grace of baptism, nor are they suffered to draw near unto salvation, though our Saviour tenderly cried out on their behalf, 'Suffer,' &c. O most unhappy people! at the voice of an heretic all the voices of the prophets and apostles are silenced, who, from one spirit of truth, have declared that the

1140

---

[3] Mosh. Hist. v. ii. p. 316.   [4] Claude's Def. of the Reform. v. i. c. 2, p. 27.

church is to be called by the faith of Christ, out of all nations of the world; so that the divine oracles have deceived us."[5] The archbishop of Narbon, writing to Louis the 7th, king of France, about the same time, details the desolations of the Catholic community, he says, "My Lord, the King, we are extremely pressed with many calamities, amongst which, there is one that most of all affects us, which is, that the Catholic faith is extremely shaken in this our diocese, and Saint Peter's boat is so violently tossed by the waves, that it is in great danger of sinking." Similar statements and complaints reached Bernard, respecting the prevalency of persons holding Baptist sentiments in Germany, where, in a future section we shall give particulars.[6] We can from these extracts discover the perturbed and anxious state of mind among the clergy, at the success attending Henry's preaching. At this very period, in the Catholic community, the night of ignorance," says Bishop Newton, "was so thick and dark, that there was hardly here and there a single star to be seen in the whole hemisphere."[7] Yet such was the disposition of the supporters of establishments at this time, that they would have extinguished every star, had not Providence thrown its *ægis* around it. We may discover in these Pædobaptists the prevailing of a false charity, for while they express their solicitude for the rising race, they can turn from those chitty acts of kindness, and with reviling and denouncing language, assign the parents, with all dissidents from the infant rite, to the regions of misery and death.

1146   10. To recover the strayed flocks, Bernard, with other clergy of note, visited those parts

---

[5] Allix's Albig. Ch. C. 14, p. 127, and c. 11, p. 117, and c. 20, p. 185.   [6] See on Sect. 12, § 4.   [7] Diss. on the Prophe. v. ii. p. 170.

of France, which were most infected with Henry's sentiments. Henry was found in the territory of the Earl of St. Giles, and though he fled and remained secreted for some time; yet it is supposed he was afterwards arrested by some Catholic bishop. What end Henry came to is unknown, though Allix remarks, it is said he was a martyr at Toulouse.[8] Henry's views are recorded under eleven heads by the Magdeburghs, who declare with Mosheim that he denied baptism to children.[9] Peter de Bruys and Henry denied baptism to children, and verbally and practically administered the ordinance only on a profession of faith.[10] "Peter and Henry were two Antipædobaptist ministers,' says Dr. Wall.[1] Henry's followers, the Henricians, are said by Catel, to have been the forerunners of the Albigenses.[2] Henry and Peter de Bruys were two principal doctors of the Albigenses.[3] Bernard says, "the Albigenses were called Henricians, from this person;" "they boast," he adds, "that they are the true successors of the apostles, and the faithful preservers and followers of their doctrine: they are simple men, and rude in their manners, yet many clergymen, bishops, and lay princes condescend to favour them.[4]

11. From the zeal and assiduity of Gundulphus and Arnold in Italy, with Berenger, Peter de Bruys, and Henry in France; the followers and disciples of these reformers became sufficiently numerous, to excite alarm in the Catholic church, before Waldo, of Lyons, appeared as a reformer. They were in different kingdoms known

---

[8] Wall's Hist. pt. 2, p. 254, and Allix's Albig. Ch. c. 14, p. 128.
[9] Danver's, p. 293. Ec. Hist. v. ii. p. 316. [10] Stennett's Ans. to Rus. p. 83. [1] Hist. Inf. Bap. pt. 2, c. 7, § 8. [2] Allix's Albig. Ch. c. 18, p. 172. [3] Mezeray's Fr. Hist. p. 276. [4] Facts, &c., 45.

1160 by different names, and are supposed at this period to have amounted to *eight hundred thousand* in profession.[5]

The success of these reformers may suggest the inquiry, how they gained so firm a footing in so dark a period, and in the face of all opposing powers. We know they, like the Paulicians,, went forth, regulated by the precepts and promises of the New Testament, with a simple and humble dependence on the SPIRIT of truth for direction and support. Their living together in large mansions, in social and brotherly compact, enabled them to carry on their secular work and religious duties unobserved. In all those associations, their great object was, the promotion of undefiled religion. They were very assiduous to their callings, all their leisure hours being spent, either in the instruction of youth, or about necessary things. The ministers ("for they had a regular succession of elders,"[6] who emanated from these colleges or churches) did not content themselves in exhorting their hearers on the Sabbath-days, but went all the week to instruct the people in the neighbourhood, preaching also in the fields to the keepers of flocks.[7] They considered every Christian as in a certain measure qualified and authorized to instruct, exhort, and confirm the brethren in their Christian course. All orders of teachers were to resemble exactly the apostles of our Saviour, and be like them, poor, and throw their possession into a fund for the support of the sick; while the healthy were to pursue some trade, to gain a daily subsistence.[8] To effect the greater good, many of them led a wandering life throughout the various provinces of

---

[5] Bap. Mag. v. i. p. 435. Wall's Hist. pt. 2, p. 228. Clark's Martyr. p. 76.   [6] Allix's Pied. Ch. c. 24, p. 242.   [7] Perrin's Hist. p. 16.   [8] Mosh. Hist. v. ii. p. 321.

Europe, and such itinerants realized considerable success in gaining the affections of the multitude, while some in their travels were called to martyrdom.[9] Various colonies were sent out from these old interests, particularly from Italy, who spread like an inundation through all the European provinces.[10] They consequently formed in different parts a vast number of religious assemblies, whose discipline and officers were the same as found in the primitive church,[1] who adhered tenaciously to their doctrines.[2] The success and number of dissidents, with the desolated state of the Catholic community, prior to the Lyonese reformer, are admirably shown by by Dr. Allix, in his remarks on the ancient churches of the Albigenses.[3]

12. Not being able to ascertain the inward arrangements of the Albigensian mansions, the popes complained of them as not being under their regulation, and concluded they must be seats of sin, like their own abodes, and therefore, sent forth their expressions of pious detestation in repeated anathemas; consequently, measures were now adopted of a vigorous character, to stop the growing evil. The censures of men, the bulls of popes, and the decrees and anathemas of councils, which shall

---

[9] Mosh. Hist. v. ii. p. 224. [10] Id. p. 226. [1] Allix's Albig. Ch. c. 20, p. 183. [2] Mosh. Hist. C. 11, p. 2. ch. 5, § 2. [3] C. 14, pp. 117—120. If we allow *eight hundred thousand persons* to profess the Berengarian faith (Bap. Mag. v. i. p. 435), and allow to each professor three adherents, these two numbers, 800,000, and 2,400,000, make 3,200,000, persons holding evangelical views; but if we allow infants to share in this calculation, it at once lowers the credit of the evangelical party, and places them in practice on a level with the Catholic church, while it would leave them sadly behind in enumeration; but there is *no proof* of pædobaptism, at this time, out of the Roman and Grecian hierarchies, while these professors were of the Berengarian class, i. e., holding only believers' baptism.

be given hereafter, follow now in rather close succession, at the same time, *all bearing* their expressions of strong aversion towards those who deny the rite to infants. The councils we allude to, were held in different parts of Europe; it must appear strange that those assemblies should all express themselves so strongly and decidedly against antipædobaptists, unless persons did exist to a considerable extent, holding those sentiments.

13. Whilst anarchy and confusion awfully prevailed in the Roman community, strife, rebellion, and conflict between popes and emperors, cardinals, clergy, and councils on the claims of contending pontiffs, a person was called by divine grace to advocate the cause of truth.

1160.

PETER, an opulent merchant of Lyons, in translating from Latin into French, the four gospels, perceived that the religion which was taught in the Roman church, differed totally from that which was originally inculcated by Christ and his apostles. Struck with the glaring difference, and animated with a pious zeal for religion, he abandoned his mercantile vocation, distributed his riches among the poor, and formed an association with other pious men. He adopted the sentiments of the Waldenses of Piedmont, and from them borrowed those reforming notions, which he diffused so successfully over the continent.[4] In 1165, he assumed the character of a public teacher in the city of Lyons.[5] He maintained at his own expense several persons, who were employed to recite and expound to the people those translations of the Scriptures he had made,[6] which proved of unspeakable service to the cause he espoused. The rules of practice

[4] Mosh. Hist. v. ii. p. 321, note. Dr. Allix's Albig. Ch. c. 11, p. 114, and Pied. Ch. c. 19, p. 182. Leger's Hist. Tom. 1, p. 12, &c.   [5] Jones's Lect. v. ii. p. 235.   [6] Gilly's Narrative, p. 20.

adopted by Peter of Lyons or Peter Waldo and his followers, were extremely severe. They took for their model, to regulate their moral discipline, Christ's sermon on the mount, which they interpreted and explained in the most literal and rigid manner,[7] and consequently prohibited war, law suits, and all attempts towards the acquisition of wealth; the infliction of capital punishments, self-defence against unjust violence, and oaths of all kinds.[8]

14. The followers of Waldo, like himself, renounced all worldly property and interest, making common stock with the poor of the church. From this circumstance, the enemies termed them "*the poor of Lyons*," and from the city where Waldo commenced his labours, they were named *Lionists;* but in general, they were mixed up with the Waldenses, their sentiments being the same,[9] and were known in general by that name. They are said to have been men of irreproachable lives.[10] They were the pious of the earth.[1] Their views of the ordinance were, says Reiner, "that the washing (immersion) given to children, does no good."[2] Dissenters were called by various names, as *the Poor of Lyons, Lionists, Paterines, Puritans, Arnoldists, Petrobrussians, Albigenses, Waldenses*, &c., &c., different names, expressive of one and the same class of Christians.[3] "However various their names, they may be," says Mezeray, "reduced to *two*,

---

[7] After adopting such a rigid view of the laws of Zion, *is it possible* that Waldo could practise infant baptism, which rite has no place in the New Testament? Their creed is a denial of the rite among them, and the same can be established of the churches of Piedmont. [8] Mosh. Hist. v. ii. p. 322. [9] Id. c. 12, p. 2, c. 5, § 11, note. [10] Bp. Jewel, in Facts, &c., p. 41. [1] Mosh. ubi sup. [2] Wall's Hist. pt. 2, c. 7, p. 233. [3] Allix's Pied. c. 14, pp. 122-8. Wall's Ib. p. 220, &c. Jones's Lect, v. ii. p. 276.

that is, the Albigenses (a term now about introduced), and the Vaudois, and these two held almost the same opinions, as those we call Calvinists."[4] Their bards or pastors were every one of them heads of their churches, but they acted nothing without the consent of the people and clergy. Deacons expounded the gospels, distributed the Lord's Supper, baptized, and sometimes had the oversight of churches, visited the sick, and took care of the temporalities of the church.[5]

15. The Albigenses, "whose religious views had been a considerable time established,"[6] gave their entire support to Waldo, so soon as he appeared in public. The archbishop of Lyons, with other rulers of the church in that province where the new reformer arose, opposed with vigour this new doctrine in Waldo's ministry, but their opposition was unsuccessful; for the purity and simplicity of that religion which these Lionese taught, the spotless innocence of that shone forth in their lives and actions, and the noble contempt of riches, which formed a complete contrast with other teachers; appeared so engaging to all such as had any sense of true piety, that the numbers of their disciples and followers increased from day to day.[7] In reference to the character of this class, *Jacob de Riberia*, secretary to the king of France, has these words in his collections of Toulouse. "The Waldenses or Lugdenses lived first in the diocese of Albi. They disputed more subtlely than all others; were afterwards admitted by the priests to teach publicly, not for that they approved their opinions, but because they were not comparable to them in wit. In so great honour was the sect of

---

[4] Fr. Hist., p. 273.   [5] Allix's Pied., c. 2. pp. 8, 9.
[6] Dr. Allix's Rem. Albig. Ch., c. 11, p. 116.   [7] Mosh. Hist. C. 12, p. 2, c. 5, § 11.

these men, that they were both exempted from charges and impositions (taxes) and obtaining more benefit by *will and testaments* of the dead, than the priests. A man would not hurt his enemy if he should meet him upon the way, accompanied with one of the heretics—insomuch that the safety of all men seemed to consist in their protection.[8] Reiner, in the ensuing century, bears the following testimony, "They were in manners composed and modest, no pride of apparel, because they are therein neither costly nor sordid. They transact their affairs without lying, fraud, or swearing, being most upon handicraft trades; yea, their doctors or teachers are weavers or shoemakers, who do not multiply riches, but content themselves with necessary things. These *Lionists* are very chaste and temperate both in meats and drinks, who neither visit taverns or stews. They do much curb their passions; they are always either working, teaching, or learning. They are very frequent in their assemblies and worship, &c. They are very modest and precise in their words, avoiding scurrility, detraction, levity, and falsehood. Neither will they say so much as verily, truly, nor such like, as bordering too much on swearing, as they conceive; but they usually say, Yea and Nay."[9]

16. The pontiff, on being made acquainted with the Lionists' proceedings, and the inadequacy of his clergy's opposition, anathematized Waldo and his followers. The severity of those measures adopted by his enemies compelled him to retire; leaving Lyons, he passed through different provinces, preaching the word with great acceptance. His kindness to the poor being diffused, his love of teaching and the love of many to

---

[8] Danver's Hist., p. 20, from Du Plessis, Inquisitor.   [9] Danver's Hist., p. 21.

CH. II. § 8.] EFFORTS TO SUPPRESS WALDO. 189

learn, awakened mutual solicitude and devotion, and strengthened each other's anxiety and exertion from day to day, so that a crowd came about him in every place, to whom he explained the scriptures, which his learning and piety enabled him profitably to do. On being forced from France, particularly Dauphine and Picardy, in which places Waldo had been very successful, he first retired into Germany, with many of his followers, who were called PICARDS, carrying along with him, wherever he went, the glad tidings of salvation: and at last settled in Bohemia, where he arrived safely, and where we shall mention again his name and his concluding labours.

1177

1179

In 1181, Lucius III. issued a decree, stating, "We declare all Puritans, Paterines, Poor of Lyons, &c. &c., to lie under a perpetual curse for teaching baptism and the Lord's Supper otherwise than the church of Rome."[10] In furtherance of the pope's object, Philip II. of France, is said to have razed *three hundred mansions*, and destroyed several walled towns, to stop the growth of these reforming opinions.[1] Numbers of Waldo's followers fled for an asylum into the valleys of Piedmont, taking with them the new translation of the Bible.[2] Others removed into Germany, while some of his opinions are to be traced in the Netherlands.[3] His doctrines were carried into Flanders, Poland, Spain, Calabria, and even into the dominions of the grand Sultan.[4] Consequently, it was found that Waldo and his followers had, in a few years, drawn multitudes from the bosom of a corrupt

1181

1183

---

[10] Jones's Lect., v. ii., p. 241.   [1] Lon. Ency., art. Waldo.   [2] Jones's Lect. v. ii., p. 238.   [3] Bap. Mag., v. xiv., p. 51.   [4] Lon. Ency., v. xviii. p. 447. art. Reform.

church, and their doctrines made a great noise in the world.[5]

17. By the assiduous and unceasing efforts of the elders and teachers, to instruct and qualify every member of the community, to inform the ignorant of the way of salvation; and by their system of local itinerancy, while others undertook more extensive journeys. These united efforts of *the whole body* were attended with incalculable good, and such organized exertions promised fair to evangelize the world; and if this object is ever attained, similar means must be used by men of disinterested virtue, whose love of souls shall rise superior to the love of gain and ease. From their combined endeavours to promote the knowledge of Christ, "The sects of the Catharists, Waldenses, Petrobrussians, and others," says Mosheim, "gathered strength from day to day, spread imperceptibly throughout all Europe, and assembled numerous congregations in Italy, France, Spain, and Germany. The number of these dissenters from all hierarchies, was nowhere greater than in Narbonne, Gaul, and the countries adjacent, where they were received and protected in a singular manner by Raymond, Earl of Toulouse, and other persons of the highest distinction; and where the bishops, either through humanity or indolence, allowed them to form settlements, and multiply prodigiously from day to day. They formed by degrees such a powerful party as rendered them formidable to the Roman pontiffs, and *menaced the papal jurisdiction with a fatal overthrow.*

"The pontiffs, therefore, considered themselves as obliged to have recourse to new and extraordinary

---

[5] Mosh. Hist., C. 12, p. 2, c. 5, § 14.

methods of defeating and subduing enemies who, both by their number and rank, were every way proper to fill them with terror. Innocent III. devised such methods, and executed such cruel measures against these worthy people, which occasioned the greatest astonishment in all Europe. His bold designs and achievements will come under consideration in our next section.[6]

18. The opinion conveyed by many writers is, that these dissenters in France, originated with Waldo; and even Robinson and Jones appear to admit, that the Vaudois or Puritans in France were in a low state at the time Waldo appeared as a teacher. Dr. Allix has shown with Mosheim, that these French dissenters descended from the Catharists and Vaudois; while their paucity in numbers, or laxity, is rather difficult to reconcile, with Bernard and other writers' statements, as to the desolation in the Catholic church from Peter de Bruys, Henry and Arnold's preaching, which last terminated his labours, only twenty-three years before Waldo appeared. The old Baptist interests no doubt were resuscitated and increased with members, new ones to a great extent were raised by Waldo and his worthy fellow-labourers; and these old and new interests together became formidable to the pontiff, and awakened their enemies to vigorous and barbarous measures; consequently, from this period the Vaudois became more known, and more prominent from their sufferings, and from recorded events by the catholic writers.

[6] Mosh. Hist. Cent. 13, p. 2, ch. 5, § 2, 3.

APPENDIX TO SECTION VIII.

WE shall now record some of those measures devised against the Anti-pædobaptists. " It is very remarkable," says Dr. Allix, " that Egbert, Alanus, Giraldus, and others, should accuse them of one custom, as belonging to all, if a distinction could be made.[7]

The voice and authority of the pope was feeble in the early ages of Christianity; nor was his power feared during the governments of the Goths and Lombards; but at the expiration of their dynasties, his character becomes apparent, and his pretensions are in some measure acknowledged; but in this (12th) century, the kings of the earth gave him their power, Rev. xiii. 2, and vii. 13; and the united power made war with the Lamb and his saints.

1050 In 1050, Leo IX. commanded that young children should be baptized, because of original sin.[8]

1070 In 1070, Gregory VII. decreed, that those children (foundlings) whose parents are unknown, should be baptized according to the tradition of the Fathers.[9]

1139 In 1139, Peter de Bruys, and Arnold of Brescia, were condemned by Innocent II. in a Lateran council, for rejecting infant baptism.[10]

1163 In 1163, Alexander III., in a synod, made a canon against the Albigenses, to damn that

---

[7] Ch. Pied., ch. 17, p. 155.   [8] Danver's Hist., p. 290.
[9] Id., p. 297. Rob. Hist. Bap., p. 314.   [10] Wall's Hist., pt. 2, ch. 7, § 5, p. 242.

heresy, that had so infected, as a canker, all those parts about Gascogne.¹ "These heretics," says Mezeray, "held almost the same doctrines as the Calvinists, and were properly Henricians and Vaudois."²

1175 In a council held at Lombez, in Gascogne, 1175, the good men of Lyons, or Albigenses, were condemned; one reason assigned was, they held that infants are not saved by baptism.³

To suppress the heresy that was strengthened by Waldo's ministry, the pontiff sent a cardinal and three **1176** bishops, in 1176, as commissioned inquisitors against the believers—Lionists, Paterines, good men, &c., with a creed requiring all persons, suspected of heresy, to subscribe to its contents. One of its articles ran thus: "We believe that none are saved, except they are baptized; and that children are saved by baptism, and that baptism is to be performed by a priest in the church."⁴ Many Albigenses, refusing the terms, were burnt in different cities in the south of France.⁵ The commissioners, on examining those people, found them to deny the utility of infant baptism.⁶

1176 In the same year, a Gallican council was called to convict and condemn the Albigenses. In the third canon, they were judged and condemned of heresy, for denying baptism to children.⁷

---

¹ Danver's Hist., p. 299. ² Fr. Hist., p. 248. 40. King.
³ Jones's Lect., v. ii., p. 240. ⁴ Hovenden's Ann. fol. p. 319, 6. A.D. 1176. In all ages, persons have been found in every community ready on the appearance of trials to compromise their professed principles, with their opposers on the terms of relief. Such was the case with very many on these occasions and examinations; but more anon. ⁵ Jones's Hist. of the Christian Church, v. ii., p. 21. ⁶ Milner's Ch. Hist., cent. 12, ch. 4.
⁷ Danver's Treat., p. 300.

K

1177 In 1177, the kings of France and England, from a desire to stop heresy, first resolved to attack the Albigenses by military force, but afterward thought it would be more prudent to send preachers first; accordingly, the archbishops of Berry and Narbonne, with Reginald, bishop of Bath, and others of figure, appeared among these people. These preaching commissioners exacted an oath of the Catholics, that they should give information of and against the Albigenses. Great numbers were in consequence discovered; and, on being cited before these bishops, a confession of the *Catholic faith* was submitted to them, and they were required to swear to their belief of it; but the Albigenses refused to swear or take any oath. Consequently, the Albigenses, Paulicians, or Waldenses, in Gascogne and Provence, were excommunicated; and all persons under the fear of the pontiff were forbidden to entertain them to their houses or country. The severity of this measure drove many into other kingdoms, others were led to abjure their opinions, and the rest the princes were requested to banish out of their dominions.[8]

1178 In 1178, Cardinal Chrysoginus was sent as an inquisitor among the heretics about Toulouse, that had evil sentiments about the sacraments.[9] He called a synod the same year, which was held at Toulouse, and the Albigenses were condemned to expulsion.[10]

1179 In 1179, Alexander III., in a council, condemned and anathematized the Puritans about

---

[8] Mezeray's F. Hist., p. 250. Allix's Albig., ch. 15. Collier's Ecc. Hist., v. i., b. 5, p. 389. Miln. Ch. Hist., C. 12, c. 4.
[9] Danver's Hist., p. 300. [10] Jones's Lect., v. ii., p. 240.

Gascogne, Albi, and other parts of Thoulouse, for denying baptism to children: and Favin, in his history, confirms the testimony of their Anti-pædobaptist views, by declaring that the Albigeois do esteem the baptizing of children superstitious.[1]

1181 In 1181, Pope Lucius III. held his general council at Verone; at which the Albigensian sect and heresy were damned, for teaching otherwise than the Church of Rome about baptism.[2]

1199 In 1199, Innocent III., in answer to a letter from the bishop of Arles, in Provence, represented the heretics as teaching " that it was to no purpose to baptize children, since they could not have forgiveness thereby, as having no faith, charity," &c.[3]

Extracts of evidence taken from the acts of the inquisition of Toulouse support these views of their denominational character.[4]

These severe methods prove dissidents to have been a powerful body; and though these measures disturbed their local establishment, yet they did not impair the main body, since they remained sufficient to menace the papacy with a *fatal overthrow*. There could be no propriety in every synod, council, and assembly, making severe rules to enforce baptism on infants, unless a considerable body of Anti-pædobaptists existed, to thwart this vestige of the man of sin, which rite his holiness evidently considered as a palladium to his interest.

At the same time, it would be difficult to trace the extent of those persons in the early ages among the

---

[1] Danver's Hist., p. 301.   [2] Ib.   [3] Wall's Hist. of Inf. Bap., pt. 2, ch. 7, § 5, p. 242.   [4] Allix's Albig. Ch., ch. 18, p. 161, &c.

Albigenses, who held the truth unsophisticated ;[5] yet, amidst all the diversity of names and opinions charged upon them, *no early author records infant baptism as practised among them;* indeed, every early testimony charges them with the error of Anti-pædobaptism and Ana-baptism.

Section IX.

CHURCHES IN FRANCE CONTINUED.

Here is the patience and the faith of the saints.—*Rev.* xiii. 10, xiv. 12.

1. The thirteenth and fourteenth chapters of Revelations should be read in connexion with the history of these churches; and though we cannot give a full detail of their sufferings, we will essay to epitomize the statements given by different historians, while we acknowledge our obligations principally to Mr. Jones, and at the same time say, with John, "Here is the patience of the saints:" heré are they that kept the commandments of God, and the faith of Jesus.

2. The severity of the pope's measures forced Waldo from Lyons. In the same year, a synod was convened at Tours, at which all the bishops and priests in the country of Toulouse were strictly enjoined "to take care, and to forbid, under pain of excommunication, every person from presuming to give reception, or the least assistance to the followers of this heresy; to have

---

[5] Allix's Pied. Ch., c. 2.

no dealings with them in *buying and selling*, that thus, being deprived of the common necessaries of life, they might be compelled to repent of the evil of their way." The measures caused many of the Albigenses to seek asylums in other kingdoms: the influence of these measures of the pope on sovereigns, was such as to occasion their first succumbing, and then uniting to support the constuprated sanctuary of Rome. The power embodying at this period to support the beast, is enough to make all stand amazed. Louis VII., of France, and Henry II., of England, became equerries to the pope, holding the bridle of his horse, and afterwards walking, one on the one side of him, the other on the other, as royal grooms to his holiness. Here the submissive state of things to the man of sin may be viewed, and the prevalency of his voice, who was obeyed and feared more than God. Lucius III. issued a decree, confirmatory of previous measures, in which was stated, "We declare all Catharists, Paterines, Poor of Lyons, Passignes, Josephists, Arnoldists, to lie under a perpetual anathema." These intolerant proceedings drove many of those people, against whom they were directed, to leave France, cross the Pyrenean mountains, and take up a residence in Spain.

1181

3. Innocent III. ascended the pontifical throne in 1192. Many popes did badly, but this exceeded all in cruel turpitude. The man of sin had been progressive in his character, actions, and inventions; but now, if his Satanic majesty was ever incarnate, or had one agent on earth that more resembled him in spirit, design, and executive mischief, there can be no doubt of Innocent *being the man*. He appears matured in the mystery of iniquity; he exhibits in full view the man fully grown in sin; and in his public character, handed round to the kings of the earth

1192

the cup of abomination, from which they drank into the same spirit and designs, participated in the fellowship of crimes, and became intoxicated or glutted with his iniquitous measures and sanguinary proceedings.

He judged that the church ought to keep no measures with sectaries, or heretics; and that if it did not crush them, if it did not extirpate their race, and strike Christendom with terror, their example would soon be followed; and that the fermentation of mind which was every where manifest, would shortly produce a conflagration throughout the whole of Europe. As incapable of temporising as he was of pity, the pope formed his plans without delay; and this lovely and delightful region of France, inhabited by the followers of the Lamb, was given up to destruction.

1193 4. In 1193, the pope sent Guy and Reinier, two legates, into France, with instructions of the most sanguinary description. Instead of making converts of the heretics, their orders were to burn their leaders, confiscate their goods, and disperse their flocks. They were not equally successful in every province; the pope, therefore, instigated the inert inhabitants of those provinces where the legates were least successful, to persecute the Albigenses; consequently, many of the leading persons among them perished in the flames, for a succession of years.

The measures now used against these people, were found partly paralyzed by many lords and barons, who had adopted their opinions, and consequently, instead of consenting to persecute, protected this inoffensive people. From different causes, a protection was cast round those persons whom his holiness had doomed to destruction. Innocent, not gaining his end, laid under an anathema such lords and barons as should refuse to seize the heretics. Finding his influence not sufficient in the locality of those poor disciples, he addressed letters to the king of France, reminding him that it was his duty to take up arms against heretics. As an additional stimulus, the pope offered the whole territory the heretics possessed, and exhorted others of his own community to take possession of all the Albigenses held. The legates laboured, both by exhortations and actions, in the extirpation of heresy. These champions, in traversing the country to preach down error, had one favourite text upon which they could delightfully descant—"*Who will rise up for me against the evil doers? or who will stand up for me against the workers of iniquity?*" Psalm xciv. 16. Though their preaching did not bring all to see as they wished, it is said to have occasioned vast multitudes repairing to the Catholic churches.[1] Public disputations were held with the Albigenses, but the Catholics could always carry by clamour those points they were incapable of demonstrating by argument, so that the victory was always claimed by one party. To what extent these missionaries succeeded, as these means were continued for some years, we do not know; but it is certain a remnant was not defiled by the woman's doctrines, for they remained virgins, and kept the commandments of God, and the faith of Jesus.

5. The temporary lodgment those harassed people sought in Spain was disturbed. Ildefonsus, king of Arragon, published an edict, 1194, commanding all "Waldenses, Poor of Lyons, and other heretics, who cannot be numbered, being excommunicated from the holy church, adversaries to the cross of Christ, violators and corruptors of the Christian religion, *to depart* out of our kingdom, and all our dominions."

---

[1] Collier's Gr. Hist. Dict., art. Albig.

And "whosoever, from that day forward, should presume to receive or harbour them, or to afford them *meat* or *favour*, were to be punished for high treason." This cruel edict was to be published in all churches, in every city and town in the Spanish dominions.

Such was the general state of things towards this people at the end of this century, which may serve to prepare us for the appalling scenes of slaughter which followed.

6. Yet, notwithstanding these inhuman proceedings, both in France and Spain, in the year 1200, the **1200** city of Toulouse, and eighteen other principal towns in Languedoc, Provence, and Dauphinè, were filled with Waldenses and Albigenses. This was owing, under a kind Providence, to the lords, barons, viscounts, and others of the French nobility. Their numbers and importance had awakened the jealousy of the pope, who now felt additionally angry at the protection given to those people. To those bulls and anathemas mentioned, the influence of the legates in exciting the clergy to duty, and the inhabitants to revenge the pope's cause, much importance was attached; but the desired effects of the commission were not so extensively realized: Rainer the Monk, and Pierre de Castelnau, archdeacon of Maguelone, were charged with the ghostly com-
1206 mission. In 1206, the missionaries were strengthened by the Spaniard Dominic uniting with them; and soon after, the order of preaching friars was established, whose business it was to go through all towns and villages, to preach the Faith; but secretly to obtain information as to the dwellings of those who were obnoxious to the pope's vengeance. When these heresy-hunters had purged different provinces of the enemies of the Roman faith, the pontiff became sensible of the value of their services; and in a few years he placed in

those towns, whose inhabitants had the misfortune to be suspected of heresy, missionaries of a like nature, though the people showed the greatest reluctance to such institutions.²

7. By the adoption of such measures against the Albigenses, the populace had been excited; many of them compromised their principles on the terms of life, while for years many had suffered martyrdom in many towns of France, from 1198 and onwards: but Innocent III. perceived that the labours of the inquisitors were not attended with the success he at first anticipated: he consequently solicited Philip, king of France, in 1207, with the leading men of that nation, by the most alluring promises of indulgence, to extirpate heresy by fire and sword. This appeal does not appear to have had the desired effect, as new exhortations were repeated with fresh promises of favour. Raymond VI., the reigning count of Toulouse, was, in the spring of this year, on the borders of the Rhone, engaged in a war against the barons of Baux, and other lords of those countries, where the pope's legate, Peter of Castlenau, above named, undertook to make peace between them. He first made application to the barons, and obtained their promise, that if Raymond would acquiesce in their pretensions, they would employ all their forces to exterminate heresy. After settling matters with them in the form of a treaty, for the extirpation of heretics, the legate repaired to the count of Toulouse, and required him to sign it. The latter was no way inclined to purchase, by the renunciation of his rights, the entrance of an army, already hostile, into his estates, who were to pillage or put to death all those of his vassals whom the Roman clergy should fix upon as

1207

² Mosh. Ecc. Hist., Cent. 13, p. 2, ch. 5, § 3, 4.

the victims of their cruelty. He therefore refused his consent; and Peter, the legate, in his wrath, excommunicated him, laid his country under an interdict, and wrote to the pope to ratify what he had done.

8. The pope was gratified at the circumstance, being aware that his agents were insufficient to destroy the heresy encouraged in Raymond's dominions. He wrote an insolent letter to the count, dated May 29, 1207, confirming the sentence of excommunication. Raymond, terrified, signed the terms of peace, engaging to exterminate all heretics from his territories. The count not keeping peace with the legate's zeal against heresy, was reproached by him in no moderate language; and was again, by him, excommunicated. Raymond was excessively provoked, and threatened Castlenau for his insulting conduct.[3] Through these agitating periods, it appears, the Albigenses had discussed the merits of the points between the hierarchy and themselves. One of the principal debaters on the Albigensian side was Arnold Hot, with whom the Catholic bishops felt themselves entangled. A circumstance, mysterious in its consequences, now occurred. Raymond, as observed, on parting with Castlenau, had threatened to make him pay for his insolence with his life. They parted without reconciliation, January 14, 1208. On the fifteenth, after mass, one of Count Raymond's friends, who appears to have known of the legate's insolence, entered into a dispute with him respecting heresy and its punishment. The legate never spared the most insulting epithets to the advocates of toleration; and the gentlemen, irritated by his language, not less than by his quarrel with Raymond, his lord, drew his poignard, struck Castlenau in his side, and killed him. The intelligence of this mur-

---

[3] Lect. on Ecc. Hist., W. Jones, v. ii., p. 380-1.

der roused the pope to the highest pitch of fury. He instantly published a bull, addressed to all counts, barons, and knights, of the four southern provinces of France. He laid under an interdict all places which should afford a refuge to the murderers of the legate: he demanded that Raymond of Toulouse should be publicly anathematized in all churches, and "that we must not observe faith towards those who keep not faith towards God, or who are separated from the communion of the faithful." All persons were relieved from their oaths of allegiance, they were to pursue his person, and take possession of his territories.

9. The first bull, as if taking little effect, was followed by another: the pope at the same time solicited the king of France to carry on the sacred war in person, and to destroy all the wicked heresy of the Albigenses. The legates and monks, at the same time, received powers from Rome to publish a crusade among the people, offering to those who should engage in this holy war of plunder and extirpation against the Albigenses, the utmost extent of indulgence, which his predecessors had ever granted to those who laboured for the deliverance of the Holy Land.[4] The ignorance of the times

---

[4] The oppressions felt by the Asiatic churches from the Mahometans, and a desire among the clergy to enlarge the territories of the church in that quarter, had occasioned the pope's suggesting a variety of means for the attainment of that object. [Peter the Hermit, on visiting Palestine, in 1093, was grieved to see holy places and persons in the power of infidels. His zeal led him to travel through Europe, sounding an alarm of war, and calling on princes and nations to rescue the holy spot. After difficulties and delays were overcome, he got together an innumerable multitude of all ranks who volunteered for this sacred expedition. These were named *Croisade*, from wearing a cross. One argument used was, "We read that God said unto Abraham, 'Unto thy seed will I give this land:' we Christians are heirs of the promise, and the

permitted these different means to be but too successful. The people from all parts of Europe hastened to France to enrol themselves in this new array, actuated by superstition and their passions for wars and adventures. They were on their arrival, immediately placed under the protection of the holy see, freed from debts, and exempted from the jurisdiction of all tribunals; and so were *lawless*, yet their services were to *expiate* all the vices and crimes of a whole life :—awful delusion!

This lovely and delightful region, in a state of growing prosperity, was delivered to the fury of countless hordes of fanatics. The conferences on the different points between Arnold Hot and the bishops, were broken up by the bishop of Villeneuse, declaring that nothing could be determined, because "*the army of the Crusaders was at hand.*"

1209 10. In the year 1209, a formidable army of cross-bearers, of forty days' service, was put into motion, destined to destroy all heretics. This army consisted of, some say, 3, others 500,000 men. At their head, as chief commander was, let every Englishman blush, Simon de Montford, Earl of Leicester. The cruelties of these Crusaders appear to have had no parallel; in a few months there were sacrificed about *two hundred thousand lives*, and barbarities practised before unheard of, all which met the approbation of Innocent the 3rd.[5] Two large cities, Beziers and Carcassone, were reduced to ashes, and thousands of victims perished by the sword; while thousands of others, driven from their burning houses, were wandering in the woods

Holy Land is given to us by covenent, as our lawful possession." Against these *federal* claims the *Albigenses and Waldenses* wrote, declaring such crusades unlawful. *Such crusades* were now invited against these people. Mosh. v. ii. p. 128, and C. 11, pt. 2, c. 1, § 9, note. [5] Lon. Ency. v. x. p. 461.

and mountains, sinking daily under the pressure of want.⁶

11. In the fall of the same year, the monks preached up another crusade against the more northernly provinces of France. To stir the nation, they opened to all volunteers the gates of paradise, with all its glories, without any reformation of life or manners. The army raised from these efforts, was directed in the ensuing spring, 1210, by ALICE, Simon de Montford's wife. With this army, a renewal of last year's cruelties commenced. All the inhabitants found were hung on gibbets. A hundred of the inhabitants of BROM had their eyes plucked out, and their noses cut off, and then were sent, under the guidance of a man with one eye spared, to inform the garrisons of other towns, what fate awaited them. The destruction of property and life must have been very great, from the sanguinary character of those who managed these cruel measures. The most perfidious conduct was conspicuous in the leaders of the Catholic cause, pope, bishops, legates, and officers of the army; whatever terms were submitted to availed the persecuted nothing, when in the hands of their enemies. On the 22nd of July, the Crusaders took possession of the castle of Minerva. The Albigensian Christians were in the meantime assembled, the men in one house, the women in another; and there, on their knees, resigned to the awaiting circumstances. A learned abbott preached to them, but they unanimously cried, "We have renounced the church of Rome—we will have none of your faith; your labour is in vain; for neither death nor life will make us 'renounce the opinions that we have embraced." An enormous pile of dry wood was prepared, and the abbott thus addressed

---

⁶ Simondi's History of the Crusades, &c., p. 6, &c.

the Albigenses, " Be converted to the Catholic faith, or ascend this pile;" but none of them were shaken. They set fire to the wood, and brought them to the fire, but it required no violence to precipitate them into the flames. Thus, more than one hundred-and-forty willing victims perished, after commending their souls to God. The sacrifice of human life under this crusade, cannot be computed.

1211 12. In 1211, another army was mustered, and measures were adopted for reducing all places suspected of heresy; but it appeared now the desire of Montford to be fully rewarded with the territories subdued, and it was found no easy matter to set bounds to his ambition. Cruelties of different degrees of atrocity, were committed by this army; but they met with a salutary check, and an ultimate dispersion by the vigorous measures of Count Raymond. We are not prepared to say why Raymond did not act with vigour before, whether from timidity, or rather, perhaps, from the well-known principles of the Albigenses, *who allowed of no retaliation*. It is certain that oppression may goad men, until they lose sight of their principles, and become wildered into forced measures.[7] Simon de Montford now began to experience a decline of fortune, Count Raymond regained all the strong places of Albigeois, and in more than fifty castles, the inhabitants either expelled or

---

[7] " The most furious and desperate rebels," says Gibbon, " are the sectaries of religion *long* persecuted, and at length provoked. In a holy cause they are no longer susceptible of fear or remorse: the justice of their arms (cause) hardens them against the feelings of humanity; and they revenge their fathers' wrongs on the children of their tyrants." This view is illustrated in the History of the Nonconformists in England, the Anabaptists in Germany, the Hussites in Bohemia, the Calvinists in France, the Albigenses under Raymond, the Paulicians in Armenia and in Bulgaria, and the Donatists in Africa. See Rom. Hist. ch. 54.

massacred the French garrisons, to surrender themselves to their ancient lord. The demon of discord at this period began to influence the leaders of the crusading army. The legate grasped at the most conspicuous and profitable places. This conduct gave many to view the massacres of the Albigenses by the monks and their incited armies, only to allow them to take possession of confiscated property; the leaders became jealous of each other, and that union among the chiefs, which had occasioned such awful devastation, was dissolved; true it is, they had held together sufficiently long; its cities were ruined; its population consumed by the sword; its commerce destroyed, and the lamp of heavenly light, which had shone so resplendent throughout the whole region, was totally extinguished.

1212 13. The monks recommenced, in 1212, their preaching throughout Christendom, with more ardour than before. The army was renewed four times this year, each army professedly serving forty days. The country was now found almost destitute of victims; Montford resolved therefore, to take advantage of his army, and conducting them against Agenois, whose entire population *was Catholics*, he made the surviving inhabitants pay a sum of money as a ransom for their lives. The crusaders contenting themselves with *this service*, as fulfilling the conditions of enlisting; the **1213** pope began to suspect the designs of the leaders, and in 1213, quite changed his tone towards his tools of mischief, charging them with *murder, usurpation, cupidity,* &c. It is supposed, the King of Arragon, brother-in-law to Raymond, had by negociation turned the tide of affairs. But Montford, and all those monks who had reaped the advantage of his cruel enterprise, now set aside the pope's authority, and refused to listen to an infallible voice, declaring, it was necessary to destroy Toulouse, and extirpate its inhabitants, which they compared to Sodom. The pope at first wavered, and then veered round to Simon's measure against Raymond; war was again preached by the officers of religion, but the pope's party was now opposed by the King of Arragon, in union with the Counts of Toulouse, Foix, and Cominges. In the first encounter, the king lost his life, and his army was routed. This battle of MURET was the death-blow to the Albigensian party in Languedoc.

1215 In 1215, the prince Louis, son of the King of France, performed a pilgrimage against heretics. He appeared before Lyons[8] with a considerable force, and performed a duty of forty days against **1216** the remaining Albigenses. In 1216, Innocent paid his debt to nature and justice. Honorius, his successor, pursued his cruel policy. The **1218** war was renewed in 1217 and 1218, but in this last year, Montford was killed at Toulouse, by the fall of a stone. The death of Simon produced a momentary truce, and afforded these harassed people a period to breathe. Louis of France became Simon's successor in sanguinary proceedings, and proved himself to be behind no servant of the pope, in zeal

---

[8] Perhaps in no city have Christians suffered so repeatedly and severely, as in Lyons. In A.D., 177, they realized every indignity. In 202, they experienced barbarities too indecent to record, and in almost every persecution, the inhabitants suffered death in every form; and now, the Albigenses were called to share in a like treatment. It is said, the blood of twenty thousand martyrs has been shed in this city! What an awful vengeance and repayment did this city realize in 1793, under the direction of the national convention, when 70,000 persons perished by every cruel means which could be devised by an enraged military force, and when France drank generally from the retaliating cup of blood, Rev.xvi. 6. See Seymour's Hist. of the Fr. Revol. v. i. 210.

against heresy. The most sanguinary conduct, in cold blood, was displayed by the bishops and soldiers under him.9 Misfortunes had now fully awakened Raymond to his situation; he, the nobility, and magistrates, united in one cause their persons and their property, and for a time, gave a check to brutal encroachment. The king, Louis, retired from the siege of Toulouse, quite dispirited. The clergy became disgusted with the crusaders, the bishops could no longer succeed in exciting fanaticism. Much blood had been spilt, yet all things had returned to their ancient masters. However drunk, or glutted, or weary the kings of the earth were with these measures, the pope and his emissaries were still athirst and unsatisfied. The pope endeavoured to arouse the king of France, but he could not be moved. Bishops and others were called upon to commit heretics to the flames, but all parties were inert, and nearly tired of the conflict. The murdering appeals of the pope awakened some enemies in the northern provinces, from which the Albigensian refugees were forced to move, and these directed their steps into Languedoc, where they experienced some respite. This mortifying state of affairs to the papal party, was felt by Cardinal Bertrand, who, to remedy this almost hopeless state of affairs, set himself as the pope's legate, to establish a body of men more completely devoted to the destruction of *heretics and the lukewarm.*

1221 Sanctioned by the pope, he, in 1221, instituted "*the order of the holy faith of Jesus Christ,*" for the defence of the church, and the destruction of heretics. The crusading armies were again put in mo-

9 "The image of the beast," Rev. xiii. 15. The interest of the beast was supported principally by the kings of France, and these appear to have had more of his *image*, in spirit and in conduct, than any other set of men possessing imperial power. See Bicheno's Signs of the Times, p. 26.

tion in this and the ensuing year, 1222, but they generally realized adverse fortune.

14. The Albigensian church was now drowned in blood; their race for the present disappeared; their opinions ceased to influence society. Hundreds of villages had seen all their inhabitants massacred with a blind fury, and without the crusaders giving themselves the trouble to examine whether they contained a single heretic!!! It is impossible to ascertain the number, who, from frenzied zeal, engaged in this war of extirpation. But we know armies arrived for seven or eight successive years, more numerous than were employed in other wars. These considered it as their right to live at the expense of the country, and therefore, with a rapacious hand, seized all the harvests of the peasants, and merchandise of the citizens. No calculations can ascertain the quantity of wealth dissipated, or the destruction of human life, which resulted from these crusades. "I have," says Mr. Jones, "traced the total extermination of the Albigenses, and with it, the extinction of the cause of reformation, so happily introduced in the 12th century. The slaughter had been so prodigious—the massacres so universal—the terror so profound, and of so long duration, that the church of Rome appeared completely to have attained her object. The churches were drowned in the blood of their members, or everywhere broken up and scattered—the public worship of the Albigenses had every where ceased. All teaching was become impossible. Almost every pastor or elder had perished in a frightful manner; and the very small number of those who had succeeded in escaping the edge of the sword, now sought an asylum in distant countries, and were enabled to avoid new persecutions, only by preserving the most studied silence respecting their opinions. The private members who had not perished by

either fire or sword, or who had not withdrawn by flight from the scrutiny of the inquisition, knew that they could only preserve their lives by burying their creed in their bosoms. For them there were no more sermons— no more public prayers—no more ordinances of the Lord's house—even their children were not to be made acquainted, for a time at least, with their sentiments."[10] "The visible assemblies of the Paulicians or Albigeois," says Gibbon, "were extirpated by fire and sword; and the bleeding remnant escaped by flight, concealment, or catholic conformity. But the invincible spirit which they had kindled, still lived and breathed in the western world. In the state, in the church, and even in the cloister, a latent succession was preserved of the disciples of Paul (Paulicians), who protested against the tyranny of Rome, embraced the Bible as a rule of faith, and purified their creed from all the visions of a false theology."[1] The timid who remained in the land, were subject to the severities of the inquisitions; these escaped only by frequently denying their belief. Terror became extreme, suspicion universal, all teaching of the proscribed doctrines had ceased, the very sight of a book made the people tremble, and ignorance was for the greater number, a salutary guarantee. So complete was the triumph of the Catholic party, that the persecutors, in confidence of victory, became divided, made war reciprocally on each other, and were thereby weakened and ruined. Aug. 6, 1221, Dominic died.

15. The Albigenses, who had been compelled to return into Languedoc, found themselves, with successive accessions, sufficiently numerous in 1222, in the places wherein their fathers had suffered, to

1222

---

[10] Lect. on Ec. Hist., Lect. 41 to 44. Mosh. Ec. Hist., v. ii., p. 432. [1] Ro. Hist. c. 54, v. x., 170.

animate them with a hope of renewing their instructions and re-organizing their churches. The monks and inquisitors, from some cause, being at this period destitute of aid from the secular arm, were reduced to the necessity of *only noting* the following: " About one hundred of the principal Albigenses held a meeting at a place called Pieussau Rasez, at which Guillabert de Cashes presided." He was one of the oldest of their preachers, and had escaped the researches of the fanatics. This assembly provided pastors or teachers for the destitute churches, whose former office-bearers had perished in the flames, by the sword, or gibbet. Not only was there a languishing in the conduct of bishops, clergy, and the army; but even young Montford, who possessed from his father the confiscated estates, saw himself without money or men, and those few castles he held only waited a favourable opportunity to welcome their old landlords. So desperate were Montford's affairs, that he offered all his blood-bought patrimony *as a gift* to the king of France, and the pope sanctioned the donative, provided the king would still prosecute the war against the Albigenses, and extirpate the newly-arisen heresy, but which the king declined.

1224 16. On Louis VIII. ascending the throne, he entered into the spirit of extirpation, and the aspect of affairs became exceedingly dark; but some circumstances in the affairs of Frederick the emperor interrupted the enemy's designs. The Albigenses were too insignificant now to give the pope any disquietude, but yet there was Raymond's vineyard, which the French king had a desire to possess. Animated by Honorius, the French king took the field with an army of *fifty thousand horse*, to annihilate *Raymond* and **1226** *heresy*. The terror which this formidable army inspired is not to be described. All those persons who made conscience of religion sought an asylum in the neighbouring countries, bordering on the Pyrenean mountains; in the valleys of Piedmont; and probably in some of the German States; which former places became early filled with Dissenters from the Roman church; those who travelled farther, carried with them the germ of reformation through nearly all the provinces of Christendom. This army was very formidable; fear became extreme; the bonds of society, of relations, and of affection, were now dissolved. A nobleman who had married a daughter of Raymond VII. sent her back to him, declaring that, after the summons of the king and the church, he broke off all connexion with him. Thus the pope's voice opposed and exalted itself, and prevailed against a divine ordinance, supported by the strongest and most tender ties.

17. Submissions were made by part of those States the king came to conquer; but some he found with Raymond disposed to hold out. Raymond knew he could not encounter the enemy in the field, therefore hoped that the elongation of the war would perhaps give his embarrassed affairs a favourable turn. On the 10th of June the siege of Avignon was commenced, which proved more difficult than was first anticipated. Famine, disease, a fever, and other causes, removed vast numbers of horses and men in the crusading army; the stench of the dead infected the army; unhappily, the besiegers consented to a capitulation on the 12th of September, which terms were shamefully violated. Fifteen days after the capitulation, a terrible inundation of the river Durance covered all the space which had been occupied by the French camp. Had not the soldiers previously taken up their quarters within the walls, they would certainly have been swept away by the water, with their tents and baggage.

1226

The next enterprise of the crusading army was against Toulouse, but their utmost efforts only produced *one heretic*, an old man and infirm preacher, named PETER ISARN: he was committed to the flames, with the parade of a great triumph. This *one life*, this *one heretick*, had cost the king the amazing amount of 20,000 men, besides horses and money. The king, under considerable disappointment in not attaining his object, returned to his court, and, from grief or infection, died Nov. 8th, 1226. These severities and harassings in Languedoc led a section to seek an asylum in the province of Gascony, which district at that time depended on the kings of England, but where the authority of the government was nearly disregarded.

1227 18. In 1227 a new army was raised against Jews and heretics, personally enumerating as heretics Raymond, the Count of Foix, and the Viscount of Beziers. They first attacked the castle of Becede, in Lauraquais. The Archbishop of Narbonne, with the Bishop of Toulouse, hastened to aid in the siege. Part of the besieged made their escape, the rest were either knocked on the head, or put to the sword. It is said the Bishop of Toulouse saved several from the violence of the soldiers, that he might be gratified in seeing them perish in the flames. Similar instances of cruelty were exhibited during all the period of this crusade, though the spirit of fanaticism was considerably abated. During the minority of Louis IX., the management of affairs devolved on his mother *Blanche*, who was by birth a Spaniard, and in the estimation of her church *very religious*. She was what the age *made her*, which, according to historians, exempts her, with Calvin and Luther, and all persecutors, from condign reproach; 'the fault of the times' has relieved the criminal, on the grounds of custom! The queen-mother had *the* *talent* to terminate the conquest of the Albigenses, and to gather the fruits of this long-cultivated ACELDAMA. Against the queen's army, Raymond now took the field,

1228 1228, flattering himself that the civil wars, risings and revolts of the barons, which threatened the queen's affairs, and the enthusiastic among the crusaders being engaged against the Holy Land, allowed him some grounds to hope he should recover his possessions. His trials had now driven him to fury, and the cruelties of his soldiers and party disgrace the page of history. Those who fell into his hands were mutilated with *odious* cruelty. From the moment of his adopting this cruel policy, the tide of affairs changed, his success and prospects ended with his clemency.

19. Fouquet, Bishop of Toulouse, had never quitted the crusaders; he surpassed all his compeers in sanguinary zeal, by which zeal he obtained the cognomen of "Bishop of Devils." To meet Raymond's opposition, many bishops preached up a crusade, and by the middle of June a numerous and fanatical army was brought before Toulouse. The citizens, affrighted, shut themselves up within the walls, abandoning the surrounding country, and flattering themselves with the hope of wearying the besiegers. The crusading army, under Fouquet and a lieutenant, drew the troops up near to the city every morning, and then retiring by different routes each day to the mountains, they destroyed, through all the space they passed over, every vestige of fruit, corn, and vegetables, with vines, trees, and houses; so that there remained no traces of the industry or the riches of man. For three months the army without interruption continued thus methodically to ravage all the adjacent country. At the end of the campaign, the city was only surrounded by a frightful desert; all its richest inhabitants, whether catholic or otherwise, were

ruined; and their courage no longer enabled them to brave such a merciless warfare. Several lords, hitherto friends, now abandoned them, submitting their castles to the king of France; and nearly at the same time, Raymond listened to proposals of peace. Raymond appears to have been so overwhelmed with terror, as well as his subjects, that he no longer preserved any hope of defending himself. Independent of those that fell by the sword, or were committed to the flames by the soldiers and magistrates, the inquisition was constantly at work, from 1206 to 1228, and produced the most dreadful havoc among the disciples of Christ. In this last year, the Archbishops of Aix, Arles, and Narbonne found it necessary to intercede with the monks of the inquisition, to defer a little their work of imprisonment, until the pope could be apprised of the immense numbers apprehended,—numbers so great, that it was impossible to defray the charge of their subsistence, or even to provide stone and mortar to build prisons for them.

1228 On Dec. 10, 1228, Raymond gave full powers to the Abbot of Grandselve to negociate with the courts of France and Rome. He demanded neither liberty of conscience for his subjects, nor the preservation of his sovereignty. He abandoned all thoughts of maintaining any longer his independence.

1229 On the 12th of April, 1229, Raymond abandoned to the king all his French possessions, and to the pope's legate all that he possessed in the kingdom of Arles. He was now required, in order to prove the sincerity of his submission to the Roman see, to make war on his friend, the Count of Foix: Raymond preferred being a prisoner, or serving five years in a crusade to the Holy Land. He submitted to the most humiliating penance. He repaired with his feet naked, and with only his shirt and trowsers, to the church of

Notre Dame, at Paris, where a cardinal, after administering the discipline upon his naked back, conducted him to the foot of the grand altar, and on account of *his humility and devotion*, he pronounced absolution, on condition of fulfilling his treaty at Paris. Raymond remained six weeks a prisoner, his daughter was taken under the queen's care, and his territories were passed into other hands. The inhabitants, his late subjects, appeared to be resigned to all impending ill; they only asked for *liberty of conscience*, but this was denied them; and in the ensuing November, the council of Toulouse established the inquisition to complete the work of heresy; and in the year 1229, first forbade the use of the Scriptures in the vulgar tongue.[2]

1229

20. Driven from their homes, the Albigenses had migrated into Germany, Switzerland; some crossed the Alps, and found an asylum in the valleys of Piedmont, which were under the clement sceptre of the dukes of Savoy; while the Pyrenean mountains afforded a convenient retreat to thousands of these exiles. In Gascony some sojourned, while others visited the churches in Italy, where Gregory IX. called for aid, in order to their extirpation. This call had been supported by Frederick, who denounced all Catharines, Paterines, poor of Lyons, and other heretics. By this edict the emperor commanded all magistrates and judges immediately to deliver to the flames every man who should be convicted of heresy by the bishops, and to pull out the tongues of those to whom the bishops should show favour, that they might not corrupt others by justifying themselves. Even Raymond no longer refused to per-

---

[2] At Toulouse it is said the first society in France was formed for circulating the Bible in the vernacular tongue.

secute his unhappy subjects, being led to expect, on this condition, the restoration of part of his property.

1232 In 1232 Raymond united with the bishop of Toulouse, and surprised by night a house, in which they discovered nineteen men and women, probably assembled for worship, whom they committed to the flames. The infamous conduct of the inquisitors, under Gregory's directions, disgusted many who were friendly to the Church of Rome; and the opposition to that tribunal was so great in Languedoc, that the inquisition was at last, Nov. 5, 1235, expelled from the city. The inquisition, by an order from the court of Rome, remained in a state of total inactivity from 1237 to 1241, which was supposed to arise from the combination of various cities formed for its destruction.

1240 The unhappy Raymond now cultivated the friendship of the emperor of Germany, and, hoping to gain his lost property, managed to assemble an army for the recovery of Provence. The people revered the names of their ancient lords, and rose in arms; he recovered a few small places; but the prompt measures of Louis, and the forces he brought into the field, filled Raymond with apprehensions of seeing the crusades against the Albigenses renewed in all their horrors; he therefore humbled himself to all the terms **1241** of the Roman court; but in the following year he made another effort to free himself and his **1242** country from the chains of slavery. A war between France and England gave some grounds to anticipate success, and a great many barons promised their aid; and the country, hoping the hour of deliverance had arrived, flocked to his standard. Several ecclesiastics and monks were surprised and cut in pieces, which so effectually awakened the ire of the pope, that his thundering measures occasioned a defection among Raymond's allies, his courage drooped, and he unconditionally submitted to Louis; and the whole territory of the Albigensian churches was delivered over to the will of the pope and king, which latter, in January, 1243, received a personal acknowledgment of Raymond's homage, and the land became quiet.³ Thus terminated all hope with the extinction of *one million of inoffensive lives.* Yet after all this waste of life, it is asserted, on good authority, that the Gospellers, or Berengarians, amounted to 800,000 persons in 1260.—Clark. Martyr.

1243

1260

21. Having brought the outlines of the Albigensian history to the period of their church's destruction, and the transfer of the territory to the see of Rome, we shall now submit a few observations and testimonies on their denominational aspect.

The purity of their lives, and inoffensiveness in character and conduct of these *witnesses of the truth,* with the soundness of their religious creed,⁴ through the domination of the man of sin, has occasioned almost every class of modern Christians to claim them as their predecessors, but proofs are required to support claims, and these only will satisfy the impartial inquirer.

First, It has been fully admitted by all creditable historians, that the Albigenses were originally called Puritans, from the Novatian, Paulician, and Paterine

---

³ See Jones's Christian Church, vol. ii. ch. 5, § 6, p. 119, &c.; also his Ecc. Hist., lect. 46. Dr. Bray's Usurpation and Tyranny of Popery, with Perrin's History, translated. Chandler's translation of Limborch's Hist. of the Inquisition. Bishop Newton on Prophecies. ⁴ Toplady's Hist. Proofs, vol. i. p. 151, &c. Dr. Cave's Prim. Christianity, and Collier's Hist. Dict., art. Albigenses.

dissenters,[5] whose sentiments have passed under review.

Secondly. The constitution of all those dissenting churches left on record, viz., Novatianists, Donatists, Paulicians, with the Albigenses,[6] was strictly on the terms of " believers' baptism indispensable to church fellowship."

Thirdly. After Novatian, Novatus, and Constantine, appeared as reformers, Gundulphus, Arnold of Brescia, Berenger, Peter de Bruys, Henry of Toulouse, and Peter Waldo, who all equally renounced infant baptism, with those who were called after their names, which subject we shall refer to in a future section.[7]

Fourthly. The productions of their pens, their creed, or confession of Faith, the Noble Lesson, and What is Antichrist, are in accordance with anti-pædobaptist views, as already exhibited.

Fifthly. When severe measures were used by the dominant party, those examined denied the utility of infant baptism.

Sixthly. The decrees of popes, the canons of councils, with the testimony of enemies, are plain proofs that the Baptists' views did widely prevail for centuries; and we believe it would be difficult to find a community existing at this period deserving the name of Christian,

---

[5] Mosh. Ecc. Hist., Cent. 12, p. 2, ch. 5, § 4, with notes and references, and C. 13, p. 2, c. 5, § 7 note. Gibbon's Rom. Hist., vol. x., p. 170, c. 54. Miln. Church Hist., Cent. 3, ch. 13. Jones's Ecc. Lect. vol. ii., p. 276. [6] Dr. Allix's Rem. on Anc. Ch. Pied., c. 2, p. 6. Ency. Brit. art. Alb. [7] The controversy in the 11th century about single and trine immersion, decides the early mode; see Mosh. Eccl. Hist., C. 11, p. 2, c. 3, § 11. Dr. Wall says, the Latins never made three immersions essential to baptism, Hist. Inf. Bap., pt. 2, p. 384.

whose views were not in accordance with the anti-pædobaptists. The submission of a creed, containing a belief of the infant rite, and an injunction to practise it, shows the jealousy of the dominant party towards the Albigenses on this subject.

22. The testimonies of avowed enemies and friends we take leave to record.

1160 Dr. *Ecbertus* says, the principal reason the Arnoldists bring against infant baptism, is Matt. xxviii. 19, and Mark xvi. 16. The Albigenses say, concerning the baptizing of children, that through their incapacity it nothing profiteth them to salvation; and that baptism ought to be deferred till they come to years of discretion, and when they can with their own mouth make a profession of faith.[8]

Erbrardus, a great doctor of that time, says, The Puritans do deny baptism to children, because they want understanding.[9]

1017 The citizens of Orleans, the first Albigenses, denied baptismal grace.[10]

Dr. *Wall* records that the Lionists, or followers of Waldo, say that the washing given to children does no good.[1] They condemn all the sacraments of the Catholic church.[2]

"Baptism added nothing to justification, and afforded no benefit to children."[3]

1192 *Alanus* affirms that some of the Puritans believed that baptism was no use to infants, but only to those of riper age, and that others saw no use in baptism at all.[4]

---

[8] Danver's Bap. p. 292-7.   [9] Idem.   [10] Milner's Ch. Hist., Cent. 11, ch. 2, from Usher.   [1] Hist. Inf. Bap., p. 2, 233.   [2] Jones's Ecc. Lect., vol. ii., p. 486.   [3] Dr. Allix's Rem. Pied. ch. 11, p. 95.   [4] Id., ch. 17, p. 155, and Dr. Wall, pt. 2, p. 240. The anti-baptismists and

Favin the historian says, "the Albigeois do esteem the baptizing of infants superstitious.⁵

Izam the troubadour, a Dominican persecutor, says, "*they admitted another baptism,*" to what the church did,—that is, believers' baptism.⁶

Chassanion says, "I cannot deny that the Albigeois for the greater part were opposed to infant baptism; the truth is, they did not reject the sacrament as useless, but only as unnecessary to infants."⁷

Other testimonies will be given under the Waldensian section.

Section X.

BAPTISTS IN BOHEMIA.

"Behold, I have set before thee an open door, and no man can shut it."—*Rev.* iii. 8.

1. THE kingdom of Bohemia is, in point of territorial surface, the most elevated ground, the most mountainous, and by nature the strongest in Germany. The country is about three hundred miles long, and two hundred and fifty broad, and is almost surrounded with impenetrable forests and lofty mountains. Bohemia derived its name from BOHMEN, which signifies the country of the BOII, a tribe of Celts, who retired into

---

the Anti-pædobaptists are allowed by Wall and others, but these writers cannot, at this period, establish pædobaptism out of the church of Rome and Greece. ⁵ Danver on Bap., p. 301.
⁶ Rob. Ecc. Res., p. 463.   ⁷ Facts opposed to Fiction, p. 48.

590 the Hercynian forest, from Gaul, to avoid the Roman yoke. The ancient inhabitants are represented by contemporary historians, as a people of a ruddy complexion, and of enormous stature and muscular strength.¹

A. D. 55
65
2. We have authentic evidence in the writings of the apostle Paul that *he preached the gospel of Christ in Illyricum*, and that Titus visited Dalmatia; hence the Bohemians infer that the gospel was preached in all the countries of Sclavonia in the first ages of Christianity. They also say, that Jerome, who was a native of Stridon, a city of Illyricum, and was a presbyter in a church in
378 Dalmatia,² translated the Scriptures into his native tongue, and that all the nations of Sclavonian extraction, the Poles, the Hungarians, the Russians, the Wallachians, the Bohemians, and Vaudois, use this translation to this day.³

3. For want of records, we are necessitated to pass over the early state and history of this people. It is not improbable, that some of the Vaudois, who left
714 Spain on the invasion of the Moors, reached Bohemia, since reference is often made to their descendants, and their manner of attending the ordinance.⁴ The persecution experienced by the
845 nonconformists in Greece, occasioned many of the Baptists to migrate, and Gibbon says,⁵ "they effected an entrance into Europe by the German caravans," though Mosheim maintains, that it was from Italy the Bulgarians or Paulicians spread themselves,

---

¹ Jones's Ch. Hist., vol. ii. p. 195. ² Vide sup. ch. 1, sect. 4, § 4. A.D. 378. ³ Robinson's Res., pp. 475—479.
⁴ Taylor's Hist. of the Gen. Bap., vol. i. p. 25. ⁵ Ro. Hist., c. 54.

950   like an inundation, through the provinces of Europe.⁶ That such a people were found at an early period in this kingdom, becomes plain from records.

4. There were two great and powerful families, who patronised the Baptists in this quarter, and manifested much attachment to them. The one was the noble family of Bozkovicz, allied by blood or marriage to almost all the grandees of the kingdom, and to several of the kings. In the reign of Uladislaus II. (1140), Lady Bozkovicz became patroness to those called heretics, and settled them on the family estate. **1140** We do not discover in history the exact source from whence these pious people at this time arose, though it is not improbable they were followers of Peter de Bruys, Henry, or Arnold of Brescia, which circumstance is supported by the era of events, though at a later period they were named *Picards*. These Baptists obtained this influence over ladies of dignity, in a manner highly to their honour. They kept a school for young ladies, and the mode of education and the purity of their manners were in such high repute, that the daughters of a very great part of the nobility of Bohemia were sent thither to be educated; and their bitterest enemies say, they kept the young ladies from the company of the other sex, and formed their manners with so much innocency, that there was nothing reprehensible but their heresy. Lady Boskovicz, the patroness, with other women, expounded the Scriptures to fair pupils, and performed all religious offices among them without a priest. When these young ladies were returned to their parents and married, they influenced their husbands, and children, and friends, to

---

⁶ Hist. of the Church, Cent. 10, p. 2, ch. 5, § 2.

favour a people so harmless and so useful to society, and this patronage preserved them nearly two centuries. The other family, patrons and friends of the Baptists, was the very ancient and noble house of SLAVATA. This family descended from the dukes of *Saltz*, lords of the district, where some of the first French refugees for religion are said to have settled. Lord William was chancellor of the kingdom of Bohemia. This gentleman was educated in one of the Baptist schools, until twenty years of age. Many great families protected and employed the Baptists; but when the great and noble lost their love for civil and religious liberty, they neglected or persecuted these people.[7]

1176 5. When Waldo sought an asylum in Bohemia, from the pope's measures, it is certain that kingdom was immersed in great darkness and superstition. Waldo and his friends found the inhabitants tenacious of the rites and ceremonies of the Greek church, which rites were nearly as superstitious as those of the church of Rome. By unceasing efforts, these persons from Picardy, sequently termed PICARDS, introduced more extensively among the Bohemians, the knowledge of the Christian faith in its purity, according to the word of God.[8] In this kingdom, the pious reformers and evangelists obtained permission to settle at SALTZ and LUN, on the river Eger, just on the borders of the kingdom: and near one hundred miles from Prague. A description of this people is to be found in the Bohemian records, which is satisfactory as to their denominational aspect. With these and later Puritans, it was customary to settle on the boundaries of kingdoms, so that, in case of surprise, they might be

---

[7] Robinson's Ecc. Res. pp. 532-4.
[8] Jones's Hist. of the Christian Church, vol. ii. p. 198.

able by a few steps to remove themselves out of one kingdom into another. Almost two centuries after, another undoubted record of the same country mentions a people of the same description, some of whom were burnt at Prague, and others still inhabited the borders of the country; and one hundred and fifty years later, we find a people of the same class settled by connivance in the metropolis, and in several other parts of the kingdom. Other testimonies prove their existence to a later date, so that after the twelfth century documents are extant, proving the existence of Baptists in Bohemia[9] and Poland.[10]

6. Waldo's labours in Bohemia were crowned with remarkable success. He spent his concluding years in this kingdom, promoting the cause of his Master in every commendable way, until 1179, when he was rewarded with a crown that fadeth not

1179

---

[9] Id. p. 39, and Rob. Res., pp. 480, 527. [10] It is recorded by Martin Cromer, that in very early ages great numbers of Christians inhabited the woods of Poland, Rob. Res., p. 555. Berenger's sentiments were here propagated (Id. 557), and owing to the patronage of some nobles, Poland abounded with Picards and Anabaptists. At an after period, this kingdom was visited by Jerome of Prague, and these churches made collections of money for their persecuted brethren in Lombardy. Ib.

The mode of baptizing in Poland, when the Catholic bishops visited the Poles and the Pomenarians, is stated as follows: "In the 12th century, Otho, a bishop, travelled through these kingdoms teaching and baptizing. Such as expressed a willingness to be baptized were put under tuition. After instruction, they were to fast three days before baptism. Otho caused large tubs to be put or let into the ground, and filled with water. Three such places were provided for men, women, and children, and each was surrounded with curtains like a tent. After some ceremonies, he baptized these all naked, by immersing them in water, pronouncing the usual words." See Basnage's Obs. in Rob. Hist. Bap., p. 288, &c.

away. Waldo's asylum at Saltz afforded refuge to those Albigenses who, in the ensuing century, being greatly increased in France, and becoming formidable to the pontiffs, were constrained to abandon their native soil from the cruel measures adopted against them. Bohemia, Livonia, and Poland, afforded these pious emigrants shelter from enraged enemies.

1207

7. The religious character of this people is so very different from that of all others, that the likeness is not easily mistaken. They had no priests, as a separate order of men, but taught one another. They had no private property, for they held all things jointly. They executed no offices, and neither exacted or took oaths. They bore no arms, and rather chose to suffer than resist wrong. They professed their belief of Christianity by being baptized, and their love to Christ and one another by receiving the Lord's Supper. They aspired at neither wealth nor power, and their plan was industry.[1] "The pious Picardians, as they were called, in Bohemia and Moravia," says Witsius, "valued the article of Justification, at its true price, when in their confession of faith, Art. 6, they thus write: 'This sixth article is accounted with us the most principal of all, as being the sum of all Christianity and piety. Wherefore our divines teach and handle it with all diligence and application, and endeavour to instil it into others.'"[2]

8. An inquisitor of the church of Rome says of the Bohemians, they say the church of Rome is not the church of Jesus Christ, but an assembly of ungodly men, and that it ceased to be the true church at the time Pope Sylvester (330) presided. They despise and reject all the ordinances and statutes of the church, as being too many

---

[1] Robins. Ecc. Res., p. 527.   [2] Witsius on the Covenants, vol. i., p. 391.

and very burdensome. They condemn all the sacraments of the church. Concerning the sacrament of baptism, they say, that the catechism signifies nothing; that the absolution pronounced over infants avails nothing; that godfathers and godmothers do not understand what they answer the priest. That infants cannot be saved by baptism, as they do not believe;[3] they condemn the custom of believers communicating no more than once a year, whereas they communicate every day (or every Lord's day). They deride the dress of priests; and reproach the church that she raises bastards, boys, and notorious offenders, to high ecclesiastical dignities. Whatever is preached without scripture proof, they account no better than fables.[4] With this account agrees the history of the Waldenses given by Æneas Sylvius, afterward Pope Pius II.[5]

All Bohemian writers state, that the Picards or Waldenses settled early in this kingdom, and that these people baptized and re-baptized such persons as joined their churches, and that they had always done so.[6]

1300 They are said in the 14th century to have numbered 80,000 in this kingdom.[7]

9. Two monks, in the ninth century, introduced popery into Bohemia, [after five centuries; and under Charles IV. it was fully established. Some opposition was made by two of his Majesty's chaplains, who persuaded the emperor to curb the pope and reform 1360 the church; but these friends to the cause of liberty were banished, and the advocates of reform lost all hopes of succeeding by the favour of the emperor.[8] By the banishment of those two noblemen, the voice of

---

[3] Allix's Ch. Pied., C. 22, p. 223.   [4] Allix's ut sup.
[5] Jones's Church Hist., vol. ii. p. 39.   [6] Robins. Res. pp. 506, 508, 517.   [7] Jones's ut sup., p. 119, and Allix's Pied. c. 23.   [8] Robins. Res., p. 480.

reform at court was silenced; ignorance, profligacy, and vice prevailed among all orders of men in the national church; the inquisition was introduced to enforce uniformity in matters of religion. The consequence was, that multitudes withdrew themselves from the public places of worship, and followed the dictates of their own consciences, by worshipping God in private houses, woods, and caves. Here they were persecuted, dragooned, drowned, and killed; and thus matters went on, till Huss and Jerome of Prague appeared.[9]

1375 10. In the latter part of Wickliff's life, Richard II, king of England, married Anne, sister to the king of Bohemia, and consequently opened a free intercourse between the two kingdoms. Peter Payne, Principal of Edmund Hall, in the university of Oxford, who became obnoxious to papal violence for his opposition to the rites of that church, fled into Bohemia, to which place he brought a number of Wickliff's tracts. These were highly esteemed by Huss and Jerome, and the greater part of the university. The introduction of these writings into the university gave great offence to the catholic clergy, and the Archbishop of Prague issued his orders for all persons possessing such books to bring them to him; consequently two hundred volumes of them, finely written, and adorned with costly covers and gold borders, were committed to the flames. This conduct in Archbishop Sbynko excited great disgust in the minds of the students of the university of Prague, and Huss in particular.[10]

11. John Huss was born in the village of Hussinetz, in 1373, of parents in affluent circumstances. He studied in the University of Prague. At the age of twenty-

---

[9] Jones's ut sup., p. 199. [10] Robin's Res., p. 480.

1394 one he was raised to the dignity of Professor, and in 1400, he was appointed to preach in one **1400** of the largest churches of that city. He was irreproachable in his life, his manners were the most affable and engaging; his talents were popular; he was the idol of the people; but, in gaining their esteem, he drew on himself the execration of the priests. He continued, like Claude of Turin and Wickliff of England, in the catholic establishment, lamenting its corruptions, while he strove to effect a reformation. He appeared in the character of a reformer so early as 1407. **1407** He was distinguished by erudition, eloquence, and his assiduity to his pastoral functions. He is said to have embraced the sentiments of the Waldenses.[1] He openly advocated the reforming doctrines of Wickliff. His bold position in the cause of reform, his appeal to the pope from the mandate of the archbishop, in burning Wickliff's books, proves his connexion, while it led his Holiness to understand how deeply the reformers' writings had taken root in Bohemia; in consequence of which, the pope issued a bull against the new doctrine. Huss and the members of the university entered **1410** a protest against the proceedings of the archbishop, who had sent out processes against four eminent members, for refusing to deliver up the proscribed works. In sequence, Huss was cited before the pope; but he excused himself from visiting Rome, and was supported in his plea by all the leading persons in the kingdom, excepting the clergy. Huss was excommunicated by the pope for contumacy, and all his followers were involved in the same censure. He, however, realized protection for some time from the king, queen, and nobility of Bohe-

---

[1] Chamb. Dic., Art. Huss.

1415 mia; but in 1415, he was shamefully betrayed, and afterwards tried for heresy, convicted, and burnt. It is difficult to say what his religious views were. His sermons are full of anabaptistical errors, as they were so called, and many of his followers became baptists.[2] His views found a prepared people in Bohemia, in the persons of the Waldenses, Picards, or Beghards, of which party he has often been considered the head.

12. Though we cannot decide on Huss's views, yet his followers are easily deciphered, from a letter written by Erasmus, wherein he states, that " the Hussites renounced all rights and ceremonies of the catholic church, they ridicule our doctrine and practice (as reformers) in both the sacraments, *they admit none until they are dipped in water*, and they reckon one another, without distinctions of rank, to be called brothers and sisters ;"[3] which accords with what is said of the early Waldenses in Bohemia, as detailed by Dr. Allix.[4] These Hussites prevailed in Hungary, Silicia, and Poland ;[5] though his followers were most numerous in those cities of Germany that lay on the Rhine, especially at Cologne,[6] where anon we shall find the Lollards.

13. After Huss's death, we are informed by Sleidan, " that the Bohemians were divided on the articles of religion into three classes or sects. The *first* were such as acknowledged the pope of Rome to be head of the church, and vicar of Jesus Christ; the *second* were those that received the Eucharist in both kinds, and in celebrating mass, read some things in the vulgar tongue, but in all other matters differed nothing from the church

---

[2] Robins. Res., pp. 481-2.   [3] Ivimy's Hist. of the Eng. Bap., vol. i. p. 70.   [4] Ch. Pied. c. 22, p. 214.   [5] Lon. Ency., Art. Huss and Reform.   [6] Mosh. Hist. vol. ii. p. 509.

of Rome; the *third* were those who went by the name of Picards or Beghards; these called the pope of Rome and all his party antichrist, and the whore described in the Revelation. They admitted of nothing in the affairs of religion, but the Bible; they chose their own priests and bishops, rather than teachers; denied marriage to no man; performed no offices for the dead; and had but very few holy days and ceremonies." It is obvious, from what has been stated, that the latter class alone were the genuine Waldenses,[7] to whom we constantly refer.

14. Jerome of Prague was the intimate friend and companion of Huss, inferior to him in age, experience, and authority, but his superior in all the liberal endowments. He was educated in the university of his native city. When he had finished his studies, he travelled into many countries of Europe, where he was admired, particularly for his graceful elocution. During his travels he visited England, where he obtained access to Wickliff's writings, which he copied out and returned with them to Prague. He had distinguished himself by an active co-operation with Huss in all his hostility to the abominations of the times, which caused him to be cited before the Council of Constance on the 17th of

1415 April, 1415, at the time his friend Huss was confined in a castle near that city. Hearing how his friend had been used, when he got near Constance, he prudently retraced his steps to Iberlingen, an imperial city, from whence he wrote to the emperor and the council, requesting a safe conduct; but not obtaining one to his satisfaction, he was preparing to return into Bohemia, when he was arrested at Hirsechaw, and conveyed to Constance. Huss and Jerome were tried

---

[7] Hist. of the Reform., b. iii. p. 53.

by the same council, and afterwards burnt by their order. Huss suffered, July, 1415. He sustained his sentence with the most heroic fortitude, praying for his persecutors. The dread of suffering at first intimidated Jerome, which caused his sentence to be delayed. His enemies took the advantage of those symptoms, in hopes of gaining him over; but he recovered his wonted vigour, and avowed his sentiments in the most open manner, and

1416 supported them with increasing confidence to the last. He expired in the flames, singing, "Hanc animam, in flammis, offero, Christe, tibi; i. e. This soul of mine, in flames of fire, O Christ, I offer thee."[8]

15. Poggius, who was secretary to the pope, a frank ingenuous man, saw and heard Jerome in the council, and wrote, in a letter to his friend Leonard Aretin, an eulogium on him, in a spirit of admiration and love. The letter being interesting, we subjoin a copy, somewhat abridged. He says, "Since my return to Constance, my attention has been wholly engaged by Jerome, the Bohemian heretic, as he is called. The eloquence and learning which this person has employed in his own defence, are so extraordinary, that I cannot forbear giving you a short account of him. To confess the truth, I never knew the art of speaking carried so near the model of ancient eloquence. It was, indeed, amazing to hear with what force of expression, with what fluency of language, and with what excellent reasoning, he answered his adversaries. Nor was I less struck with the gracefulness of his manner, the dignity of his action, and the firmness and constancy of his whole behaviour. It grieved me to think so great a man was labouring under

---

[8] Jones's Christian Ch., vol. ii. p. 205. Robin. Res., p. 513. Clark's Lives, p. 116.

so atrocious an accusation. Whether this accusation be a just one, God knows: for myself, I inquire not into the merits of it; resting satisfied with the decision of my superiors. But I will just give you a summary of his trial. After many articles had been proved against him, leave was at length given him to answer each in its order; but Jerome long refused, strenuously contending that he had many things to say previously in his defence, and that he ought first to be heard in general, before he descended to particulars. When this was over-ruled, 'Here,' said he, standing in the midst of the assembly, 'here is justice—here is equity! Beset by my enemies, I am pronounced a heretic—I am condemned before I am examined. Were you Gods omniscient, instead of an assembly of fallible men, you could not act with more sufficiency. Error is the lot of mortals; and you, exalted as you are, are subject to it. But consider, that the higher you are exalted, of the more dangerous consequence are your errors. As for me, I know I am a wretch below your notice; but at least consider, that an unjust action in such an assembly will be of dangerous example.' This, and much more, he spoke with great eloquence of language, in the midst of a very unruly and indecent assembly; and thus far, at least, he prevailed; the council ordered that he should first answer objections, and promised that he should then have liberty to speak. * * * It is incredible with what acuteness he answered, and with what amazing dexterity he warded off every stroke of his adversaries. Nothing escaped him: his whole behaviour was truly great and pious. If he were, indeed, the man his defence spoke him, he was so far from meriting death, that, in my judgment, he was not in any degree culpable. In a word, he endeavoured to prove, that the greater part of the charges were purely the inventions of his adversaries. Among other things, being accused of hating and defaming the holy see, the pope, the cardinals, the prelates, and the whole estate of the clergy, he stretched out his hands, and said, in a most moving accent, 'On which side, reverend fathers, shall I turn for redress? Whom shall I implore? Whose assistance can I expect? Which of you hath not this malicious charge entirely alienated from me? Which of you hath it not changed from a judge into an inveterate enemy? It was artfully alleged indeed! Though other parts of their charge were of less moment, my accusers might well imagine, that if this were fastened on me, it could not fail in drawing upon me the united indignation of my judges.'"

It appears from this secretary, Poggio Bracciotini, that on the third day of his trial, Jerome obtained leave to defend himself. "He first began with prayer to God, whose assistance he pathetically implored. He then referred to profane history, and to unjust sentences given against Socrates, Plato, Anaxagoras. He next referred to the Scriptures, and exhibited the sufferings of the worthies; and then he dwelt on the merits of the cause pending, resting entirely on the credit of witnesses, who avowedly hated him; and here his appeal made a strong impression upon the minds of his hearers, and not a little shook the credit of the witnesses. "It was," says the secretary, "impossible to hear this pathetic speaker without emotion. Every ear was captivated, and every heart touched. But wishes in his favour are vain; he threw himself beyond a possibility of mercy. Braving death, he even provoked the vengeance which was hanging over him. Through this whole oration, he showed a most amazing strength of memory. He had been confined almost a year in a dungeon, the severity of which usage he complained of, but in the language of a great and good man. In this horrid place, he was deprived of books and papers; yet notwithstanding this, and the constant anxiety which must have hung over him, he was at no more loss for proper authorities and quotations, than if he had spent the intermediate time at leisure in his study." In his defence, "his voice was sweet, distinct, and full; his action every way the most proper, either to express indignation or to raise pity, though he made no affected application to the passions of his audience. Firm and intrepid, he stood before the council, collected in himself, and not only contemning, but seeming even desirous of death. The greatest character in ancient story could not possibly go beyond him. If there is any justice in history, this man will be admired by all posterity. What I admired, was his learning, his eloquence, and amazing acuteness. God knows whether these things were the ground-work of his ruin. * * * * With cheerful countenance, and more than stoical constancy, he met his fate; fearing neither death itself, nor the horrible form in which it appeared. * * *" He suffered martyrdom, May 20, 1416.9

1416

16. It is recorded of Jerome, that he was baptized by immersion, by some of the Greek church. This view of Jerome's, with his being a laymen, will account for many historians omitting his name altogether. The neglect of some writers has been amply repaid by the secretary's statement, which we felt called on to detail. Jerome held almost the same doctrines as Wickliffe had taught, and took unwearied pains to convince the common people that they might, without any authority from the pope or the clergy, read, judge, and explain the Holy Scriptures; that any one who could might

---

9 Jones' Hist. of the Ch. vol. ii., pp. 207—11.

preach, baptize, and administer the Lord's Supper, and that these exercises were as effectual to answer all the ends for which they were instituted, in the hands of the laity as in those of the clergy. He travelled into Russia, Poland, Silicia, and Lithuania for the same purpose, and was every where heard with admiration and respect. He was one of the most eminent of the reformers, though little is said of him in history.[10] Huss and Jerome both taught those errors charged on the Anabaptists. This accusation can be brought against those reformers, who advocated a separation from worldly establishments, and a liberty to choose the way of preferring devotion to the great Head of the church. It is true some reformers, as Claude, Wickliff, Huss, stated Christian liberty, but these, with others, set forth no example of its value, or the duty involved in the command, by coming out of corrupt communities; while other reformers left the Roman church, and formed new associations, on the same principle, and with similar materials, to the one from which they had seceded. A few were found at different periods, who left the hierarchy, and these carried their views and principles into practice before the world, and are now denominated by historians *witnesses for the truth*, though they encountered the odium of heresy from Rome, and the stigma of anabaptism from their German brethren and their successors.[1]

17. The Baptists, from the time of their early settlement, lived about the forests and mines. These people were now multiplied by accessions from other kingdoms, and by those converted under Huss and Jerome. These people were of different sentiments on doctrinal subjects, but in general they entertained the same ideas of

---

[10] Robins. Res. p. 513.   [1] Id. p. 482.

religion as *the old Vaudois did*. They were all indiscriminately called Waldenses and Picards, and it is said they all re-baptized. Huss, while in prison, wrote a letter to a friend at Prague, in which he said, "Salute also my brother teachers in Christ, shoemakers, tailors, and writers; and tell them to attend diligently to the Holy Scripture." The effects of Huss and Jerome's instruction were now visible in the multitude, in the disregard they paid to relicts and the Catholic priests. The priesthood suffered every indignity from these aroused people. Crato, physician to the emperor Maximilian, was one day riding with him in the royal carriage, when his imperial Majesty asked the doctor what sect he thought came nearest the simplicity of the apostles? Crato replied, "I verily think the people called Picards;" the emperor added, "I think so too."[2]

18. To resume our details: the proceedings of the Council of Constance flew like lightning all over the kingdom, and Bohemia was all in an uproar. The king, Winceslaus, was seldom sober, and paid little regard to the welfare of his subjects. The nation was divided into three religious bodies, and the nobles were divided into factions, some zealous to resent the insult offered to the nation by the council, and to repel the forces of foreigners, who had been excited by the pope to visit and suppress heresy in Bohemia, and to oblige that fierce nation to establish uniformity in religion. The king put himself under the emperor, and the latter gave his support to the Catholic party, promising to suppress heresy, and settle the affairs both of church and state. The measures now adopted by the priesthood to suppress heresy aroused all men, particularly the patriot and plebeian. These were changed from a

[2] Robins. Res. pp. 508—21.

harmless inquisitive multitude into a resentful community. Feeling their importance, and seeing the union of efforts in order to suppress their privileges, they gathered together in multitudes in the country, about five miles from Prague, where the people met for worship: they elected their own preachers, who administered to this company of various sentiments the Lord's Supper, at three hundred tables (boards laid on casks),

1240 to forty thousand people. The conflict now commenced between the Hussites and Catholics; confusion ensued, riots and murders were frequent. In the city of Prague, the enraged citizens threw twelve imperial officers out of the windows of the council-chamber. The emperor entered Bohemia with an armed force, while the Protestants, to defend their rights, *took up arms*, and chose Ziska as their general.

19. The Protestant army was made up of different parties, uniting in one common cause of defence from various causes; but it would appear that the Vaudois, Waldenses, or Picards did not enter Ziska's army during the war. We know their principles were opposed to war, and they do not seem to have borne arms at any time. During such commotions, it is said of them, that 'they were always going and coming, retiring from the cities while others were coming to reside. When they were persecuted in one city, they fled to another. They do not seem to have had any regular (i. e., separate class) minister.[3] A portion of this people, called Waldenses, came down from the mountains to live in peace under the protection of Ziska. This state of civil discord lasted upwards of twelve years. The agitated state of the kingdom for so many years must have been very injurious to the cause of undefiled religion.

[3] Robins. Res. p. 517.

1433 The Council of Basil, in 1433, took great pains to bring the Protestant delegates to submit implicitly to the council; but they utterly refused. After many intrigues by the Catholics, a division was effected among the Protestants, consequently their importance became lessened. The affairs of the kingdom remained in a very unsettled state even to the middle of this century, about which time Rokyzan, archbishop of Prague, tired with contentions, advised the advocates of reform to retire to the lordship of Latitz, about twenty miles from Prague, a place desolated by war, where they might establish their own way of worship, choose their own ministers, introduce their own discipline and order, according to their own consciences and judgments. Numbers adopted the suggestion, and embraced the privilege, and in 1457 they formed **1457** themselves into a society. This body being made up of persons entertaining religious views wide of each other, they chose the name of UNITAS FRATRUM, or THE UNITED BRETHREN, though they were generally called Picards. These brethren bound themselves to a vigorous discipline in church affairs, and not to defend themselves with the sword, but suffer the loss of all for conscience' sake.[4] In 1459 these godly people, **1459** made up of all classes, obtained from their king, Pogiebracius, a place to worship in, where they established a society on the model of primitive simplicity.[5] These brethren re-baptized all such as joined themselves to their congregation.[6]

---

[4] Robins. Res. pp. 498-9.   [5] Clark's Martyr. p. 127.
[6] Buck's Theo. Dict. 4 Ed. Lon. Ency. art. Bohem. Brethren. The brethren in their writings retain the early mode. Trobe says of Christ's baptism, externally his body was washed with pure water, nay, *even dipped into it*, and as it was, buried by the ministry of a servant of Christ. § 138. Again, "The dipping or

20. Three years had scarcely elapsed before their numbers were considerable; pious persons flocked to them, not only from different parts of Bohemia, but even from every distant quarter of the whole empire; and churches were gathered every where throughout Bohemia and Moravia. Many of the old-fashioned Waldenses, who had been lurking about in dens and caves of the earth, as well as upon the tops of mountains, now came forward with alacrity, joined themselves to the " United Brethren," and became eminently serviceable to the newly-formed societies, in consequence of their more advanced state of religious knowledge and experience. Many persons who had previously held infant baptism renounced those views, and the ministers baptized them before they received them into church communion.[7] The multiplication of these brethren raised a clamour among the Catholic priesthood; the archbishop was censured, and reproached with the terms used to signalize the brethren; consequently he changed his course of conduct towards them. Three years had scarcely elapsed from their establishment in religious freedom, when a terrible persecution broke out against them, and which trial was calculated to prove what spirit they were of. They were declared by the state unworthy the common rights of subjects; and in the depth of winter, expelled from their homes in towns and villages, with the forfeiture of all their goods. Even the sick were cast into the open fields, where numbers perished through cold and hunger. Every kind of indignity was

1460

1462

---

overstreaming with water cannot of itself procure us salvation, see 1 Pet. iii. 21; but the participation of the death of Jesus, *which faith lays hold of, is that upon which all depends in baptism.* § 139. Exposition of the Christian doctrine of the United Brethren, by Benj. La Trobe.   [7] Robins. Res. p. 449.

realized by these inoffensive people, with the loss of all that was dear. Many retired into the woods, caves, &c., so that almost every society of these people in the kingdom became scattered. In the ensuing reign, the dispersed brethren were suffered to return to their homes, to occupy their lands, and were allowed ease and prosperity. They now took such deep root, and extended their branches so far and wide, that after this settlement it was impossible to extirpate them. In **1500** 1500, there were two hundred congregations of the united brethren in Bohemia and Moravia. Many counts, barons, and noblemen joined their churches, who built them meeting-houses in their cities and villages. These Baptists got the Bible translated into the Bohemian tongue, and printed at Venice: when that edition was disposed of, they obtained two more, printed at Nuremberg. Finding the demand for the Holy Scriptures continuing to increase, they established a printing-office at Prague, another at Bunzlaw, in Bohemia, and a third at Kralitz, in Moravia, where at first they printed nothing but Bohemian Bibles.[8]

21. The disposition of the king of Bohemia might be perceived from the import of the prayer he preferred morning and night. His anxiety for peace in his empire led him to offer these words continually: "Give peace in my time, O Lord." The Catholic clergy were unceasingly teazing him to suppress heresy. He in return ordered them to converse with the Picards, in order to convince them of their errors. Taking hold of the queen's gravid situation, they thought it a favourable opportunity to move his fears, in which they were but too successful; for at length they obtained an edict for the suppression of the Picards. The king, on the recol-

[8] Robins. Res. p. 502.

lection of what was done, was grieved at his conduct, and professedly sought forgiveness of God for his act.

1507 The edict became law four years after, when the brethren were prohibited from holding any religious assemblies, public or private; commanding that all their meeting-houses should be shut up, and **1510** that within a given time the Picards or Brethren should all hold communion with either Calixtines or Catholics.9 The clergy could not prevail with

---

9 It is said that some of the brethren, to ward off this law, had presented to the king, while in Hungary, a confession of their faith. This confession is called Waldensian by the Pædobaptists, and was presented in 1508. The confession is entitled, A Confession of Faith of the Waldensian Brethren, and is addressed to king Uladislaus, in Hungary. It begins with informing the king, that they were not Waldenses, though they were persecuted under that name. It goes on to speak of their sufferings, and the reason for laying before him the most sacred articles of their religion, which they say were revealed by the Holy Spirit, and deposited in the Holy Scriptures, and are perfectly agreeable to the apostles' creed, and the faith of the primitive church. Then follows the creed, which consists of fourteen short articles. The 6th is on baptism, viz.: " Whoever, having arrived at years of discretion, hath believed by hearing the word, and hath acquired power over sin by renewing and enlightening of his mind, ought to profess the inward cleansing of his mind by exterior washing, and is to be baptized into the unity of the holy church, in the name of, &c. This our profession extends to children, who, by an apostolic canon, as Dionysius writes, ought to be baptized." On this confession we observe, there were *eight editions* in twenty-five years; each was improved; and the last was prefaced by Luther, when their anabaptism ceased. The brethren complained that their creed was translated into German by some one who knew not the Bohemian language, and who had *altered* some things, and *added* others. There was apparently no Hungarian king in the 16th century of the name of Uladislaus, and the petitioners deny being Waldenses. Now we believe this creed emanated from the Calixtines, a mixed body of professors, while the confession indi-

all to pursue their cruel measures, though many of the brethren were called to severe sufferings. Some of them emigrated, others retired into the forests and caves, worshipping God in private. Those detected in their devotions were arrested and brought before priests, who required them to own them as their shepherds. They replied, "Christ is the Shepherd of our souls;" upon which they were convicted and burned. In this confused and suffering state the affairs of the brethren continued, until Luther appeared as a reformer in Germany. So wearied were the United Brethren of sufferings, that they had been meditating a compromise with the Catholic church; and when the reformer appeared, they actually wrote to him for his advice on the subject. Luther's admonitions in the end brought them to submit their creed to him, who revised it, and prefaced it with praises for orthodoxy, admiring the agreement of this modern creed with their ancient church. They now, under his protection, agreed to leave off re-baptizing, which should in future be called ana-baptism. Luther said, "He had formerly been prejudiced against the brethren called Picards; though he had always admired their aptness in

1516

1522

rectly confirms this view, since it is expressive of believers' and unbelievers' baptism. Dr. Allix's Ch. Pied. c. 24; and this date and society in 1440 agree with Uladislaus' reign. The Picards or Brethren ever boasted of their Waldensian ancestors, and were ever found regulating all their religious affairs by the Scriptures *alone*, discarding the writings of the Fathers as fables. It is recorded at a later period, that the Bohemian brethren, or the successors to these people, were comprehended in the Lutheran church, when they consented to leave off re-baptizing; but re-baptizing and Pædobaptism have ever been at variance. Rob. Res. pp. 503 & 507. Osiander in Danver's, pp. 328, &c. See Dr. Allix's Ch. Pied. p. 241. See Appendix to the Waldensian History.

the Holy Scriptures; and it was no wonder they had expressed themselves obscurely, because the learned languages had been little understood in general, and as these people had entertained such an aversion to the subtleties of the school." To this creed and people we shall again refer.[10]

22. It is certain that the ancient Waldensian church subsisted at the Reformation, and that they left off baptizing adults on their profession of faith. Whether all those churches of the brethren ultimately fell into the Lutheran community, and consequently were comprehended by imperial law, cannot be positively decided. It is plain here that the patience of the saints was worn out. Dan. vii. 25. It appears the assistance rendered them by able divines, and which enabled them to conclude there was no need to re-baptize, regulated the conduct of many; yet the Baptists were still a scattered community, and were named now Anabaptists[1] and Picard Calvinists. The emperor expressed his astonishment at their numbers, and horror at their principal error, which was, that, according to the express declarations of Scripture, *they were to submit to no human authority*, 1 Cor. vii. 23. Some of them kept schools, and preached; others practised physic. Luther strongly objected to those Anabaptists, who taught and followed a worldly calling. These people lived in forty-five divisions, called colleges, exactly as their ancestors had done previously to their banishment from France, about four hundred and fifty years before. But their views of liberty occasioned the emperor's displeasure, he consequently banished all Anabaptists from his dominions on pain of death;[2] though it was found very difficult to get rid of these Baptists.

1526

---

[10] Robins. Res. ch. 13.   [1] Ency. Brit. Art. Anab.
[2] Jones' Church Hist. vol. ii., c. 5.   Robins. Res. c. 13.

They must be comprehended in future in the term Anabaptist, since this term, which originated in Germany among the reformers, was given to all those who denied infant sprinkling.[3] The Moravians contend that they are the descendants of these churches of the *unitas fratrum*.[4] See Anabaptists, sect. 12, § 19.

Section XI.

BAPTISTS IN PIEDMONT.

" Because thou hast kept the word of my patience, I will also keep thee," &c.—*Rev.* iii. 10.

1. There is a range of mountains, the highest in Europe, extending from the Adriatic to the Mediterranean Seas, and separating Italy from France, Switzerland, and Germany. The principality of Piedmont derives its name from its locality, being situated at the foot of the Alps; *pede,* foot—*montium,* mountains. It is an extensive tract of rich and fruitful valleys, containing a superficial extent of thirteen thousand square miles, and is embosomed in mountains, which are encircled again with other mountains higher than they, intersected with deep and rapid rivers, and exhibiting in strong contrasts the beauty and plenty of Paradise, in sight of frightful precipices, wide lakes of ice, and stupendous mountains of never-wasting snow. The whole country is an interchange of hill and dale, moun-

---

[3] Good and Gregory's Cyclop. art. Anap.   [4] Dav. Crantz's Hist. of the Brethren. Bost. Hist. of the Brethren.

tain and valley, traversed with four principal rivers; namely, the Po, the Tanaro, the Stura, and the Dora, besides about eight-and-twenty rivulets, great and small —which, winding their courses in different directions, contribute to the fertility of the valleys, which make the land, on a map, to resemble a watered garden. Such was the surrounding scenery of those people who were, at different periods, driven into the wilderness—Rev. xii. 6. May we not conclude, they had not only chosen the better part, but were directed to an earthly Eden to enjoy it?[1]

2. The origin and character of the people who at an early age inhabited these valleys, has been shown;[2] but such details have no interesting connexion with our history. The same writer has proved, in a most satisfactory way, that the class of people called Waldenses derived this name from inhabiting valleys. In Spain, these people were termed *Navarri;* in France, *Vaudois* (vaux); in Lombardy, ecclesiastical writers named them *Valdenses*, simply from their living in valleys.[3] "They call themselves *Valdenses*, because they abide in a valley of teàrs."[4] It is certain these valleys, at an early period in the Christian era, became an asylum to the worshippers of the Redeemer; who, at the remotest period, were known by the term *Credenti*, believers.[5] However remote their antiquity, no records exist as to any of these churches being apostolical:[6] though the fact is beyond all contradiction, that early and late dissidents in religion were found in these valleys, and in other

---

[1] Lon. Ency. art. Pied. Lady Morgan's Letters. Rob. Ecc. Res., p. 458. Jones's Ecc. Lect., vol. ii. p. 416.   [2] Robins. Res., p. 425.   [3] Robins. Res., p. 302.   [4] Bp. Newton's Diss. on the Proph., vol. ii. p. 248; and Maps of Piedmont in Gilly's Narrative.   [5] Robins. Res., p. 461.   [6] Allix's Ch. of Pied., c. 1, p. 2.

provinces, who were never in communion with the Church of Rome.⁷

3. Though we have no document proving apostolic foundation for these churches, yet it becomes evident that some communities did exist here in the second century, since it is recorded they practised believers' baptism by immersion.⁸ Whether these societies were gathered by the apostles, or their successors, or whether they originated with those emigrants who left the cities under the persecuting edicts of Marcus Aurelius Antonius, we have no means of deciding. We have already observed⁹ from Claudius Seyssel, the popish archbishop, that one LEO was charged with originating the Waldensian heresy in the valleys, in the days of Constantine the Great. When those severe measures emanated from the emperor Honorius against re-baptizers, the Baptists left the seats of opulence and power, and sought retreats in the country and in the valleys of Piedmont—which last place in particular became their retreat from imperial oppression.¹⁰ The assumption of power by the Roman priesthood occasioned multitudes of private persons to express publicly their abhorrence of clerical vice and intolerance, and particularly of the lordly ambition of the Roman pontiffs. In the sixth and seventh centuries, many withdrew from the scenes of sacerdotal oppression, ignorance, and voluptuousness. These sought refuge in Piedmont, and were called Valdenses: they abhorred popery.¹ Here the Valdenses were more at liberty to oppose the tyranny of those

---

⁷ Robins. Res., pp. 425, 440, 448.   ⁸ D. Belthazar in Bap. Mag., vol. i. p. 167.   ⁹ See above, ch. 2, s. 1, § 7.   ¹⁰ Sabast. Frank, in Bap. Mag., vol. i. p. 256. A. Keith's Signs of the Times, vol. ii. ch. 22, p. 64, &c.   ¹ Jortin's Rem., vol. iii. p. 419.

imperious prelates.² The prevalency of Arianism in Lombardy was equally afflictive to these *Credenti;* since some of the believers, or Valdenses, were deprived of their ministers by persecution, while others were led, from the severity of the trial, to compromise the affair by taking their children to the Arian establishment for immersion.³

4. The antiquity of the Valdenses, or believers, is asserted by their friends, and corroborated by their enemies. Dr. Maclaine, in Mosheim's history, says, "We may affirm, with the learned Beza, that these people derived their name from the valleys they inhabited; and hence Peter of Lyons was called, in Latin, *Valdus,* because he had adopted their doctrine." Reiner Sacco speaks of the Lionists as a sect that had flourished above five hundred years (back to 750); while he mentions authors of note among them, who make their *antiquity remount to the apostolic age.*⁴ Theodore Belvedre, a popish monk, says, that the heresy had always been in the valleys.⁵ In the preface to the first French Bible, the translators say, that they (the Valdenses) have always had the full enjoyment of the heavenly truth contained in the holy Scriptures, ever since they were enriched with the same *by the apostles;* having in fair MSS. preserved the entire Bible in their native tongue, from generation to generation.⁶

5. The old, or primitive Waldenses, were distinguished by the doctrine and practice of Christian liberty.⁷ They held priesthood in abhorrence. It is not clear that the ancient Waldenses had any clergy as distinct from laity. Females were allowed to teach, as well as

---

² Mosh. Hist., vol. i. p. 445.   ³ Perrin refers to these people, Allix's Ch. Pied., ch. 24, p. 242.   ⁴ Ecc. Hist., vol. ii. p. 320, note.   ⁵ Danver's, p. 18.   ⁶ Moreland's Hist., p. 14. Gilly's Life of F. Neff.   ⁷ Robins. Res., p. 311.

men; they laughed at the different classes of the priesthood. They took no oaths, but used a simple affirmation. They believed in the doctrine of the Trinity, and baptized believers.[8] They refused baptism to infants, when it came into use in other churches:[9] and were consequently reproached with the term re-baptizers, or Anabaptists.[10] "They admitted," says Dr. Allix, "the catechumi, after an exact instruction, and baptized them on Easter-day, and Whitsunday, and prepared them for receiving of that sacrament by long-continued fasts, in which the church used to join * * * they were to make confession of their sins in token of their contrition before they received baptism * * * after which they were admitted to the eucharist."[1] The mode of administering the ordinance is proved from the account and description we have of their baptisteries.[2] The churches, at an early period, to which a baptistery was annexed, were called baptismal churches: these were resorted to by all persons living in that district for baptism; these baptismal churches consequently became mother churches, and, when possessed by the Catholics, cathedrals; and even a shadow of this was to be found among the reformed churches of Piedmont.[3] It is a fact, however superstition may have disguised it, that the forming of Christian congregations in the established church of Piedmont and Savoy, began, like the gospel itself, with baptism.[4]

6. Knowing the people we are deciphering have had many claimants to affinity, we shall subjoin, before we proceed with their history, a few testimonies as to the

---

[8] Robins. Res., pp. 446, 461.   [9] Id., p. 462.   [10] Id., pp. 310, 315, 467, 513.   [1] Ch. in Pied., ch. 2, p. 7.   [2] Rob. Res., p. 468.   [3] Robins. Hist. of Bap., p. 357; and Res., pp. 405, 468.   [4] Id., p. 468.

oneness of the Waldenses in views, with those Baptists whose histories have been already given.

Eckbertus and *Emericus*, two avowedly open and bitter enemies of the Waldenses, do assert, that the new Puritans (Waldenses) do conform to the doctrines and manners of the old Puritans (i. e., the Novatianists).[5] *Beza* affirms * * * the Waldenses were the relics of the pure primitive Christian churches; some of them were called "the poor of Lyons."[6] *Paul Perrin* asserts, that the Waldenses were time out of mind in Italy and Dalmatia, and were the offspring of the Novatianists, who were persecuted and driven from Rome, A.D. 400 (rather 413); and who, for purity in communion, were called Puritans.[7] The name of Paterines was given to the Waldenses; and who, for the most part, held the same opinions, and have therefore been taken for one and the same class of people, who continued till the Reformation under name of Paterines or Waldenses.[8] There was no difference in religious views between the Albigenses and Waldenses.[9] All those people inhabiting the south of France were called, in general, Albigenses; and, in doctrine and manners, were not distinct from the Waldenses.[10] *Bossuet*, bishop of Meaux, says, as to the Vaudois, they were a species of Donatists, and worse than the ancient Donatists; they formed their churches of only good men; they all, without distinction, if they were reputed good people, preached and administered the ordinances.[1] The celebrated *Matthew Franconitz* says, the Waldenses scent a little of anabaptism.[2] The Waldenses were, in religious

[5] Danvers on Bap., p. 273; and Jones's Lect., vol. ii. p. 178. [6] Danvers, ut sup., p. 18. [7] Id., p. 273. [8] Allix's Ch. Pied., ch. 14, pp, 122, 128. [9] Mezeray's Fr. Hist., p. 278. Maclaine in Mosh. Hist., vol. ii., p. 320, note. [10] Miln. Ch. Hist., Cent. 13, ch. 4. [1] Rob. Res., p. 476. Id., p. 311.

sentiments, substantially the same as the Paulicians, Paterines, Puritans, and Albigenses.³—See appendix to this section.

7. Having stated their antiquity, and proved their affinity to other classes of early dissidents, we now come to describe the people, which originally were called simply *believers*. These were distinguished from others by their faith, while some professors were known principally by pleading virtue; but these Christians distinguished themselves by the soundness of their faith, of which the apostles' creed was their standard; and though they were not indifferent to virtue, yet virtue was a secondary object, or, as it is now called, *a fruit of faith*. They did not dissent from Rome on account of the doctrines taught in that church, but on account of ceremonies, rejecting the popes, prelates, and all its religious orders, with councils and traditions, and adhering to Scripture *alone* as a rule of faith, and by refusing all the papal ceremonies of baptism and the Lord's Supper:⁴ the attempts of these *believers*, therefore, were not intended by way of imposing or proposing new articles of faith to Christians; all they aimed to do was, to reduce the form of ecclesiastical government to that amiable simplicity, and primitive sanctity, which characterized the apostolic ages. The government of their churches was committed to elders, presbyters, and deacons. Their elders, or bards, were every one ministers or heads of their churches; but these could proceed in no spiritual affair without the consent of the brethren, teachers, and people. Deacons expounded the gospel, distributed the eucharist, baptized, and sometimes had the oversight of churches, visited the sick, and took

---

³ Mosh. Hist., vol. ii., pp. 224, 226, 432, notes. Jones's Lect. vol. ii. p. 371-6.   ⁴ Robins. Res., p. 461.

care of the temporalities of the church.⁵ They considered that these orders should be like the apostles;—poor, illiterate men, without worldly possessions, and qualified to follow some laborious trade in order to gain a livelihood. Their elders and officers do not appear distinguished from their brethren by dress or names, but every Christian was considered as capable, in a certain measure, of instructing others, and of confirming the brethren by exhortations. Their elders were the seniors of the brethren, while the presbyters were the whole body of the teachers, whether fixed or itinerating.⁶ Their rules of practice were regulated by a literal interpretation of Christ's sermon on the mount. They sequently prohibited wars, suits at law, acquisitions of wealth, capital punishments, self-defence, and oaths of all kinds. The body of believers was divided into two classes; one of which contained the *perfect*, the other the *imperfect* Christians. The former gave up all worldly possessions, the latter were less austere, though they abstained, like the graver sort of Anabaptists in later times, from all appearances of pomp and luxury.⁷ These people contended that a church was an assembly of believers, faithful men, and that of such a church the Lord Jesus Christ is head, and he alone; that it is governed by his word, and guided by the Holy Spirit; that it behoves all Christians to walk in fellowship; that the only ordinances Christ hath appointed for the churches, are baptism and the Lord's Supper; that they are both symbolical ordinances, or signs of holy things, "visible emblems of invisible blessings," and that believers are the proper participants of them.⁸

⁵ Dr. Allix's Rem. Ch. Pied., ch. 2, pp. 8, 9. ⁶ See Camp. 4th Lect. on Ecc. History, p. 72. ⁷ Mosh. Hist., vol. ii. p. 321, &c. ⁸ Jones's Lect., vol. ii. p. 455. The first writers against the Vaudois, never censured their mode of

8. On the Saracens invading Spain, near the middle of the eighth century, many thousands of the Spanish Vaudois, with their wives, children, and servants, under cover of a large army, emigrated over the Pyrenèes, from the Spanish to the French foot of the mountains. As the French provinces became also invaded, it is very probable many of the emigrants would seek a refuge in Piedmont, during those military commotions. It is recorded, that the parts which remained freest from the vices and contagion of those marauders, were Savoy, Piedmont, and the southern parts of France; and it is equally remarkable, that when the Saracens approached to those parts inhabited by the Vaudois, they were defeated with great slaughter, in several engagements by the famous Charles Martel.[9]

732

9. At a period when ignorance, superstition, and iniquity almost universally prevailed, and the members of the Catholic community were locked up in a moral slumber, one character, of respectability and importance, was raised up in this community; Claude of Turin,[10] who successfully raised his voice against prevailing corruptions. He was a Spaniard by birth, and a disciple of Felix, of Urgel, the Arian; who, in 794, published a work on the adoption of Jesus by the Father.[1] Churchmen say, Claude rejected tradition in matters of religion, and that he entirely conformed to the sense of the ancient church![2] How this could be, while he re-

817

baptizing; for in those times all parties administered baptism by dipping, except in cases of danger. Rob. Res., pp. 447, 468-9.

[9] Mezeray's Fr. Hist., p. 82. Bp. Newton on the Proph., vol. ii., p. 207. [10] Claude lived and died a Catholic, and most probably an Arian. He was a brave general, as well as a bold preacher, and headed his own troops. In his days, those children *who could ask* for baptism received it. Robins. ut sup. [1] Mezeray's Fr. Hist., p. 105. [2] Allix's Ch. Pied., ch. 9, p. 61. Newton, as above, p. 239.

mained in a community that was a sink of lewdness and uncleanness,³ we have yet to learn. His views are considered evangelical. He asserted the equality of all the apostles, and maintained that Jesus Christ was the only head of the church. His labours were very beneficial to the interests of religion in the valleys. He lived and died in the Catholic church; he gave no encouragement to others to separate, or form distinct communities, indeed he was an enemy to schism. His continuing to labour in a church so awfully corrupt for twenty-two years—his military enterprises—his association with the bishop of Urgel, leave his orthodoxy doubtful: he was in life beloved, and after death his memory was revered by his disciples.⁴ It is stated by Gilly, that Independent churches were first formed at the time of Claude.⁵ The bishop of Turin gave no encouragement to such societies; nor do we know what is to be understood by these *first Independent churches*, since such churches existed among dissidents from apostolic days. Probably, after Claude's death, his followers, who could not unite with the Baptists, or Vaudois churches, attempted something of the kind, and formed societies, similar to the Calixtines after Huss's death: but of this we have no records. That the old interests of the believers realized considerable accessions from Claude's labours, there is no doubt:⁶ and many more of corresponding features might have been formed, but of this we can only conjecture.

10. It becomes very plain, that early dissidents, both in the east and west, adopted the system of itinerating through kingdoms. This system was well suited to the

---

³ Mezeray ut sup. and pp. 112, 115.   ⁴ Jones's Lect., vol. ii. p. 192.   ⁵ Narrative, p. 82.   ⁶ London Ency., art. Reform. Rob. Res., pp. 447, 467.

850 state of the world in the eighth and ninth centuries, when the genuine religion and spirit of the gospel was utterly unknown to the doctors of the first rank in the catholic church. What aid the Piedmontese churches had from the Spanish Vaudois, or the Paulicians in Armenia and Bulgaria, we are not able to state. It was in the ninth century that the Paulicians flourished most, and acquired astonishing strength. As their religious views were at an early period propagated " beyond the Alps," it is not unreasonable to conclude, that they held some correspondence with these believers. Robinson asserts, that Greece was the parent of the Vaudois, while Piedmont was the jailer.[7] There is no room to question but that Savoy became the fostering friend of these dissenters. But to resume; the perfect class among the Vaudois was well calculated for a migratory life. While dispossessed of earthly possessions, and living celibate, such a mode of existence would be rendered comparatively easy. Such excursive undertakings, on such commissions, always left their return precarious.

The different ministers of eminence raised up in their churches, or brought over to their party from other communities, were considerable helps to the interests gene**1020** rally. Such was Gundulphus in Italy, who espoused their views, and was successful in gaining a great many disciples. The persons who were thus converted were instructed in the main points of religion, and were sent through various provinces to disseminate the truth; and it is allowed they were successful in withdrawing many from the Roman church.[8]

While other kingdoms and provinces barbarously used all dissidents, the valleys of Piedmont for ages afforded

---

[7] Eccles. Researches, p. 320. [8] Dr. Allix's Ch. Pied. c. 11, p. 91.

an asylum (Rev. iii. 10) for all the disaffected, towards the church and state union. Blessed here with security and liberty, and free from the impurities of the menstruous harlot, they breathed their devotions in one of the purest regions under heaven, while surrounded by the corruptest elements. Their minds were fettered with no human forms—their knees bowed to no delegated authority—their devotion was guided by no adjusted rules—their lips made no professions, but such as were stimulated by choice, and that choice was the response of divine benevolence, aided by a glowing gratitude, and presented alive to the author of all their mercies, in an acceptable way, through the blood of the Lamb. When their hearts became warm with spiritual kindlings, and their torch lighted up by a celestial flame, they marched forth, unaided and unabetted by the plenitude of modern favours, into the surrounding and distant territories, to enlighten the regions of darkness, to awaken men from the slumberings of a moral death, and to exhibit, in all the glow of heavenly benevolence, a fountain opened for the pollutions of a world, and an ample and sufficient balm for the sicknesses and moral diseases of a perishing universe. Such were Novatian and Novatus, with Constantine, Sylvanus, and Sergius of old; and such were Gundulphus and his coadjutors, with Arnold, Valdo, Berengarius, Henry, and Peter de Bruys.

These worthy men, who went forth with their lives in their hands, were the only moral means, in those ages, of renovating the corrupt inhabitants of this world; and no doubt, the success attending their efforts will be evident in the great day of decision, when many stars will be seen studding their crowns.

11. The attention paid by these Christians to the cultivation of the mind in the word of God and spiritual things, is highly commendable. The department of

teaching devolving on all believers, made the church an efficient resource of moral means for the necessary instruction of every class, within and without its community. Their enemies lay to their charge, that "they were very zealous, that they (men and women) never cease from teaching night and day."[9] "They had the Old and New Testament," says an inquisitor, "in the vulgar tongue; and that they teach and learn so well, that he had seen and heard a country clown *recount all Job*, word for word; and divers, who could perfectly deliver all the New Testament; and that men and women, little and great, day and night, cease not to learn and teach." It is natural for us to conclude, that these people, from their attention to the divine oracles, were able to give a scriptural reason for the hope within them, and to vindicate their peculiarities, by a direct appeal to the source of all authority in affairs of the soul. Indeed their habitude with the Scriptures appears to have been their boast, as they would say "there was scarcely a man or woman among them, who was not far better read in the Bible, than the doctors of the church." The advantages arising to them from having the Scriptures in their vernacular tongue, were incalculable; and their attention to its contents deserves the highest praise, while it presents to us an example eminently worthy of our close imitation.

One rule among this people, already recorded, was, that every Christian was in a certain measure qualified and authorized to instruct, exhort, and confirm the brethren in their christian course. This arrangement educed every talent among the brotherhood, and their gifts being exercised in the church, became an excellent means of qualifying every gifted brother for more gene-

---

[9] Jones's Lect., vol. ii. p. 274.

ral usefulness. This mode of proceeding would operate as a stimulus to spiritual acquirements, and a beneficial end must have been realized in all the community, especially since the gifted brethren's minds were richly laden with the inestimable pearls of sacred truth. Thus qualified with mighty weapons—clad with a spiritual armour, many whose hearts expanded with divine benevolence for the welfare of immortal souls, travelled through whole kingdoms, and became known by the name of the *Wandering Anabaptists*.[10] To effectuate the object of their mission, they carried with them a basket of portable wares, as our pedlars do, which often gained them access to persons of great respectability, when, if an opportunity offered, they would introduce some part of the history of John or Jesus. Reiner, the Judas among them, gave a full detail of their mode of instruction, and their views of the catholic church. Father Gretzer, who edited Reiner's works in the fifteenth century, affirms that this description of the Waldenses was a true picture of the heretics of his age, particularly of the Anabaptists.[1] This plan in the proceedings of these pious and benevolent people, will remove one difficulty, as to their maintaining their numbers and influence over almost whole provinces, when we are assured their enemies on every side for ages combined all their energies for their annihilation.

1025

This is the key to the success of Gundulphus and Valdo, who had many disciples, with Berenger, Valdo's friend and follower.[2] Each believer's gifts and talents were brought into requisition, and a multiplication of adherents ensued.

1100

It is recorded, that so early as 1100, the religion of the Waldenses had spread itself almost

[10] Rob. Res., pp. 467, 513.   [1] Id. p. 314.   [2] Id. p. 303.

in all parts of Europe, even among the Poles. That their doctrine differed little from the first protestants, and their numbers were such as to defeat all power that opposed it.[3] They were described nearly in the following language : "If a man loves those that desire to love God and Jesus Christ, if he will neither curse, nor swear, nor lie, nor whore, nor kill, nor deceive his neighbour, nor avenge himself of his enemies, they presently say, he is a Vaudois—he deserves to be punished."[4]

12. The centuriators of Magdeburgh, under the twelfth century, recite from an old manuscript, the outlines of the Waldensian creed : viz. "In articles of faith, the authority of the Holy Scripture is the highest authority; and for that reason it is the standard of judging; so that whatever doth not agree with the word of God, is deservedly to be rejected and avoided. The sacraments of the church of Christ are two, baptism and the Lord's supper. That is the church of Christ which hears the pure doctrine of Christ, and observes the ordinances instituted by him, in whatever place it exists."[5]

1110 About the same period, *Peter de Bruys* appeared as a public teacher. He was one of the chief doctors of the Vaudois. He stands first on the list of those pastors or bards of the valleys of Piedmont.[6] His views have been already given.[7]

1120 In 1120, the Vaudois put forth a confession of their faith; from which we give the following statements :—Art. 11. We hold in abhorrence all human inventions, as proceeding from antichrist, &c. Art. 12. We do believe, that the sacraments are signs of the

---

[3] Danvers on Bap., p. 24, and Jones's Lect., vol. ii. p. 429. from Sieur de la Popeliniere, see above, c. 2. s. 8, § 11.   [4] Allix's Pied. Ch., c. 18. p. 163.   [5] Jones's Hist. of the Ch., vol. ii. p. 56.   [6] Jones's Lect., vol. ii. p. 207.   [7] Vide above, c. 2, s. 8, § 6.

holy things, or as visible emblems of invisible blessings. We regard it as proper, and even necessary, that believers use these symbols or visible forms, when it can be done. Notwithstanding which, we maintain, that believers may be saved without these signs, when they have neither place nor opportunity of observing them.[8]

1130 13. The united labours of Arnold of Brescia, Peter de Bruys, and Henry of Toulouse, must have been productive of an amazing amount of good. These good men held corresponding views of religion, which we have already noticed; and their united services gave considerable encouragement to dissenters. Their numerous followers were called locally, for a considerable period, after the names of their leaders, or their country; yet, in the course of time, they were all known from inhabiting the valleys, under the generic term of Waldenses.[9] The success of Henry and others have been recorded in a previous section; the complaints of Bernard and his fraternity, with the united endeavours of the pontiff, the patrician, and the plebeian, to stay their increase, were unsuccessful; "for the purity and simplicity of that religion which these good men taught, the spotless innocence of their lives, their neglect of riches and honours, with an agreeable conversation, appeared so engaging to all who had any true estimate of piety, as secured the increase of numbers to their interests from time to time.[10]

1160 To aid the cause of real religion, a tract was sent forth by the Puritans, about this period, in the language of the ancient inhabitants of the valleys, entitled, *The noble Lesson*. The writer, supposing the world was drawing to a conclusion, refers to the scrip-

[8] Jones's Hist. of the Ch. vol. ii. p. 55. Gilly's Narr. app. 12.
[9] Jones's Lect., vol. ii. p. 214. [10] Mosh. Hist., C. 12, pt. 2, c. 5, § 12-13.

tures as a rule of guidance, and exhorts his brethren to prayer, watching, and renouncing of the world. He speaks with energy of death and judgment, the different issues of godliness and wickedness; and, from a review of the scripture history connected with the experience of the times in which he lived, concludes that there are but few (in comparison of the world) that shall be saved. In speaking of the apostles, it is observed, "they spoke, without fear, of the doctrine of Christ; they preached to Jews and Greeks, working miracles; and those that believed, they baptized in the name of Jesus."[1] This poetic effusion, with others from the Puritans, was supported by the poets of the age, called Troubadours, who united with the Vaudois in condemning the reigning vices of the times: their satires were chiefly directed against the clergy and monks, whose crimes were exposed in no measured terms. These Troubadours resorted to, and were great favourites in different courts; and their productions, written in the ancient language of Provence, were read by the inhabitants of Italy and Spain.[2] These circumstances, with the persecution of Waldo and his followers at Lyons, many of whom fled for an asylum into the valleys of Piedmont, with the new translation of the Bible, combined to increase dissenters, and strengthen the interests of religion in these abodes of peace. Their numbers became so formidable, says Mosheim, as to menace the papal jurisdiction with a fatal overthrow; which has been before

---

[1] Moreland's Hist., B. 1, c. 6, pp. 99, 116. Date of the *noble lesson*, says J. R. Peyrin, is from 1170 to 1190. The 1100 years in that work does not refer to the *lesson*, but to the time elapsed since John wrote. Rev. ii. 18. Hist. Def., &c. p. 147.   [2] Mc. Crie's Hist. of the Reform. in Italy, p. 15, &c. Mrs. Dobson's History of the Troubadours.

stated, with the evils resulting to the Albigensian churches from the crusading armies. A catechism, bearing date this century, says, "By the holy catholic church is meant, all the elect of God, from the beginning to the end, by the grace of God, through the merits of Christ, gathered together by the Holy Spirit, and fore-ordained to eternal life." This creed has no allusion to baptism.

1208

14. It has been observed, and the thing is worthy of notice, that at a period when all the potentates of Europe were combined to second the intolerant measures of the court of Rome, the Dukes of Savoy, who were now become the most absolute monarchs in Christendom, should have allowed their subjects *liberty of conscience*, and protected them in the legitimate exercise of their civil and religious principles; and Rev. iii. 10 appears remarkably accomplished in this state of things. Secluded in a considerable degree from general observation, and taught by their religion to lead " quiet and peaceable lives in all godliness and honesty;" the princes and governors of the country in which they lived, were continually receiving the most favourable reports of them, as a people simple in their manners, free from deceit and malice, upright in their dealings, loyal to their governors, and ever ready to yield them a cheerful obedience in every thing that did not interfere with the claims of conscience; and consequently, the governors constantly turned a deaf ear to the solicitations of priests and monks, to disturb their tranquillity. The tolerant principles of the dukes, with the sequestered habitations of these people; the difficulties of approaching their territories; their little intercourse with the world, connected with their rusticity of manners, were favourable circumstances to all the pious of the glens of Piedmont, while it afforded nothing inviting to strangers and the polite.

Consequently, these people appear to have enjoyed a considerable share of tranquillity, while their brethren in the south of France were experiencing the fury of papal vengeance. It is natural, therefore, to conclude, that, when persecution raged against the churches of France, the disciples of the Saviour in the French provinces would seek an asylum among the Alps on the one side, and the recesses of the Pyrenèes on the other. These mountains, at all trying seasons, afforded a retreat to all the sons of civil and religious freedom. Those Albigenses who retired before the crusading army visited France, lived long in the interior parts of the country, in obscurity, and busied themselves, says Voltaire, in the culture of barren lands. They had no priests, nor had they any quarrels about religious worship. From various accessions, the Waldenses had about this period, so greatly multiplied in the valleys, as to require fresh abodes and territories in order to support their rising families.

15. The zeal and activity of the Waldenses were not cooled or checked by the destruction of the Albigensian brotherhood, but they continued in their vigour, promoting the interests of religion. In 1223, they had good and extensive churches in many provinces and kingdoms.[3] In 1229, they had spread themselves in great number throughout all Italy. They had ten schools in Valcamonica alone, which were supported by contributions from all their societies. In 1250, Reiner Sacco, who had lived seventeen years among them, left the Waldenses, and went over to the Catholic party, and from his persecuting propensities, was raised to the office of inquisitor. He

---

[3] Danver's Hist., p. 23. M'Crie's Italy, p. 5, &c.

wrote an account of this people, and their heresy; he says in his time there was an innumerable multitude of Waldenses. He has stated their antiquity with their sentiments on the ordinances.⁴ Their increase and stability in the valleys occasioned an effort to be made so **1252** early as 1252, to introduce the inquisition into Piedmont; but the sanguinary proceedings of those officers of his holiness, against the Languedocians, had sufficiently opened the eyes of the inhabitants to the spirit and design of that infernal court; besides, it was found to interfere with the duties of the magistrate; it also came into conflict with resident bishops and priests of the same community, which occasioned considerable opposition from various quarters; but the Piedmontese, like some others, townsmen and citizens, wisely resisted its establishment among them at this early period.⁵ These pious inhabitants of the valleys maintained evidently their footing, in the face of all opposition; since Perrin esti**1260** mates their number in 1260, at eight hundred thousand persons.⁶ It is true, they had sus-

---

⁴ Wall's Hist. of Inf. Bap., pt. 2, p. 246.

⁵ In 1270 this office of inquisition was matured. The inquiry after heretics and their property in 1208, led to the organization of a society for the destruction of the liberties, properties, and lives of all persons suspected of incredulity towards the Roman hierarchy. Wherever the holy office was established, terror was inspired to such a degree, that suspicion seemed there to have a sovereign reign. Ignorance, and a servile conduct to the officers of the order, appeared the only palladium to life or property. Religion was not the *only object* promoted by this machine. Beauty and money had charms, and were interwoven in its movements. Millions were ruined, and millions were banished by it. Limborch's Inquis. ab. ed. 1816. Gavin's Master Key to Popery. Jones's Ecc. Lect., vol. ii. p. 355.   ⁶ Hist. of the Old Wald., b. 2, c. 11.   Benedict, in his History of the American Baptists, computes *seven adherents to each communicant;* suppose

tained in France and Germany, within this century, by deaths in every form, the loss of innumerable multitudes; yet, such were their number and remaining strength, their churches were still found to exist in Albania, Lombardy, Milan, in Romagna, Vicenza, Florence, Val Spoletine, and Constantinople, Philadelphia, Sclavonia, Bulgaria, Diagonitia; at after periods they were found in considerable numbers in Sicily, and posterior to their persecution in Picardy, they dispersed themselves into Livonia and Sarmatia, spreading themselves over other provinces and kingdoms.[7]

1300   16. In 1300, many of the Waldenses emigrated; some went into Provence, and settled in the district of Avignon, where they laboured and lived in credit; others obtained grants of land in the marquisate of Salucis; many took up their residence on the river Dora; while the greater portion of emigrants, at an after period, went into Calabria, in the extremity of Italy on the east, to which place they were invited by the lords of the soil; and where arrangements were made for their enjoying civil and religious privileges. Here they erected villages, and the colony prospered for a considerable time; of which success we have already spoken. The Waldenses, in their emigrations, went off from the main body in the valleys, in sufficient numbers to form colonies in other parts, of different dimensions, and in their newly-acquired places, they were not only mutual aids in the common concerns of life, but, carrying

---

we say *three* to each communicant of this name, this would make the adherents *alone* to these churches, amount to nearly *two millions and a half*; these, added to the members or communicants, 800,000, produce 3,200,000 persons, possessing evangelical views. This number will quadrate by and by, with the *moving shoals of Anabaptists* in Germany and other kingdoms.   [7] Jones's Lect. vol. ii. pp. 255, 430, 488.

with them the enkindled ember, they lighted up the lamp and altar, as companions and safeguards to their tents; assembled themselves as a church, and so diffused the sacred *illumination* all around. As expressive of their characters and designs, they selected a lamp ignited, with the motto, "the light shineth in darkness." In this capacity, in the new region, this people formed a *nucleus*, around which the materials of the district were collected, and under the smiles of their Redeemer were gathered in, and impregnated with the same particles of sanctity as dignified the founders of the interest.

17. For one hundred and thirty years after the destruction of the churches in France, the Waldenses in these valleys experienced a tolerable portion of ease, and a respite from the severity of a general persecution; all which time they multiplied greatly, and were as a people whom the Lord had evidently blessed; *they took deep root, they filled the land, they covered the hills with their shadow, and sent out their boughs unto the sea, and their branches unto the river.* Yet they were occasionally troubled by the inquisitors, who severely used those who

1320 fell into their hands, as was experienced in some parts of Germany. In Picardy, the severity of their afflictions drove many into Poland, but

1330 here they were disturbed in 1330, by the inquisitors. "In 1370," says M'Crie, "the
1370 Vaudois who resided in the valleys of Pragela, finding themselves straitened, sent out a colony to Calabria, where they flourished for nearly two centuries.

1390 Towards the latter end of this century, some of the Waldenses suffered in Paris from the monks.

1400 18. About the year 1400, a violent outrage was committed upon the Waldenses inhabiting the valley Pragela, in Piedmont, by a Catholic party residing in the neighbourhood. The attack, which seems to have been of the most furious kind, was made towards the end of December, when the mountains were covered with snow, and thereby rendered so difficult of access, that the peaceable inhabitants of these valleys were wholly unapprised that any such attempt was meditated; and the persecutors were in actual possession of their caves ere the owners seemed to have been apprised of any hostile design against them. In this pitiable strait, they had recourse to the only alternative which remained for saving their lives—they fled, though at that inauspicious season of the year, to one of the highest mountains of the Alps, with their wives and children; the unhappy mothers carrying the cradle in one hand, and in the other, leading such of the offspring as were able to walk. Their inhuman invaders pursued them in their flight, until darkness obscured the objects of their fury. Many were slain before they could reach the mountains. Overtaken by the shades of night, these afflicted outcasts wandered up and down the mountains covered with snow; destitute of the means of shelter from the inclemency of the weather, or of supporting themselves under it, by any of the comforts which Providence has destined for that purpose; benumbed with cold, some fell asleep, and became an easy prey to the severity of the climate; and when the night had passed away, there were found in their cradles, or lying upon the snow, fourscore of their infants, deprived of life; many of their mothers were dead by their side, and others just on the point of expiring. During the night their enemies had plundered their abodes of everything that was valuable. This seems to have been the first general attack made by the Catholic peasantry on the Waldenses. They had been hitherto sheltered from the pontiff's measures, by the Dukes of Savoy, so that the rage of their enemies had been restrained to a few solitary cases of arrested heresy; but this kind of assault, planned, no doubt, by the clergy, was of a novel character; and so deeply impressed were the minds of these people with the circumstances of the sufferers, as to speak of it for a century after, with feelings of apparent horror. We have rather minutely detailed this affair, in order to show its influence on the minds of the Waldenses, and to account, in some measure, for the change which took place soon after, in their views and conduct.

19. The combination of enemies and powers against this people, becomes now more ostensible. The valleys Fraissiniere, Argentiere, and Loyse, seem to have abounded with Waldenses in 1460; at which **1460** period, a Franciscan monk, armed with inquisitorial power, was sent on a mission of persecution, and to drive the inhabitants from the neighbourhood. Such was the ardour with which this zealot proceeded in his odious measures, that scarcely any person in those valleys escaped being apprehended, either as heretics, or as their abettors. The King of France, on application, interfered on behalf of the inoffensive Vaudois, but his majesty's instructions were so interpreted as to give sanction to additional acts of cruelty; and to every remonstrance this emissary of evil turned a deaf ear.

20. At this period, 1480, Claudius Seisse- **1480** lius, Archbishop of Turin, resided in the valleys; from his situation and office, he must have known something of these people. He says of the Waldenses, "Their heresy excepted, they generally live a purer life than other Christians. They never swear but by compulsion, and rarely take God's name in vain. They fulfil their promise with punctuality, and live, for the most part, in poverty; they profess to preserve the

apostolic life and doctrine. They also profess it to be their desire to overcome only by the simplicity of faith, by purity of conscience, and integrity of life; not by philosophical niceties, and theological subtleties. In their lives and morals they are perfectly irreprehensible, and without reproach among men, addicting themselves with all their might to observe the commands of God. All sorts of people have repeatedly endeavoured, but in vain, to root them out; for, even yet contrary to the opinion of all men, they still remain conquerors, or at least wholly invincible."[8]

1484 21. Innocent the 8th, was promoted to the Tiara in 1484. This pontiff, in the spirit of his predecessor, of infamous notoriety, Innocent III., issued his bulls for the extirpation of the Waldenses, and appointed officers to carry the same into effect. " We have heard," said the pope, "and it is come to our knowledge, not without much displeasure, that certain sons of iniquity, followers of that abominable and pernicious sect of malignant men, called ' *the poor of Lyons,*' or Waldenses, who have so long ago endeavoured, in Piedmont and other places, to ensnare the sheep belonging to God," &c. These indications of vengeance, and the ensuing measures, had considerable influence on them. Whether the halcyon days of these people had permitted them to subside into a Laodicean state, or whether they were terrified by the pope's threats we cannot ascertain, but one thing is certain, their line of policy subsequently adopted, of defending themselves with the sword, was a wide departure from their early creed, which suggests their degeneracy, and their wavering faith in the divine promises.

22. The pontiff's menaces were not vapour. An

---

[8] Jones's Hist. of Christian Ch., vol. ii. pp. 47, 79.

army was soon raised by 'Albert, the pope's legate, and marched directly into the valley of Loyse. The inhabitants, apprised of their approach, fled to their caves at the tops of the mountains, carrying with them their children, and whatever valuables they possessed, as well as what was thought necessary for their support. The lieutenant, finding the inhabitants all fled, and that not an individual appeared with whom he could converse, had considerable trouble in discovering their retreats; when, causing quantities of wood to be placed at the entrance of their caves, he ordered the same to be set on fire. The consequence of this inhuman conduct was, four hundred children were suffocated in their cradles, or in the arms of their dead mothers, while multitudes, to avoid death by suffocation, or being committed to the flames, precipitated themselves headlong from their caverns upon the rocks below, where they were dashed to pieces; if any escaped death by the fall, they were immediately slaughtered by the brutal soldiers. It appears more than three thousand men and women, belonging to the valley of Loyse, perished on this occasion. Measures equally ferocious, were adopted against the inoffensive inhabitants of other valleys, and with a like cruel success. Sentences were now publicly given against them in various churches. Innocent VIII. appeared as resolved at this period to free the world of these dissenters, as Innocent III. had been in the thirteenth century, to rid Languedoc of the Albigenses. The pontiff was himself filled with terrible apprehensions of danger. The Turks threatened Europe generally on the one hand, and dangers were seen to await the church from dissidents, on the other. The pope strongly exhorted European princes to put a stop to the progress of both. In order to have pecuniary means adequate to the expenses of these undertakings, indulgences to sin were sold by the servants of the church, and pardons for crimes past, or to be committed, could be purchased of those Panders of hell. So effectual were the papal measures, that the inhabitants were wholly extirpated in the above-named valleys, and these abodes were afterwards peopled with new inhabitants.9

1487 In 1487, scenes of barbarous cruelty awaited those long privileged people, who inhabited other districts of Piedmont, and in the ensuing year, to complete the work of destruction, an army of eighteen thousand men marched into those sequestered parts. The early Waldenses forbade war, and even prohibited self-defence, but their patience was now *worn* out, Dan. vii. 25, and they now departed from their ancestors' creed. They armed themselves with wooden targets and cross-bows, availing themselves of the advantages of their situation and country, every where defended the defiles of their mountains, and repulsed the invaders. The women and children, an affecting sight, were on their knees during the conflict, and in the simplest language, arising from overwhelming distress, and the prospect of losing all (their religion and their lives), entreated the Lord to spare and protect his people. Such were the feelings inspired in the bosoms of this people, by the sanguinary and brutal conduct of the inquisitors and soldiers, that FEAR led them to avoid public worship, and in time their worship was observed wholly in private. Some of the Waldenses found it expedient occasionally to conform to that communion which their ancestors had ever viewed as the harlot in the Apocalypse. Evidences now increase, and become but too apparent of a dege-

---

9 See Lady Morgan's Letters, for the present state of the valleys.

neracy from their primitive purity and practice. A succession of adverse circumstances awaited the Waldenses. The inquisitors, who lay in ambush, issued out their processes daily against them, and as often as they could apprehend any of them, they were delivered over to the secular arm for punishment. The sanguinary proceedings of Rome appeared either to have triumphed over its enemies, or to have exhausted its malice. The heretics, or Waldenses, were destroyed or driven into obscurity, and the state of the Catholic church at the

1500 beginning of the sixteenth century was unusually calm and tranquil. The witnesses ceased to trouble the church.[10]

23. Under cover of convincing them of their errors, and preventing the effusion of blood, a monk was deputed to hold a conference with them; but the monk returned in confusion, owning that, in his whole life, he had never known so much of the Scriptures as he had learned, during those few days he conversed with heretics. Others visited them by the bishop's appointment, and returned with similar views and convictions. The king of France, Francis I., being informed of the charges brought against the Waldenses in Provence, deputed a nobleman to inquire into their characters and mode of living. The report of the nobleman to his Majesty, reflected great credit on the Waldenses. Louis XII., in 1498, deputed two confidential servants to investigate and report on accusations brought against these people. On their return to court, they said, "their places of worship were free from those ornaments found in Catholic churches. They discovered no crimes, but on the contrary, they keep the sabbath-day, observe the ordinance of baptism according to

[10] Jones's Lect., vol. ii. pp. 490-8.

the primitive church (not as the Catholic church), instructed their children in the articles of the Christian faith, and the commandments of God." Consequently the king understood they were innocent and an inoffensive people, and that they were persecuted in order that their enemies might possess their property.[1] "The first lesson the Waldenses teach those whom they bring over to their party," says Reiner, "is, as to what kind of persons the disciples of Christ ought to be; and this they do by the doctrine of the evangelists and apostles; saying that those only are followers of the apostles who imitate their manner of life,"[2] and that a man is then first baptized (i. e. rightly baptized) when he is received into their society.[3] So effectual was their mode of instruction, that many among them could retain in their memories most of the New Testament writings. The celebrated president and historian Thuanus, says, " their clothing is of the skins of sheep, they have no linen; they inhabit (A. D. 1543—1590) seven villages: their houses are constructed of flint stone, having a flat roof covered with mud. In these they live with their cattle, separated however from them by a fence.[4] They have also two caves set apart for particular purposes, in one of which they conceal their cattle, in the other themselves, when hunted by their enemies. They live on milk and venison, being, through constant practice, excellent marksmen. Poor as they are, they are content, and live in a state of seclusion from the rest of mankind. One thing is very remarkable, that persons, externally so savage and rude, should have so much moral cultivation. They can all

---

[1] Mezeray's Fr. Hist., p. 948. [2] Jones's Lect, vol. ii. pp. 469—475. [3] Allix's Pied. Ch., c. 20, p. 190.
[4] Very similar to the Irish peasantry of this day.

read and write. They know French sufficiently for the understanding the Bible, and singing of psalms. You can scarcely find a boy among them who cannot give an intelligent account of the faith which they profess. In this, indeed, they resemble their brethren of the other valleys. They pay tribute with good conscience, and the obligation of this duty is particularly noted in their confessions of faith. If, by reason of the civil wars, they are prevented from doing this, they carefully set apart the sum, and, at the first opportunity, pay it to the king's tax-gatherers." This great man was a candid enemy.

24. The schism which took place in the Roman community, through the public preaching and writing of Luther and his associates, must have been a source of infinite satisfaction to the persecuted Waldenses. When the barbs, or pastors of the valleys, became acquainted with the reformation in Germany, they deputed, in 1526, persons to visit and inquire into its truth. The deputation returned with some printed books to the brethren. "The Vaudois took encouragement," says Mezeray, "to preach openly from Luther's appearing in the character of a reformer, but these zealous advocates for religion were punished by a decree made by Anthony Chassaue, and massacred.[5] It was found by the Waldenses in their communications and conferences with Luther, that their views were not in unison with his on the ordinances, but that they were more conformable to the sacramentarians, or those who deny the real presence.[6] Other brethren made a like visit into Germany, and conferred with Œcolampadius, Bucer, and others, who from the statement given, exhorted them to remedy certain evils

1526

[5] Fr. Hist., p. 618. [6] Id., p. 948.

which they perceived to exist among them; viz.—First, In certain points of doctrine; Secondly, In church order; and Thirdly, In irregular conduct of members, who mingled with Catholics in worship. After these preliminaries, the Waldenses appear, during 1530, to have been employed in paving the way for a more unreserved intercourse between themselves and the reformers. Their Laodicean state will easily account for their conformity, when we know their spiritual condition occasioned Œcolampadius to say, "We understand that the fear of persecution hath caused you *to conceal and dissemble* your faith—but those who are ashamed to confess Christ before the world shall find no acceptance with God," &c. &c. Those who could dissemble their faith, could as easily change it, which we find was the employment of many of these churches in different provinces during the year 1532. After much difficulty, many conferences, and a world of trouble, to mould these dissidents into conformity, *a creed* was made, ratified, and confirmed, in 1533, and the Waldensian brethren were comprehended and relieved from the ban of re-baptizing, while it was widely announced, that the Waldensian creed had ever been, in orthodoxy, one with the reformers'.[7] Calvin, who began in 1534 to preach the reforming doctrines, was found in his views more in accordance with the sentiments of the sacramentarians, or anabaptists, than Luther. "His views overthrew all ceremonies," says Mezeray, "and, consequently, the Waldenses left Luther's orthodoxy for communion with the reformed churches under Calvin.[8] Some of those churches, or

---

[7] Rob. Res., pp. 423-4.   Jones's Lect., vol. ii. pp. 499, 507.
[8] Fr. Hist., pp. 597, 948.

state communities under Calvin, amounted in a few years to *ten thousand members* in each, but whether infants are included or not, is not expressed. If not, it proves the vast numbers received into the corporations of those persons who had for ages sustained nonconformity. From this period, all dissenters from the Catholic church were called Lutherans in France and other provinces, though improperly. Some called them Sacramentaries, because they denied the real presence, but in 1560 they were called *Huguenots*, because they held their assemblies at midnight, at a gate called *Hugon*, or rather, because of their being in *league* with each other.[9] The favour the Italian protestants entertained for the reformed church, allow us to concede the comprehension, during this and the ensuing age, of the greater portion.[10]

25. One of the Waldensian bards, George Morell, who formed part of the deputation to Germany in 1533, and who published Memoirs of the History of their Churches, states, that at the time of his writing, there were *more than eight hundred thousand persons professing* the religion of the Waldenses. As to the extent of Puritanism among them, it cannot be ascertained, since, from the severity of the times, many in these valleys had occasionally or entirely conformed. It seems difficult, after the destruction of these people in Piedmont, to admit Morell's statement, unless in the term Waldenses he includes the Anabaptists, who abounded in Holland and Germany, which shall be shown anon. Hitherto these people had been obliged to confine themselves to manuscripts; and *in the Waldensian tongue*, they seem not to have generally pos-

---

[9] Mezeray's Fr. Hist., p. 667. Browning's Hist. of the Huguenots of the 16th century. [10] Jones's Ecc. Lect., No. 50.

sessed an entire version of the whole Bible, but the New Testament only, and some particular books of the old. They now (1535), however, contracted with a printer in Switzerland, for an entire impression of the whole Bible in French, for the sum of fifteen hundred crowns of gold.

26. Agreeably to the advice received from the reformers, the Waldenses opened again their places of worship, and their ministers appeared openly as teachers of the people adopting every spiritual means to resuscitate their drooping communities; but this bold and commendable position being reported to the duke of Savoy awakened his displeasure. It is now but too ostensible that the hitherto tolerant dukes listened to the proposals and facinorous measures of the court of Rome. The sovereign of Savoy raised an army to suppress the dissenters in those places over which his predecessors had for eight centuries extended their protection. The army surprised the people, but, recovering from the panic, each left his employ, and, by means of slings and stones, they compelled the army to retire without booty. From this defeat the duke gave them up to all the cruelties of the inquisitors.[1] An Observantine monk, preaching one day at Imola, told the people that it behoved them to purchase heaven by the merit of their good works. A boy who was present, exclaimed, "That's blasphemy! for the Bible tells us that Christ purchased heaven by his sufferings and death, and bestows it on us freely by his mercy." A dispute of considerable length ensued between the youth and the preacher. Provoked at the pertinent replies of his juvenile opponent, and at the favourable reception which the audience gave them,

---

[1] Jones's Lect., vol. ii. lect. 50..

"Get you gone, you young rascal!" exclaimed the monk, "you are just come from the cradle, and will you take it upon you to judge of sacred things, which the most learned cannot explain?" "Did you never read these words, 'out of the mouths of babes and sucklings, God perfects praise?'" rejoined the youth; upon which the preacher quitted the pulpit in wrathful confusion, breathing out threatenings against the poor boy, who was instantly thrown into prison, "where he still lies," says the writer. Dec. 31, 1544.[2]

27. "In this year, 1544, the Waldenses put forth a confession," says Sleidan, "expressive of their religious views." In Art. 4th, they say, "We believe that there is one holy church comprising the whole assembly of the elect and faithful, that have existed from the beginning of the world, and shall be to the end thereof." Art. 7th; "We believe in the ordinance of baptism, the water is the visible and external sign, which represents to us that which, by virtue of God's invisible operation, is within us, namely, the renovation of our minds, and the mortification of our members through the faith of Jesus Christ; and by this ordinance we are received into the holy congregation of God's people, previously professing and declaring our faith and change of life."[3] This creed was probably sent forth to show the reasonableness of their views, and to moderate the prejudices of the duke to whom they had been misrepresented. Though many of their brethren had taken shelter in the establishment, and consequently gave support to the sprinkling of infants, now first adopted as to healthy children at Geneva,[4] yet, in this confession there is no compromise

---

[2] M'Crie's Italy, p. 117, &c. Ch., vol. ii., ch. 5, § 3, pp. 59, 60.
[3] Jones's Hist. Chris.
[4] Dr. Wall's Hist., pt. 2, c. 9, § 2, pp. 365-6.

of the subject, it is sufficiently plain that pædobaptism had no encouragement from the persons from whom these articles emanated.

1561 28. In 1561, these Dissenters sustained another fierce and formidable attack, but they again defeated their opponents. Calvin and Beza, with a benevolence in accordance with their eminent piety, on hearing of these good men's distresses, obtained a liberal supply from various sources, to meet their temporary wants. Harassed incessantly, and always liable to the fury of the holy office, occasioned some of the brethren to migrate, while others, influenced perhaps from various motives, were led to unite with the churches of France and Geneva.[5] Whether the Waldenses embraced the reformed religion, from a hope of mitigating their sufferings, or were drawn over by the kindness of Calvin, or whether they from conviction saw differently to their former declarations, we leave; but *the change* of their belief was pleaded by the Bishop of Meaux, for recalling the edict of Nantz.[6] It does not appear, that any great difference existed between the Sacramentarians or Anabaptists, and Calvin's doctrinal views, but the principal points of discrepancy were on the *church's constitution and discipline;* but to these things they became familiar, and with a state church, they embraced for its defence, a state sword.[7] Such were the accessions which these

---

[5] Mosh. Hist., vol. iv. p. 69.   [6] Allix's Pied. Ch., pref.
[7] The Waldenses in France and other provinces, who embraced Calvin's views, found their enemies active and malicious. The persons, under the names of Sacramentarians, Huguenots, or Calvinists, devised a plan to secure their chief enemies in France, viz., **1560** the Duke of Guise and others, 1560, by force of arms ; but the plan was discovered, and they were defeated and hung. The **1562** violence of the Catholics drove the Reformers to arms ; wherever the Huguenots were masters, they abolished the Catholic

churches realized, that in 1571, the year before the general massacre, they amounted to 2,150, and some of which contained 10,000 members.[8]

29. Though the reformed churches embraced a great portion of the Waldenses, after infinite pains had been taken to quadrate their minds to the reformer's sentiments, "and then," says Robinson, " equal pains were taken to prove that they had always subsisted in the uniform orthodoxy of the reformed church ;[9] yet

1590 all the Vaudois did not yield their faith to the mandate of hierarchists. There were some remains of the Vaudois, or poor of Lyons, in the valleys of Dauphine, who had pastors, and held their assemblies apart; they were a little independent republic, as well for matters of religion as for government." The pope caused this abode of happiness to be stormed, and the Vaudois were destroyed or driven out of those valleys.[10] Others who were banished from the soil, had never heard the name of Luther,[1] and down to 1630, some retained their

1630 puritanical views.[2] But at this period those circumstances and changes did take place among this people, that each writer admits of a general degeneracy.[3]

---

religion, and broke their images; adopting a system of odious
1563 retaliation; for when they met with monks or clergy, they cut off their ears and their *virilia*, and did vast mischief by way of reprisals, so that, in tormenting the monks and priests, they rendered themselves execrable to the people! Mezeray, pp. 665, 681, 957—959. This conduct in the Calvinists led to the Bar-
Aug. 22, tholomew massacre! This picture of Pædobaptists, ob-
1572 scures Munster madmen: autem, comparationes odiosae sunt. [8] Lon. Ency., vol. xviii. p. 458, Art. Reform.
[9] Resear. p. 423. [10] Mezeray's Fr. Hist., p. 948. [1] Jones's Hist. Christian Ch., vol. ii. and Jones's Lect., vol. ii. 647, note. Mosh. Hist., vol. iii. p. 295. [3] Gilly's Narr. pp. 76, 249.

1655 30. In 1655, the Waldenses were called to sufferings of the most serious character, which awakened all the protestant princes of Europe; and Oliver Cromwell, on hearing of their persecution, 'rose like a lion from his lair,' and Sir Samuel Moreland was deputed by him to visit the valleys, to intercede with their oppressors, and to render such aid as would relieve their present wants.[4] By way of exhibiting the reasons of their choice in divine things, the inoffensiveness of their lives and doctrine, and to enlist the attention of Protestants to their case, as well as disarm their enemies of any grounds for misrepresentation, they published a confession of their faith, from which the following articles are taken: Art. 25. That the

1655 church is a company of the faithful, who, having been elected before the foundation of the world, and called with a holy calling, come to unite themselves to follow the word of God, believing whatsoever he teacheth them, and living in his fear. Art. 26. And that all the elect are upheld and preserved by the power of God in such sort, that they all persevere in the faith unto the end, and remain united in the holy church, as so many living members thereof. Art. 28. That God doth not only instruct and teach us by his word, but has also ordained certain sacraments to be joined with it, as means to unite us unto Christ, and to make us partakers of his benefits; and that there are only two of them *belonging in common to all the members of the church under the New Testament*, to wit, baptism and the Lord's Supper. Art. 29. That God hath ordained the sacrament of baptism to be a testimony of our adoption, and of our being cleansed from our sins by the blood of Christ, and renewed in holiness of life.[5]

---

[4] Jones's Lect., No. 53.   [5] Gilly's Narr., Appen. 12.

31. It is pleasing to discover a remnant of the Vaudois still witnessing, as their ancestors had done, the faith and practice of the gospel, though it is not in our power to say to what extent churches supporting the above views, then existed. In 1685, Oct. 8, **1685** the edict of Nantz was repealed, by which act, no toleration could be allowed to Dissenters from the Catholic church. Fifteen days were allowed to Protestant ministers to leave the kingdom; two millions of persons were condemned by this instrument, and banished from their native soil. This cruel instrument ruined the Protestant churches, and freed France and other kingdoms from the witnesses of the truth. If any remained, it was at the peril of life and liberty; yet some braved the danger, and worshipped unseen and unheard by malicious foes. "Pious females, **1686** shrouded by the night, bent their way amidst darkness and danger, towards the spot assigned for their religious services,—a dark lanthorn guided their perilous steps; arrived at their temple, amidst the rocks, two walking-sticks hastily struck in the ground, and covered with a black silk apron of the female auditors, formed what was called the pulpit of the desert. To such an assembly how eloquent must have appeared the lessons of that preacher, who braved death at every word he uttered; how impressive that service, the attending of which, incurred the penalty of fetters for life. These were the glorious days of Protestantism in France; these were her proudest triumphs; she could then boast of valour of which the world was not worthy; her martyrs then bore testimony to their faith, at the fatal tree, or were chained for life to the oar of the galleys; and women, with the same noble feelings, in the same sacred cause, shrank not from perpetual imprisonment in the

gloomy tower that overhangs the shores of the Mediterranean."⁶

1686 32. The severity of the measures used by the armies of France and Savoy, exceed this year in cruelty, those of 1655. The Swiss cantons sent deputies to the Duke of Savoy, who, now tired with human carnage, at their entreaty, set open the prison-doors, and those who survived were ordered to leave in peace.⁷ The Swiss government not being able to procure of France or Savoy any toleration for the Waldenses or Huguenots, led Henry Arnaud and about **1689** 400 of these exiles in 1689, to try to recover their native land, with sword in hand. These men did and suffered much of a marvellous character, and after fighting and suffering, were permitted to settle in their native soil.⁸

33. How far these men and their posterity can be considered the genuine successors of the old Vaudois, we leave with Dr. Gilly and others. We admit, they soon became regular in their education and ordination, agreeably to the rubric of the state. Their frockless and stipendless bishops, Napoleon enrolled among the Catholic clergy.⁹ These modern Waldenses are not Calvinists, they are not professed Puritans, they partake of the amusements and diversions of the world, they

---

⁶ Life of Claude prefixed to his Def., p. 54. Oct. Claude's Complaints of Protestants. Dr. Gilly's Narrative, and Bap. Mag., vol. viii. p. 89. A.D., 1816. ⁷ Jones's Lect., vol. ii. p. 644, Lect. 56. ⁸ Glorious recovery by the Vaudois, of their Valleys, &c., by H. D. Acland, London, 1827. Authentic Details of the Waldenses in Piedmont, &c., London, 1827. Dr. Beattie's Waldenses, &c. ⁹ The church, clergy, and state were brought under the Justinian code, 533,—1260 years after, 1793, the government of France dissolved the connexion, and the sovereign of that nation *killed the remaining witnesses in sackcloth*, by incorporating them with the Catholic clergy!

communicate in state order four times a year. Dr. Gilly, who evidently felt the tenderness of the ground he explored, says, in 1823, " they do not object to infant baptism," but he gives no early date to prove an early practice. Alas! how is the gold become dim![10]

[10] It is remarkable that the church clergy should claim succession to the Waldenses, and yet plead apostolic ordination through the regular line of popes, JOAN, *Alexander,* Leo, &c., in the Roman Church, when these different interests were always religious *antipodes.*

Appendix to the Waldensian Section.

Doctrinal and Denominational Sentiments of the Waldensian Churches.

1. Since the publication of Perrin's history of these people, in 1619, many able pens have been employed to rescue their names from reproach, while each writer has, from the character of these Vaudois, been desirous of finding their religious creed in alliance with his own. Bishop Bossuet says, "Provided any person complained of any doctrine of the church, and especially, if he murmured against the pope, whatever he were in other respects, or whatever opinions he held, he is put into a catalogue of predecessors of Protestants, and judged worthy to support the succession of their churches. As to the Vaudois, (whom you claim) they were a species of Donatists, and worse than the ancient Donatists of Africa." Again he says, "You call Claude of Turin one of your apostolical church; you adopt Henry and Peter Bruys; both of these every one knows were Anabaptists." Rob. Res. p. 476. We shall sequently submit the testimonies of accredited writers on these debateable points, and *prove our affinity* from other assertions.

2. The following statements establish their doctrinal views.

Genebrard asserts that the Henricians, Petrobrussians, Arnauldists, Apostolicis (Fathers of the Calvinists), with the Waldenses and the Albigenses, were similar in doctrinal views with Luther and Calvin. Leger's Hist., p. 155. Dr. Allix's Albig. Church, ch. 18, p. 172.

Reiner says, " the Lionists believe in the Trinity, as the church does." Rob. Res. p. 445.

Lindanus, a Catholic bishop asserts, Calvin inherited the doctrines of the Waldenses. Jones's Lect., vol. ii. p. 456.

Gaulter, a monk, shows the Waldensian creed was in accordance with the Calvinistic views. Ibid.

Æneas Sylvius, (Pope Pius II.) declares, the doctrines taught by Calvin to be the same as those of the Waldenses. Ibid.

Ecchius reproaches Luther with renewing the heresies of the Albigenses and Waldenses of Wickliff and Huss, which had been long condemned. Ibid.

Sieur de la Popeliniere, a French historian, says, the principles of the Waldenses extended throughout Europe, even unto Poland and Lithuania. These doctrines, which may be traced from A.D., 1100, differ very little from the Protestants of the Reformation. Danver's Hist., p. 25.

Mezeray, the historian of France, observes, the pope, at the Council of Tours, made a decree against heretics, i. e., a kind of Manicheans, who held almost the same doctrines as the Calvinists, and were properly Henricians and Vaudois. The people who could distinguish them, called them alike names with Cathares, Paterines, Boulgres, &c., p. 248, under 40 King. Calvin's doctrines were more conformed to the Anabaptists in the valleys, than Luther's, Ib. Toplady's Hist. Proof., vol. i. p. 151.

3. The subjoined extracts prove the denominational views of these people.

The fact is,—the forming of Christian congregations

in the established church of Piedmont and Savoy, like the gospel itself, began with baptism. Rob. Res., p. 468, and Hist., Bap., p. 581.

250 The people, the ancestors of the Waldenses, were termed *Vaudois*, (Id. Res., p. 299.) *Puritans*, (Mosh. Hist., c. 12, p. 2, c. 5, § 4, note.) *Paterines*, (Allix's Ch. Pied., c. 14, p. 128.) *Lyonists*, (Mosh. Hist., Id., § 11, Jones's Lect. 2, 238.) *Petrobrussians*, (Wall's History, part 2, c. 7, § 3, p. 220.) *Arnoldists*, (Facts op. to Fict., p. 46, from Platina.) *Berengarians*, (Wall, ut sup.) These, with the *Paulicians*, were one and the same people, (Jones, Id., p. 276. Mosh. Hist., Id. 224. Wall, Id. 230.)

650 and so far as information can be obtained, were all Anti-pædobaptists, which has been previously proved in their respective sections. These all agreed in one article of discipline, they *re-baptized* all such as came into their communion from the Catholic church, hence were called Anabaptists. Jones's Lect. vol. ii. p. 410.

660 In the seventh century, we have A LITURGY of Bobbio, near Genoa, but this directory contains no office for the baptism of children, nor the least hint of pouring or sprinkling; on the contrary, there is a directory for making a Christian a pagan, *before* baptism, and for washing the feet after it; and there is the delivery of the creed in Lent, with exhortations to competents, and suitable collects, epistles, and gospels, as in other ordinals, preparatory to baptism, on holy Saturday. The introductory discourse of the presbyter before delivering the creed, runs thus, " Dear brethren, the divine sacraments are not so properly matters of investigation, as of faith, and not only of faith, but also of fear, for no one can receive the discipline of faith, unless he have for *a foundation, the fear of the Lord.* * * * You are about to hear the creed, therefore, to day, for without that, neither can Christ be announced, nor can you exercise faith, nor can baptism be administered. * * * After the presbyter had repeated the creed, he expounded it, sentence by sentence, referring to trine immersion, and closed with repeated observations on *the absolute necessity of faith, in order to a worthy participation of baptism.* Rob. Res. pp. 473, 4.

670 The Gothic LITURGY, used in France, at this period, (670) has the manner of baptizing stated, but Dr. Allix could find no infant baptism in that document. Ch. of Albig. c. 7, p. 60, &c.

The same is asserted of the Roman, Ambrosian, Milanese, Spanish, Grecian, &c.; all these show the mode, single and trine immersion, yet nothing is said of infant baptism, but they appear composed, like all the Grecian, expressly for adult baptism. Rob. Res. 387.

774 During the kingdoms of the Goths and Lombards, the Baptists, or, as they were called by Catholics, Anabaptists, had their share of churches and baptisteries in these provinces, though they held no communion with Rome, Milan, Aquileia, Ravenna, or any **945** other hierarchy. But the laws of emperors deprived them of these edifices, and transferred them to the Catholic party. Rob. Res. p. 405.

1025 When Bishop Gerard, of Arras and Cambray, charged the Waldenses with abhorring (catholic) baptism, they said baptism added nothing to our justification, and a strange will, a strange faith, and a strange confession, do not seem to belong to, or be of any advantage to a little child, who neither wills nor runs, who knows nothing of faith, and is altogether

o

ignorant of his own good and salvation, in whom there can be no desire of regeneration, and from whom no confession of faith can be expected. Allix's Ch. Pied., c. 11, p. 95. Jortin's Rem. on Hist., vol. v. p. 27.

1120 The Waldensian confession of faith, in 1120, sets forth, "We regard it as proper, and even necessary, that believers use these symbols or visible forms (baptism and the Lord's Supper) when it can be done, * * * though we maintain believers can be saved without (Jones's Hist. of the Ch. Church, vol. ii. c. 5, § 5, p. 55), in case they have no place or means to use them (Gilly's Nar., Ap. 12). But surely, there were no difficulties in sprinkling a child, this could be done at any time, though there might be many difficulties in the way of immersing believers, and to those obstructions this confession, and an ensuing one, plainly alludes.

1139. The *Lateran* Council of 1139 did enforce infant baptism by severe measures, and successive councils condemned the Waldenses for rejecting it. Wall's Hist., pt. 2, p. 242.

1140 *Evervinus* of Stanfield complained to Bernard, Abbot of Clairval, that Cologne was infected with Waldensian heretics, who denied baptism to infants. Allix's Ch. Pied., c. 16, p. 140.

1146 *Peter*, Abbot of Clugny, wrote against the Waldenses, on account of their denying infant baptism. Ivimey's Hist. of the Eng. Bap., vol. i. p. 21.

1147 *Bernard* the saint, the renowned abbot of Clairval, says, the Albigenses and Waldenses administer baptism *only to the adults*. They do not believe infant baptism. Facts op. to Fict., p. 47.

1160 *Ecbertus Schonaugiensis,* who wrote against this people, declares, They say that baptism does no good to infants; therefore, such as come over to their sect, they baptize in a private way; that is, without the pomp and public parade of the catholics. Wall's Hist., pt. 2, p. 228.

1170 *Ermengendus,* a great man in the church, charges the Waldenses with denying infant baptism. Danvers on Bap., p. 298.

1175 At a council held in *Lombez,* the good men of Lyons were condemned: one charge was, that they denied infants to be saved by baptism. Jones's Lect., vol. ii. p. 240.

1176 The Waldenses were condemned, in conference, at Albi; when the bishop of Lyons, to convince them of their error, produced what were considered proofs for infant baptism, and tried to solve their objection from infants wanting faith, without which they said it was impossible to please God. (Heb. xi. 6, Rom. xiv. 23.) Allix's Ch. Albig., c. 15, p. 133.

1179 Alexander III., in council condemned the Waldensian or Puritan heresy, for denying baptism to infants. Danvers on Bap., p. 301.

1192 *Alanus Magnus* states, that they denied the ordinance to children. He disputes their views, and refutes their opinions. Allix's Ch. Albig., c. 16, p. 145.

The *Waldenses* admitted the catechumeni to baptism, after an exact instruction, a long fast, in which the church united, to witness to them the concern they took in their conversion, and a confession of sins in token of contrition. The newly-baptized were, the same day, admitted to the Eucharist, with all the brethren and sisters present. Allix's Ch. Pied., c. 2, pp. 7-8.

1200 *The Poor of Lyons*, for denying the sacraments, and practising otherwise in baptism than the church of Rome, were called by Baronius, Anabaptists. Danvers on Bap. p. 303.

Mezeray says, In baptism, in the twelfth century, they plunged the candidate in the sacred font, to show them what operation that sacrament hath on the soul. Hist. of France, 12 cent., p. 288.

The *Ordibarians*, or Waldenses, say, that baptism does no good to infants, unless they are perfected (by instruction first) in that sect. Wall's Hist., pt. 2, p. 233.

A catechism, emanating from the Waldenses during the thirteenth century, has no allusion to infant baptism. It says of the church catholic, that it is the elect of God, from the beginning to the end, by the grace of God, through the merit of Christ, gathered together by the Holy Spirit, and fore-ordained to eternal life. Gilly's Narr. App. 12.

Peter de Bruys and Henry, with other reformers, whose religious views we have given, were, says Mezeray, two principal doctors among these people; and yet these are said to have re-baptized all persons before fellowship. Fr. Hist. and Wall's Hist. and Bossuet. Var.

1254 *Reiner Sacco*, who, lived among the Waldenses seventeen years, and then went over to the catholic party, and was raised to the bad eminence of an inquisitor, asserts, They hold, that none of the ordinances of the church which have been introduced since Christ's ascension ought to be observed, as being of no value. (Jones's Hist. Ch. vol. ii. p. 30.) And among all the sects which ever existed, none were more pernicious to the church than the LYONISTS, from its *duration*, from its *extension*, from its show of *devotion*, as they believe rightly concerning the creed. (Bp. Newton's Diss., vol. ii. p. 250.) Some of them say that baptism is of no advantage to infants, because they cannot believe, and that a man is *then first* baptized, when he is received into their communion. (Jones ut sup.) Others were indifferent to the ordinances, whom we should class with Quakers.

We may observe, with Dr. Wall, that no man knew the Waldenses better than Reiner; yet we see the difference between the two parties *is not on doctrines*, but the ceremonies and pretensions of the Roman church. The sacraments in Piedmont and England were the apple of strife. In those bulls of popes and decrees of councils, year after year for centuries, we see the charge maintained against them, of neglecting infant baptism, without the shadow of evidence that this charge was improperly made against any portion of this people. Nor is there any document or testimony, quoted by Pædobaptists of this period, showing that the Waldenses as a body were wrongly charged in this affair. In all Dr. Wall's research, he found no document but what involved the Pædobaptists in reproach. pt. 2, p. 221, § 3.

1480 *Claudius Seisselius* says, the Waldenses receive only what is written in the Old and New Testaments. * * * They deny holy water, because neither Christ nor his apostles made it or commanded it: as if we ought to say or do nothing but what we read was done by them. Jones's Hist. of Ch. Ch., vol. ii. pp. 47—52.

1521 *Montanus*, in his *Impress* the second, says, that the Waldenses, in the public declaration of their faith to the French king, in the year 1521, assert in the strongest terms the baptizing of believers, and denying that of infants. Iwisk's Chronol., p. 930, also Meringus's Hist. of Baptism, p. 739.

The Waldenses in Italy held the unity of the Godhead, the baptism of only believers, and the right of private judgment, in which *last two all agreed*; but these the Lutherans and Calvinists abhorred. This is fully described by Reiner Sacco, being discussed freely, and the fraud of their claim to them admirably cleared by Father Gretzer. Robins. Res., p. 445, &c.

1544 In their confession of faith, dated by Sleiden, 1544, are the following sentiments :—

Art. 7. We believe, that in the ordinance of baptism, the water is the visible and external sign, which represents to us that which, by virtue of God's invisible operation, is within us; namely, the renovation of our minds, and the mortification of our members, through [the faith of] Jesus Christ. And by this ordinance, we are received into the holy congregation of God's people, *previously professing and declaring our faith and change of life*. Evan. Mag. for 1819, p. 505. Jones's Ch. Hist., vol. ii. c. 5, § 3, pp. 59, &c.

1560 *Cardinal Hossius*, who presided at the council of Trent, and wrote a history of the heresy of his own times, says, the Waldenses rejected infant baptism, and re-baptized all who embraced their sentiments. In his letters, apud opera, pp. 112—213. Bap. Mag., vol. xiv. p. 53.

1590 *Bellarmine,* a catholic writer of repute, acknowledged the Waldenses to have held, that *only adults* ought to be baptized. Facts op. to Fict., p. 42.

Father Gretzer, who edited Reiner Sacco's works, after Reiner's account of the Waldenses, and their manner of teaching, added, This is a true picture of the heretics of our age, particularly the Anabaptists. Rob. Res., p. 315.

1635 A Waldensian confession of faith dated in Gilly, 1655, contains the following views:—

Art. 28. That God does not only instruct and teach us by his word, but has also ordained certain sacraments to be joined with it, as a means to unite us unto Christ, and to make us partakers of his benefits; and that there are only two of them belonging in common *to all the members* of the church under the New Testament; to wit, baptism and the Lord's Supper.

Art. 29. That God has ordained the sacrament of baptism to be a testimonial of our adoption, and of our being cleansed from our sins by the blood of Jesus Christ, and renewed in holiness of life. Gilly's Narr. app. 12. This confession is altered by the present Protestant of the Valleys, which may be seen by comparing the above with a confession in Peyrin's Historical Defence, ed. by Rev. T. Sims, 1826, § 27, p. 463.

1670 *Limborch,* professor of divinity in the university of Amsterdam, and who wrote a history of the inquisition, in comparing the Waldenses with the Christians of his own times, says, To speak honestly what I think, of all the modern sects of Christians, the Dutch Baptists most resemble both the Albigenses and the Waldenses, but particularly the latter. Robins. Res., p. 311.

1685 *Bossuet*, bishop of Meaux, says, the sect of the Waldenses is a kind of Donatistism, (Rob· Res., p. 476, Allix's Ch. Pied., c. 20, p. 184), and their re-baptizing was an open declaration, that in the opinion of the brethren, the Catholic church had lost baptism. Robin's Bap., p. 463.

1692 Their views of baptism, says *Dr. Allix*, were, that it added nothing to justification, and afforded no benefit to children. Ch. Pied., c. 11, p. 95, and Ch. Albig., c. 18, p. 160.

1750 *Mosheim*, chancellor of the university of Gottingen, and author of the History of the Church, concurs with Limborch in the family likeness of the Waldenses with the Dutch Baptists, which shall be given in a future section. Ch. Hist., vol. ii. p. 323, and vol. iii. p. 320.

1790 The ancient Vaudois, says Robinson, are distinguished from the later inhabitants and the reformed churches, by not using any liturgy, by not compelling faith, by condemning parochial churches, by not taking oaths, by allowing every person, even women, to teach, by not practising infant baptism, by not admitting godfathers, by rejecting all sacerdotal habits, by denying all ecclesiastical orders of priesthood, papal and episcopal, by not bearing arms, and by their abhorrence of every species of persecution. This statement, he says, was made soon after the Waldenses united with Calvin. Eccles. Research., p. 461.

If the modern papers (of Perrin Moreland, Leger, &c.) describe the Vaudois' ancient customs, they baptized no infants. Id. p. 471.

Amidst all the productions of early writers, friends and foes, confessors of the *whole* truth and opposers of it, annalists, historians, recorders, inquisitors, and others, with the laboured researches of Usher, Newton, Allix, Collier, Wall, Perrin, Leger, Moreland, Mosheim, Macleane, Gilly, Sims, and others, all of the Pædobaptist persuasion, with every advantage of learning on their side, who collated councils, canons, synods, conferences, chronicles, decrees, bulls, sermons, homilies, confessions, creeds, liturgies, &c. from the private creed of Irenæus, down to the rules of Ausbergh; who examined documents at home, and explored the territories abroad,— *their united labours* could never produce a single dated document or testimony of Pædobaptism among the Vaudois, separate from the Romish community, from Novatian's rupture to the death of the execrable monster, Alexander VI., 1503.

1826 The Waldenses brought up their children in the nurture and admonition of the Lord; but they neither sprinkled nor immersed them, under the notion of administering Christian baptism. *They were*, in a word, *so many distinct churches of* ANTIPÆDOBAPTISTS. Jones's Hist. of Christ. Ch., pref. to 5th ed., 1826, p. xxvi.

We here accommodate Dr. Allix's words to this subject: "It is very remarkable, that Egbert, Alanus, Giraldus, and others, should accuse them of one custom for ages, as belonging to all, if a distinction could have been made." (Ch. Pied., c. 17, p. 155.) At the same time, all their dated documents and confessions justify the charge of neglecting the infant rite, while no testimony is produced to prove the accusation unfounded, among this numerous body, until the confession dated 1508, which states the writers to be falsely called Waldenses. See Bohemian sect.

3. Are we to conclude from these consecutive documents, that no persons bearing the name of Waldenses, saw and practised infant baptism with the Catholics? By no means. There were in those days, as in the present, persons who were found in every degree of distance from the established church. "It would be difficult to trace," says Dr. Allix, "the extent of those persons who held the truth unsophisticated." We should, from all that is written of them, divide the community into three sections. The Baptists, whose history is given; the Anti-baptismists, or Quakers; and the occasional conformists, or Pædobaptists. We shall state facts, in order that the misstatements of our opponents may be seen in their proper light.

The earliest claims which Pædobaptists can establish to any section of these dissidents as a distinct body from Rome, is from a document dated 1508. This instrument is easily explained. During the ministry of Huss and Jerome, many persons were brought into their congregations who could not forego the Roman ceremonies. After Huss's death, a great many found in Zisca's army (1433), were called Calixtines: i. e., persons who wished the cup in the eucharist restored to the laity; but in every other respect were Catholics. Another part was made up of those persons who were zealous for reform in church and state: while a third part was called Waldenses, or Picards, who interfered not in political affairs. (Rob. Res., pp. 488-92.) Osiander says, These people were a mixed society; some had lately separated from the church in the business of the cup, and were called Calixtines, Hussites, and Tharabites. (Allix's Ch. Pied., ch. 22, p. 214; and ch. 24, p. 241. Mosh. Hist., cent. 15, p. 2, ch. 3, § 5.) That many of the brethren, or Picards, opposed the baptism of infants. (Danver's Hist., p. 328.) But the Hussites, or Picards, in Bohemia, being inflamed with a divine zeal, took courage, says Allix, and separated themselves from the Calixtines, or pretended Hussites, setting up a distinct meeting in 1457, in several places, supported only by divine assistance. (Allix, ib.) Such was the unsettled state of the rest and remainder of this body, that they published nine creeds, or confessions of faith, or rather one creed *amended and improved* each time. (Robins. Res., p. 312.) The fourth, with the fifth edition improved, was presented, it is said, in 1508, to king Uladislaus, while he was in Hungary. The confession presented to the king, says in the preface, that *the petitioning party were not Waldenses*, though they were persecuted under that name. Here we leave these Calixtine Pædobaptists (Rob. ib.); and if in its mixture and unsettled condition, and without unity of spirit, it may be termed a church, it is the first church admitting of open communion which is found on record, and is certainly a model for all kindred communities.

The next document referred by Pædobaptists to prove infant baptism among the Waldenses, is *the Spiritual Almanack*. This instrument of information is without date; though, for party purposes, it is supposed to be very ancient. This is a glorious document to every tyro in school. This almanack is not referred to by any early writer: Dr. Allix does not mention it; Milner barely refers to it, but says nothing of its age or date. This spiritual almanack was written, as supposed, says Danvers, by George Moril, about 1530 (Hist., p. 328): but to this work we shall allude again.

Sir Samuel Moreland was sent by Oliver Cromwell, in 1655, into the valleys of Piedmont, with pecuniary aid, to the distressed inhabitants. His inquiries among these people led to the possession of some MSS.; extracts from which, Sir Samuel entitled, "*The ancient discipline of evangelical churches, extracted out of divers MSS., written in their own language several hundred years before Luther.*" (Evan. Mag. 1819, p. 408.) Those MSS. require a very close investigation; since Allix detected *two* to be falsely chronicled (Ch. Pied., ch. 18, p. 169); and the bishop of Meaux doubts the date of Perrin's document. (Id. ch. 20, p. 197.) But since there were divers of these MSS.—and Moreland found it easy *to age* them by centuries—we will try and quadrate their *early claims* with other discoveries. Every one interested in the merits of this discussion must be acquainted with the labours of William Wall, vicar of Shoreham, Kent, on the subject of infant baptism: for which history he obtained the honorary distinction of D.D. This man of research was very anxious to exhibit proofs of the uninterrupted practice of the infant rite from apostolic days. He has aided, in some measure, the anti-pædobaptist side of the question, without proving his own thesis. He conceded the absence of example in apostolic days; and in the middle ages, among the Albigenses and Waldenses,[1] his best efforts prove a

---

[1] Pædobaptists having in the seventeenth century used the Waldensian name as supporting their rite, H. Danvers, Esq., chal-

paucity of materials on his side of the question : and much which he has said has been demonstrated by Gale to be postulatory, with inferences falsely deduced. Yet his history is allowed to be the best in the infant question. After failing in his hands, it is not surprising to find the Pædobaptist historians of our day acknowledge the rite to be an "*inextricable maze!*" Wall's solicitude to find his views supported by a corresponding practice in the churches in the valleys, is very evident. After grappling with the subject, and belabouring through the leaden age of awful ignorance, cruel calumnies, and odious barbarities, aided by the historians of the valleys, Perrin and Leger, with Moreland's accounts fresh from the press—all advocates and coadjutors in the same cause—yet the only statement, the best account Dr. Wall could exhibit as demonstrative of the practice of Pædobaptism among the Waldenses, is the following, from Perrin; taken from *the Spiritual Almanack.* Wall quotes the Waldenses as saying—"*That their ancestors being constrained for some hundred years to suffer their children to be baptized by the priests of the church of Rome, they deferred the doing thereof as long as they could, because they had in detestation those human inventions that were added to the sacrament, which they held to be the pollution thereof. And forasmuch as their own pastors were many times abroad, employed in the service of the churches, they could not have baptism administered to their infants by their own ministers. For this cause they kept them long from baptism; which the priests*

lenged Baxter *to proof*, and to produce one single testimony of its existence among those churches. Baxter, in his "More Proofs," quoted Usher; but, says Dr. Wall, on examining Hovenden, the first writer, quoted by Usher, Danvers' cause was victorious;— Hist., pt. 2, ch. 7, § 3, p. 223. Dr. Wall has, by his concession, allowed that no proof exists of its practice in those churches.

perceiving, and taking notice of, charged them with this slander! Hist. of Inf. Bap., pt. 2, ch. 7, § 3, p. 221.

Now this is the *best proof* of Pædobaptism in the valleys, even after an examination of Moreland's divers MSS. of evangelical churches, several hundred years before Luther; and the Spiritual Almanack is often referred to as the strong fort. We ask, is this a true picture of those people whose names we revere, and whose creed we are anxious should be allied to our own, and which people we are trying to claim as our puritan predecessors? Then we yield them to Pædobaptists, and repudiate them from our pages as a people *we* cannot respect. Did Dr. Wall give this quotation to confer credit, or to burlesque the people? Does this statement reflect honour or disgrace, and which preponderates? The popish priests, perceiving the neglect and the slander incurred, are given as the reasons for complying with things they had in detestation. What particular mark did the water leave, so as to enable the priests to discriminate and reproach—save the pastoral visits of such priests to such occasional conformists, led to the inquiry and disclosure of facts? What class of dissenters would at this day, from the slander of priests, attend a ceremony *they detested*, and who would claim a sodality with them whose ancestors had sustained the same compromising character *for centuries?* And how amazingly punctilious in mental sagacity were such Pædobaptists in distinguishing between the authority for a traditional rite, and those human inventions added; when the Church of Rome owns the traditional character of the infant rite altogether, with hundreds of the literati, who confess its absence in the primitive church, while the practitioners of the present day *are divided* on *the grounds* as well as *the extent* of its practice!

But we observe, the Waldensian churches had regular

and settled pastors. "A stated ministry was always considered as a matter of great importance among the Waldensian churches. (Jones's Lect., vol. ii. p. 459. Allix's Pied., ch. 24, p. 245.) "Those barbs, or pastors, who remained at home in the valleys, besides preaching, took upon them the disciplining and instructing of the young," &c. (Danvers, p. 30, from Moreland.) And Reiner charges them with communicating every (Lord's) day, which would require a stated and settled ministry. Were these Pædobaptists, as given by Perrin and Wall, real Waldenses? I trow not.

That the Pædobaptists, in Perrin, should succeed each other for *several hundred years*, and that successive generations should suffer themselves to be constrained into a religious service, and for them to be for centuries without ministers, satisfactorily demonstrate their interest to have been very low, not 800,000, as recorded, but distinct from the Waldensian churches, and even through centuries not a thriving denomination. Indeed we shall make it appear, *that these were not a separate people*, but occasional conformists to the Roman church.

The Catholics baptized children, with the first advocates, solely on the grounds of original sin, and its accompanying salvation. Augustin had never heard of a man (practising it) who had not that view; and Dr. Wall quotes early writers largely in point, and asserts, this sense was disturbed by Calvin. (Hist., pt. 2, pp. 66, 451.) Now, in Perrin's account, given by Wall, those Pædobaptists make no objection to the Catholic doctrinal views accompanying the rite, and consequently could not be considered true dissidents from that body.

But truth is always consistent; and here we give the key to this class of professors. "The believers of Lombardy, in the time of Gregory I.," says Allix, "who were deprived of their ministers by persecutions of

Arians, carried their children to the Arian priests to have them baptized." (Ch. Pied., ch. 24, p. 242.) This conformity was the condition of peace; the place was the established church; the creed was the Arian, and by one immersion; the cause was the absence of their own minister. Again, when inquisitors were commissioned by the pope, in 1176, to visit the heretics in Languedoc, and by any and every means to bring them over to the Catholic church: they took a creed with them, to which they required the Vaudois fully to consent as the terms of peace and paradise. This creed contained the following objectionable clause: "We believe that none are saved, excepting they are baptized; and that children are saved by baptism; and that baptism is to be performed by a priest (not in a river, but) in a church." (Danvers, p. 300.)

In the thirteenth century, when the preaching monks went through the length and breadth of the land, Collier, with others, says, that on these occasions, with the above creed, multitudes repaired to the Catholic churches, and compromised their principles. (Gr. Hist. Dict. Albig.) Multitudes must have previously neglected their infant seed! A succession of such accommodating persons is plain, since Reiner says, The Waldenses pursued "the same dissembling course; they frequent our churches, are present at divine worship, offer at the altar, receive the sacrament, confess to the priests, &c. &c., though they scoff at our institutions." (Jones's Christian Ch., vol. ii. p. 34.); or, as the confession of Perrin, "they held them in detestation." These compromising Vaudois, with their remote ancestors and progeny, form evidently the class of evangelicals, whose conduct is an exact key to Perrin's account. This is supported by their state in 1530; when the churches *connected with George Moril*, to save themselves from

Catholic rage, did go to mass in Provence, and pleaded it was no great harm, provided their hearts were kept right with God. For which prevarication and hypocrisy, the reformer Œcolampadius rebukes them, and condemns the practice. (Perrin's Hist.) Such were not witnesses of the truth.

The Waldenses took the Scriptures alone for their guidance, and carefully avoided all human impositions in religious duties. The Catholics, with the Vaudois, allowed infant baptism no higher authority than the "*tradition of the Fathers*," and "*the custom of the church.*" (Milner's End of all Controv., Lect. 30. Easky discussion, p. 79.) We are sure, a people who were guided in all religious duties by a literal interpretation, as of Christ's sermon on the mount, would never adopt in their churches a human rite. The real Waldenses looked upon infant baptism to be one feature of Antichrist, since it borrowed the form of sound words to support a lie, and conferred a spiritual figure upon an alien to spiritual blessings.

The Vaudois did not practise Pædobaptism, nor receive the sign of the cross: this they called the mark of the beast. This is evident from the laws enacted to regulate commercial affairs, and which excluded those from any advantages in trade, who refused this shibboleth. The cross running through the *whole* of that system is certainly the mark of the breast. (Bp. Newton, Diss. 2, pp. 195, 289.) It was the ground model of their sanctuaries, the ornament within and without; it was placed on the forehead in baptism, and, by various digitary motions, conferred on every part of the body; it was worn on the clothes, or carried in the hand; it was the ensign of peace, or the signal of war; it was the emblazonry of the field, and the escutcheon of the mansion; it was the pope's signet, and the peasant's security; it was the talisman in private, and the Palladium of the public interest; the pontiff's tiara, the church's confidence, the community's glory and dread. This mark the Waldenses did not receive, and there was no baptism conferred on infants without it. Had they received the mark of the beast, they could not be considered free of the threatened indignation. Rev. xiv. 9. Whether infant baptism was limited, or extensively practised in the valleys, one conclusion will force itself on every impartial inquirer, that *those* who administered, and those who received the rite, would in every age be viewed by Catholics in a more favourable light, than those who denied infant baptism; consequently, those who agreed in so essential a point of salvation, would find no great barrier to communion in times of persecution, compared with those who, like the real Waldenses, abhorred every vestige of the man of sin. This is made plain by facts; for so soon as the Waldenses embraced Pædobaptism, so far they were incorporated into national churches in 1532-5. (Dr. Allix's Ch. Pied., ch. 20, p. 184. See German Section.)

4. Bogue and Bennet, in their History of Dissenters, felt convincingly the difficulty of establishing a community of Pædobaptists in the valleys separate from the Church of Rome ; and when called on to explain some harsh expressions about our denomination, gave a postulatory statement, that the dissenting interests were formed of mixed materials, and in justification said, " That no evidence has been adduced to make it evident that they (the Baptists) were *a distinct body*, which excluded others from their communion."

Any person, with Mosheim in his hand, might controvert this gratuitous assertion! We observe,

First. The church of Jerusalem is satisfactory to negative this statement; Acts ii. 41 ; with the first account of church discipline extant, which says, "This food we call the eucharist; of which none are allowed to be partakers, but such only as are true believers, and have been baptized in the laver of regeneration for the remission of sins, and live according to Christ's precepts." (Justin Martyr's Apol., Reeve's Trans., vol. i. § 86, p. 120.) Dr. Wall asserts, that "no church ever gave the communion to any person before they were baptized." (Hist., pt. 2, p. 441.)

Secondly. We have already proved in the previous sections, and shall confirm the same statements in future pages, that the *terms of communion*, in the churches of Novatian, Donatus, Constantine Sylvanus, with the Paterines in Italy, the followers of Peter de Bruys, who was a doctor among the Albigenses, were, *a profession of faith and baptism*: the latter held, "that persons baptized in infancy are to be baptized after they believe, which is not to be esteemed re-baptization, but right baptism." (Osiander, Cent. 12, L. 3, p. 262.) "The Waldenses admitted the catechumeni to baptism, after an exact instruction, a long fast, &c., and then were admitted to the eucharist after baptism." Allix's Ch. Pied. ch. 7, pp. 7, 8.

Thirdly. Robinson's works on baptism might be considered a kind of literary excursion to decry intolerance. His zeal for mental freedom led him to examine minutely every early record on the terms of communion; and his history of the controversy on this subject makes no mention of the practice in any early church. (Works, vol. iii. p. 141.) His earliest discovery bears date 1577. The Baptist churches in Poland originated in some of Waldo's disciples leaving France in the twelfth century. These, with all our churches, were established on the terms of strict communion. (Rob. Res., p. 600.) At this period, 1577, Faustus Socinus reached Cracow, and essayed to join the Baptists, but was refused without baptism. He blamed the churches for their strictness, and showed them by argument *the innocency of mental error.* (Others, perhaps, would class Antinomianism, Sabellianism, and Socinianism, in the catalogue of mental errors: *but mental error is sanction, and is virtually the grounds of the mixed system.*) Being a great and learned man, he brought many to see with himself. He soon stood a member of the church; and by zeal and charity, effected a radical change in the Baptist creed and churches. (Rob. Res., p. 607.) He is now acknowledged as the honourable head of the Socinian Baptist churches in Poland, though himself was never baptized. Our views will be again exhibited on the churches' constitution, so as to prove the Baptists to be *a distinct body*, from the great Catholic community of Pædobaptists. As great names are apt to dazzle, and even set aside facts, reason, and revelation, we caution all our readers against receiving great sounding assertions in the room of facts. There can be no proof of Pædobaptism, as practised before the sixteenth century, but among persons of the Catholic and Grecian persuasion. Prove our assertion to be wrong, and you shall have our thanks for your friendship. "Open communion arises *from a new state of things.*"—R. Hall.

Section XII.

German and Dutch Baptists.

"As concerning this sect, we know that everywhere it is spoken against."—*Acts* xxviii. 22.

1. That vast tract of land, called by the Romans Germany, extended one way from the North Sea to the banks of the Danube, and the other from Gaul to the Mæotick lake. This immense tract of forests and mountains, rivers, marshes, and plains, the limits of which cannot be exactly defined, was inhabited by a great number of different tribes, having a general likeness, but divided into several nations, in different degrees of civilization, and distinguished by different names. They were a people of large stature, fair complexion, blue eyes, and red hair. At early ages they had a simple sort of patriarchal worship; but this degenerated into idolatry, and a savage character ensued. They sent out immense multitudes on all sides to obtain settlements and support for their rising posterity, so that Germany appears, at that period, as a kind of storehouse of nations. It would be impossible to enumerate the German tribes, they are THE FATHERS of all Europe; for from this immense territory, as from a hive, they swarmed, and colonized, and overspread half the world. In the life-time of our Redeemer, the Goths were enthusiasts for liberty in their own forests. This love of freedom was cherished in the migratory tribes, and was found to characterize those Goths who took up their abode in Spain; the descend-

ants of which people inhabited the foot of the Pyrenèes, and were afterwards called Vaudois.¹

2. It is highly probable, that the gospel was preached to these people by the apostles, since it is absolutely certain that the Goths professed Christianity several centuries before their kings became Catholics. They retained their natural love of freedom, and consequently divided, at after periods, into various religious sentiments, having no national standard of faith, nor any legal civil coercion for conscience. The catholics, all through this early period, called them Anabaptists, heretics, and not Christians.²

In the third century, the gospel was preached and churches existed at Cologne, Treves, Metz, and in other places.³ We have no means of knowing whether the Novatianists in their itinerancy visited these kingdoms or not. Those who represent the German tribes as barbarous at this period offer a cruel insult to the memory of a brave and generous people, and contradict those historians who lived among them. In their religious discipline, they considered soundness of faith essential to the ordinance, yet they tolerated all others in their religious exercises. The Arian views at an early period had extensive encouragement among the Gothic tribes.

Though the German nation was divided by various denominations, yet they all agreed in one point. They baptized none without previous instruction, but such they baptized at any time. They also re-baptized all who had been baptized among Catholics, before they could be received into their churches; and for this

---

¹ Gib. Hist., vol. i. p. 317.   Robins. Res., pp. 153, 154, 199, 315, 393.   ² Robinson's Res., pp. 199, 315.   ³ Mosh. Hist., vol. i., p. 152.

reason were called Anabaptists. These views on the ordinance embraced by the Germans, regulated their conduct in their religious societies wherever they formed a colony among other people: as may be traced in Spain, Lombardy, Africa, Italy, and France.[4] Mezeray, the French historian, says, the Burgundians, a people of Germany who had received the Christian faith, visited France so early as 430, and obtained a settlement at Vienne and Lyons.

3. The freedom of religious ordinances in Germany being destroyed by Charles the Great, makes it necessary that we should digress. Cyprian, Austin, and Innocent used every means to comprehend all infants in the Christian church by baptism, on account of original sin; but these proved successful only where the mental and moral character was degenerated from apostolic simplicity. In 517, a canon was made by seven bishops at Girona, in Spain, enjoining baptism for babes if they would not suck their mother's breasts; and in which cases of danger, Gregory, the pope, allowed one immersion to be valid baptism. In 789, Charles the Great resolved to subdue the Saxons or destroy them, unless they accepted of life on the condition of professing the Christian religion agreeably to the Roman ritual. On pain of death the Saxons, with their *infant offspring*, were to receive baptism. Germany in time was subdued, and religious liberty destroyed. The king took an oath of fidelity of them and received pledges for the fulfilment of his stipulations.[5] In this way the religious privileges of these and other nations were infringed on, and by these and similar means Christianity under state patron-

---

[4] Id., pp. 99, 167, 199, 393.   [5] Mezeray's Fr. Hist., p. 103.

age, made rapid progress for ages, as detailed in the works of hierarchists. To make the conversion of these people accord with the gospel record, apostles were sent to them, but the Germans were exceedingly jealous of such bifarious commissioned ministers of religion. These apostles of Rome preached up *trine immersion*, but said nothing of infants. Success attended the imperial commands; other kingdoms were visited in virtue of the same authority, and converted from fear of the carnal weapon. The evidence of their complete conversion was made apparent by their baptism. Wooden tubs and other utensils were placed in the open air, and the new converts with their children *were immersed naked* into the profession of Christianity. This indelicacy in the mode originated with the advocates of minor baptism as already shown: it has never been practised in Baptist communities. This mandate of Charles is the first legal authority for infant baptism,[6] and we ask if the mental character must not have been exceedingly low, to enforce such terms of denudation on the female portion of candidates? We repudiate the charge, and leave the blot on those who were guilty of the practice.[7]

4. The wilds and forests of Germany would prove asylums to dissidents through the rise and assumption of the man of sin. That Germany was inhabited by persons of this description is evident, and that such persons must have been very active in disseminating the truth becomes plain, since it is recorded that the Baptist itinerant preachers, could in their travels pass, during the ninth century, through the whole German empire, and lodge every night at the

---

[6] Robins. Hist. Bap., pp. 268, 282, &c. [7] Wall's Hist., vol. ii., p. 379, and Bap. Mag., vol. i., p. 435, from Vossius.

house of one of their friends.⁸ It is very probable these travelling ministers were Paulicians or Paterines, from Bulgaria or Italy. They were termed by Catholics anabaptist preachers.⁹ Their sentiments of religion are learned, and their views of the ordinances proved, from their confession of faith, which asserts, "In the beginning of Christianity there was no baptizing of children; and their forefathers practised no such thing:" and "We do from our hearts acknowledge that baptism is a washing, which is performed with water, and doth hold out the washing of the soul from sin."¹⁰ In 1024, a company of men out of Italy visited and travelled through whole provinces preaching the gospel, and were exceedingly successful in enlightening many and drawing them from the catholic cause. These disciples of Gundulphus have been referred to, where we proved they disallowed of infant baptism.¹ It is allowed by Mosheim, that many dissenters of the Paulician character, in this century, led a wandering life in Germany, where they were called Gazari, i. e., Puritans. These good men grounded their plea for religious freedom on Scripture, and were called brethren and sisters of the free Spirit, while their animated devotion gained them the name of Beghards.² When this term first sprung up in Germany, it was used to designate a person *devout in prayer*: at after periods it was used to point out all those communities which were distinct from Rome, and thus in time it was

---

⁸ Mosh. Hist., vol. ii. p. 224. Twisk's Chro., lib. 13, p. 546. Clark's Martyr. p. 76, &c. Gillie's Historical Collection, vol. i. p. 32. Bap. Mag., vol. i. p. 454. ⁹ Robins. Res., pp. 467, 513. ¹⁰ Merning in Meringus' Hist. of Bap., pt. 2, p. 738. Junius, p. 77. ¹ Jortin's Ecc. Rem., vol. v. p. 27. ² Ecc. Hist., vol. ii. p. 224, &c.

P

given to persons who only had the garb of religion.³

1100 Twisk, upon the year 1100, asserts that the Waldenses did practise believers' baptism.⁴ We have, under date 1140, a letter written by Evervimus,

1140 of Stainfield, in the diocese of Cologne, in Germany, to Bernard, Abbot of Clairval, wherein he speaks to the following effect: There have been some heretics lately discovered here which after conference, and not being able to recover them, they were committed to the flames, which they bore with astonishing patience, and even joy. Their heresy is this: they say the church is among them, because they only follow the steps of Christ, and continue in the true imitation of the true apostolic life, not seeking the things of the world, possessing neither house, lands, nor any property, nor did he give his disciples leave to possess anything. * * * We the poor of Christ, who have no certain abode, fleeing from one city to another, like sheep in the midst of wolves, do endure persecution with the apostles and martyrs. They say much on the baptism of the Holy Ghost which they support from scripture. They call themselves elect, and say, every elect hath power to baptize others *whom they find worthy*, but they contemn our baptism * * * and give their ordinance to those only who are come to age, as they do not believe in infant baptism.⁵ "I must," says the writer, "inform you also, that those of them who have returned to our church, tell us that they had great numbers of their persuasion scattered almost everywhere; and as for those who were burnt, they, in the defence they made of themselves, told us that this heresy had been concealed from the time of the

---

³ Ecc. Hist. Cent. 13, c. 5, § 40. ⁴ Chro., lib. 11, p. 423. ⁵ Allix's Ch. Pied., c. 16, pp. 140—143.

martyrs; and that it had existed in Greece (among the Paulicians) and other countries. Bernard was exceedingly offended with these Baptists for deriding the Catholics because they baptized infants, prayed for the dead, and maintained a state of purgatory, &c.[6]

5. The severity of the pontiff's measures **1170** adopted against Peter Waldo, constrained him to leave Lyons, with a valuable portion of its inhabitants, for other kingdoms. For some time he continued to publish the gospel with great success, through Dauphiny, Picardy, and various parts of the German states, concluding a labour of twenty years in **1180** a province of Bohemia.[7] At Salt and Lun, as before observed, mention is made by Crantz of a colony of Waldenses settling.[8] The followers of Waldo visited many kingdoms with the New Testament translation, while some of this persuasion settled in the Netherlands.[9] These emigrants, coming from Picardy into Bohemia and Germany, were commonly called PICARDS by catholics and historians.[10] Of their views on Justification we have already enlarged in the Bohemian section. Wherever these people went, they sowed the seeds of reformation. The countenance and blessing of heaven attended their labours, not only in the places where Waldo had laboured, but in more distant regions. In Alsace, and along the Rhine, these doctrines spread extensively. Persecution ensued; thirty-five citizens of Mentz were consumed to ashes in one fire, in the city of Bingen, and eighteen in Mentz itself. The bishops of Mentz and Strasburg breathed nothing but vengeance and slaughter against them, and at the

[e] Jones's Lect., vol. ii. p. 247.   [7] Lon. Ency., Art. Reform.   [8] Robins. Res., pp. 479. 527.   [9] Bap. Mag., vol. xiv. p. 51.   [10] Clark's Martyr. p. 76.

latter city, where Waldo himself is said to have narrowly escaped apprehension, eighty persons were committed to the flames. Multitudes died praising God, and in the confident hope of a blessed resurrection. But the blood of the martyrs became the seed of the church : and in Bulgaria, Croatia, Dalmatia, and Hungary, churches were planted principally from the labours of one Bartholomew, of Carcassonne, which societies flourished throughout the thirteenth century.[1]

6. Whatever injury the society sustained by persecution, must have been in some measure repaired by a corresponding class coming into Germany out of Italy in the early part of the thirteenth century.

1210 These baptists, with others who had previously settled, became known by the appellation of brethren of the free Spirit, or Beghards. It was no uncommon thing, in those dark times, to reproach persons for their devotional conduct, as Massalians, Euchites, Bogomites, and Beghards, meaning "persons of prayer," which, in our view, confers on such persons the meed of praise. These accessions from Italy, with numbers of the Albigenses who escaped the sword and flames in Languedoc, taking refuge in Germany, will account for the prominency of the Beghards in the histories of those times, and the establishment of their reputation at this period.[2] They first appeared as a religious body so early as the eleventh century, probably from the labours of those men already mentioned, 1025, out of Italy; but came more particularly into reputation during this century. "Their primitive establishment," says Mosheim, " was undoubtedly the effect of virtuous dispositions and

---

[1] Jones's Lect., vol. ii. p. 238.   [2] Mosh. Hist., vol. ii. p. 299, and Robins. Res., p. 516.

upright intentions. A certain number of pious women, both virgins and widows, in order to maintain their integrity, and preserve their principles from the contagion of a vicious and corrupt age, formed themselves into societies, each of which had a fixed place of residence, and was under the inspection and government of a female head. Here they divided their time between exercises of devotion, and works of honest industry; reserving to themselves the liberty of entering into a state of matrimony, or of quitting the establishment, whenever they thought proper. All those who made extraordinary professions of piety and devotion were called *Beguines*. The first society of this kind, of which any account exists, was formed in the beginning of this century, and was followed by so many institutions of a like nature in France, Germany, Flanders, and Holland, that, towards the middle of this century, there was scarcely a city of any note which had not its beguinage or vineyard, Cant. viii. 12. Ps. lxxx. 15. This example of the women was followed by corresponding institutions for men, and these pious persons were, in the style of the age, called Beghards and Beguines, and, by a corruption of that term usual among the Flemish and Dutch, Bogards; but from others, at an after period, they were denominated Lollards. The hours not appropriated to devotion among the Beguines, were employed in weaving, embroidering, and other manual labours of various kinds. The poor, the sick, and disabled among them, were supported by the pious liberality of such opulent persons as were friendly to the order. The same religious views and purposes were adopted by the different establishments of men and women.[3]

1226

[3] Mosh. Hist., vol. ii. p. 400 note, and De Beghardis et Beguinabus Com. Rob. Res., pp. 532, &c.

7. We shall now exhibit our claim to these pious Waldenses, so far as it respects the ordinance. We own their religious views are not fully known. They thought Christianity wanted no comment but a pious walk; and they professed their belief of that by being baptized, and their love to Christ and one another by receiving the Lord's Supper.[4] Jacob Merning says that he had, in the German tongue, a confession of the faith of the Baptists, called Waldenses; which declared the absence of infant baptism in the early churches of these people, that their forefathers practised no such thing, and that people of this faith and practice made a prodigious spread through Poland (yea, Poland was filled with them[5]), Lombardy, Germany, and Holland.[6] These people re-baptized such as joined their churches, as the Waldenses had done in early ages;[7] and though a law was made against the Piçards for rebellion, yet they suffered burning in the hand, and banishment, rather than forego what they considered their duty.[8] Dr. Wall, who is a candid opponent, says, the Beghards were also called Picards or Pighards. They spread themselves over the great territory of Upper Germany; they abominated popery; they chose their pastors from among married men; they mutually called one another brother and sister; they owned no other authority than the Scriptures; they slighted all the doctors, both ancient and modern; their ministers wore no garments to celebrate communion, nor do they use any collection of prayers but the Lord's Prayer; they believed or owned little or nothing of the sacraments of the catholic church; such as came over to their church must every one be

---

[4] Rob. Res., p. 527.   [5] Id. p. 557.   [6] Meringus' Hist. of Bap., pt. 2, p. 738, and upon Cent. 13, p. 737, and Montantus, p. 86.   [7] Rob. Res., p. 506.   [8] Id. p. 518.

baptized anew in mere water; they believe that the bread and wine do only, by some occult signs, represent the death of Christ—that the sacrament was instituted by Christ to no other purpose but to renew the memory of his passion, &c. &c.[9] In this statement may be discovered a family likeness to those churches in the south of France. Their renouncing worldly possessions; their mode of living in large communities; their distinction into perfect and imperfect classes; with their allowed piety, support their claim of descent from the early Vaudois. We may be permitted to admire the *motive* and *design* of the institutors of such establishments, and particularly the *spirit* which animated, guided, and bound up these societies in *unity* for centuries. The object of its members must have been the restoring of Christianity to its native simplicity, original purity, and benign aspect. The seven concluding verses in the second of Acts appear the rule of guidance in these communities. Their extensive interests through the German empire accord with the moving shoals of the Anabaptists in a future period.

8. These dissenting communities had their respective schools, at which many of the nobility were educated. Uladislaus II. was prevailed upon in 1140 to sign an edict against the Vaudois or Picards; but the influence of the nobles rose above the sovereign, and rendered the law void.[10] In 1210 the dissidents had become so numerous and so odious to the catholic clergy, that Otho IV., at their entreaty, granted an edict against them. A severer measure was adopted by Frederick II., which extended over all the imperial cities, in 1220; and, in the hands of the inquisitors, entailed misery on the peo-

---

[9] Hist. of Inf. Bap., pt. 2, c. 7, § 4, pp. 270-1.   [10] Rob. Res., p. 532.

ple.¹ The cruel measures awakened in the lower orders of the people retaliating feelings; these received the officers of the pope with clubs, stones, daggers, and poison. The first martyr was a friar Conrad, who was killed in Germany while he was preaching against liberty in religion. No means had been left untried to rid France of the Albigenses, which had been so far successful as to destroy *one million lives*.² While the pontiff was devising means to free Gascony of a section of those heretics, he and his conclave were suddenly alarmed by the news, that the work of reform, which, according to his hope, had been so often extinguished, had now made its appearance in the very heart of Germany; and that the city of STETTIN was infected by the same heretics who, as he fondly hoped, had been extinguished in Languedoc. Gregory IX. lost no time in addressing bulls to the bishops of Minden, of Lubeck, and of Rachhasbourg in Styria, to induce them to preach up a crusade against the heretics. In order to excite greater horror against these sectaries, the pontiff represented to the people, that "a hideous toad was presented at once to the adoration and caresses of the initiated. The same being, who was no other than the Devil, afterwards took successively different forms, all equally revolting, and all offered to the salutations of his worshippers.". Such were the accusations the popes often exhibited against the Waldenses; and coming from the lips of holiness and infallibility itself, they could not fail of success. The fanatics took up arms in crowds, under the conduct of the German bishops. Those among the sectaries who were not in a condition to carry

[1228]

---

¹ Rob. Res., p. 412, and see above, sect. 6, § 13—15.   ² P. Personius in Claude's Def. preface, p. 61. Monthly Review, Feb. 1815, p. 222. Simondi's Hist. of the Crusades: *passim*.

arms, or who had not taken refuge in the strong places, were first brought to judgment; and in the year 1233, "*an innumerable multitude of heretics was burned alive through Germany; a still greater number was converted.*" The crusading army and the inquisitors, to all appearance, extinguished the heretical light. But such was the nature of this pestilence, as the court called it, that, like water which was dammed up in one place by inadequate mounds, it is sure to break out in another.[3] Though Frederick II. had, in the early part of his reign, gone into the cruel measures of the pope, by not complying with his mandate, he now incurred his holiness's displeasure. The pope excommunicated Frederick, incensed his own son to rebel against him, nominated another emperor, and thus rent the empire in twain. During the interdict, the churches were closed, the bells silent, the dead unburied: the penalty fell upon those who had no share in the offence.[4] Frederick wrote letters to all the princes of Europe, exposing the ambition of the pontiffs, and calling on all to take from the clergy the treasures they had amassed. The sufferings to which thousands were reduced in Germany, from this strife, were dreadful; yet the pope was insensible to the reigning misery. This state of affairs continued till the death of Frederick, 1250. This affray between the emperor and the pope relieved the sectaries from the cruel and oppressive designs of their enemies, and afforded these people some relief and opportunity to propagate their views. Their increase becomes apparent, since it is recorded, that in the beginning of the fourteenth century, they existed in thousands; and, as observed, in Bohemia they were consid-

---

[3] Jones's Lect., v. ii. p. 398.   [4] Hallam's Middle Ages, vol. ii. pp. 240-3.

ered as amounting to 80,000. Some of these Picards, while travelling and propagating the truth, were seized, and suffered; while persecution scattered others into various provinces and kingdoms, whose efforts and labours were apparent in the multitudes which arose at the dawn of the reformation, in this empire.[5]

1315 9. A bold and intrepid teacher was raised up among the Beghards, or Picards, in 1315, in the person of WALTER LOLLARD, who became an eminent barb or pastor among them, and from whom the Waldenses were called Lollards.[6] Clark says, Lollard stirred up the Albigenses by his powerful preaching, converting many to the truth, and defending the faith of these people.[7] Moreland asserts he was in great reputation with the Waldenses, for having conveyed their doctrines into England,[8] where they prevailed all over the kingdom.[9] Mosheim remarks, that Walter was a Dutchman, and was a chief among the Beghards, or brethren of the free Spirit.

He was a man of learning and of remarkable eloquence, and famous for his writings.[10] Walter was in unity of views in doctrine and practice with the Waldenses.[1] He was a laborious and successful preacher among the Baptists who resided on the Rhine; but his converts are said to have covered all England.[2] The Lollards rejected infant baptism as a needless ceremony.[3]

1320 In 1320, Walter Lollard was apprehended and burnt. In him the Beghards on the Rhine lost their chief, leader, and champion. His death was

---

[5] Bishop Newton's Diss. on the Prophec., vol. ii. p. 225. [6] Wall's Hist., vol. ii. p. 272. [7] Martyr., p. 76. [8] Hist., p. 30. [9] Allix's Ch. Pied., c. 22, p. 202. [10] Hist., vol. ii. p. 509. [1] Gilly's Nar., p. 78. [2] Allix ubi sup. [3] Lon. Ency., Art. Loll. Collier's Eccl. Hist., vol. i. b. 7, p. 619.

highly detrimental to their affairs, but did not, however, ruin their cause; for it appears they were supported by men of rank and great learning, and continued their societies in many provinces of Germany.[4]

1330 10. About 1330, these people were grievously harassed and oppressed in several parts of Germany, by an inquisitor, named Eachard, a Jacobin monk. After inflicting cruelties for a length of time, with great severity, upon the Picards, he was induced to investigate the causes and reasons of their separation from the church of Rome. The force of truth ultimately prevailed over all his prejudices. His own conscience attested, that many of the errors and corruptions which they charged on that apostate church really existed; and finding himself unable to disprove the articles of their faith by the Word of God, he confessed that truth had overcome him, gave glory to God, and entered into the communion of the Waldensian churches, which he had been engaged in persecuting even to death. The news of his conversion aroused the ire of the inquisitors. Emissaries were despatched in pursuit of him; he was at length apprehended and conveyed to Heidelberg, where he was committed to the flames.[5]

11. The Baptists who inhabited those cities that lay on the Rhine, especially at Cologne, had considerable **1407** accessions from the labours of John Huss, who, in 1407, became a bold champion in the cause of truth. He taught the same doctrines as Lollard and Wickliff; he was popular, and his discourses were full of those truths charged on the Anabaptists. John Huss, with Jerome, travelled and laboured for the interests of the Redeemer; consequently dissidents were multiplied in the empire, by conversions and by accessions from

---

[4] Mosh. Hist. ut sup. [5] Jones's Lect., vol. ii. p. 428.

other kingdoms. These persons, reasoning on the principles laid down by Huss and Jerome, on the sufficiency of the Scriptures to guide them in the affairs of the soul, entertained the same ideas of religion as the old Vaudois did; and with their successors, the Beghards, they became incorporated. They were indiscriminately called Waldenses, or Picards; and they all, says Robinson, re-baptized; but they entertained views widely different on other subjects.[6] The deaths of Huss and Jerome, accompanied with efforts on the part of the clergy to excite the people to destroy heretics, awakened in these people a conviction of their danger. They therefore formed the plan of leaving Upper Germany for the lower parts of the empire; but the vigorous opposition of their enemies, who learned their design, prevented them realizing their concerted object.[7] They were aroused now to defend their privileges. The emperor Sigismund, a dissolute man, was devoted to the clergy, and promised them uniformity in religion. The nonconformists of all classes, throughout the empire, saw all their religious and civil liberties at stake. John de Trocznow, commonly called Ziska, from his having only one eye, determined, as the last defence, to take arms, as already stated. Having raised his standard, Ziska found himself, in a few weeks, at the head of fifty thousand troops. See Bohemia.

1416

1457
12. In 1457, a great number of Waldenses were discovered by inquisitors in the diocese of Eiston in Germany, who were put to death. These sufferers confessed that they had among them, in that district, twelve barbs or pastors, who laboured in the

---

[6] Resear., pp. 481, 513.   [7] Wall's Hist., pt. 2, p. 272.
Mosh. Hist., r

work of the ministry. It appears, from what Trithemius relates, who lived at this time, that Germany was full of Waldenses prior to the Reformation by Luther; for he mentions it as a well-known fact, that so numerous were they, that in travelling from Cologne to Milan, the whole extent of Germany, they could lodge every night with persons of their own profession; and that it was a custom among them, to affix certain private marks to their signs and gates, whereby they might be known to each other.[8] This is allowed by the best of our historians, and conceded by Mosheim,[9] who asserts, "before the rise of Luther or Calvin, there lay concealed, in almost all the countries of Europe, particularly in Bohemia, Moravia, Switzerland, and Germany, many persons who adhered tenaciously to the doctrine of the Dutch Baptists, which the Waldenses, Wickliffites, and Hussites had maintained, some in a more disguised, and others in a more open and public manner; viz. that the kingdom of Christ, or the visible church he had established upon earth, was an assembly of true and real saints,'and ought therefore to be inaccessible to the wicked and unrighteous, *and also exempt from those institutions which human prudence suggested*, to oppose the progress of iniquity, or to correct and reform transgressors. This maxim is the true source of all the peculiarities that are to be found in the religious doctrine and discipline of the Baptists. It is evident that these views were approved of by many before the dawn of the reformation."

The emperor's opinion of the Picards, and his physician's concurrence of their views and practice, being nearer to apostolic precedent than any other religious sect, has been already recorded. Their bitterest ene-

---

[8] Danvers' Hist., p. 25. [9] Ec. Hist., vol. iii. p. 320.

mies, who were eye-witnesses of their actions, say, They resembled the ancient Donatists; their lives were blameless, but their doctrine was heretical: their simplicity, innocence, fidelity, and industry, are admirable; but their doctrines are damnable.[10] They made no figure in the world, says Voltaire; but they laid open the dangerous truth which is implanted in every breast, that mankind are all born equal.[1]

1490 13. At the conclusion of the 15th century, Germany was divided into sixteen circles, and governed by sovereign princes, whose tyrannical oppression would exceed belief, were they not well attested; consequently the peasants or boors were slaves every where! This state of oppression and beggary should be taken into consideration by the censurers of those times and people. The peasants had several times attempted in Germany, as in Switzerland, to obtain their freedom.

1491 In 1491, they aimed to recover their birth-right, but failed. In 1502, another attempt proved alike abortive.[2] The princes and ecclesiastics continued to be supreme tyrants rioting in luxury wrung from their respective peasants. The ignorance of the priests was extreme. Numbers of them could not read, and few had ever seen a Bible. Many, on oath, declared they knew not that there was a New Testament. These officers of religion held no intercourse with the laity, and their manner of giving them instruction was accompanied with a haughty superiority: " Ye that be lay people, ye shall know,—that there be ten commandments," &c., &c.[3] Yet, this ignorant and lordly class was supported at an enormous expense. The taxes of the state, the luxury of princes, and the ponderous burden of tithes for the sup-

---

[10] Rob. Res., p. 566.   [1] Rob. Bap., p. 484.   [2] Rob. Res., p. 537, &c.   [3] Rob. Bap. p. 296.

port of the church were all produced by the labour of the peasants; sequently, the situation, to a people, who from early times, had been distinguished by the love of liberty, became insufferable.[4] Besides, their present thraldom was increasingly felt, from their witnessing and hearing the successful efforts of the peasants in Switzerland. Such was the vassalage of Christendom at this period, to the church of Rome, that the pontiff appeared to feel no apprehensions of the general tranquillity being disturbed.[5] The church was made up of monsters, living in the most complicated crimes, and the greater portion of the community had become profoundly stupid.[6] Here is the climax of a state church!!!

14. The severity of the inquisitors, and the watchful conduct of the state clergy, had occasioned the detection and removal of every public champion of reforming principles, almost as soon as he avowed his sentiments, which is apparent in every part of history; and, were the records collected, the account of those of the Baptist persuasion, who have suffered martyrdom *solely* on the account of religion, would make *a large book*.[7] Under these successive losses, the Waldenses continued to disseminate the truths of the gospel by means of all the members of their community. The Baptists appear, through successive ages, opposed to worldly greatness, and always at variance with the secular maxims of securing success by human learning and tithes of distinction; they moved silently on, scattering in their walks the seeds of life. The least mental attainment in the Christian brother among them, was encouraged, and placed in requisition to the cause of truth, which awakened anger and contempt among the state clergy,

---

[4] Mosh. Hist. vol. iii. p, 50, note.   [5] Jones's Lect., vol. ii. p. 503.   [6] Rob. Res., p. 301.   [7] Bayle's Dict. Anab. F.

for desecrating the holy order. Their societies were consequently of a missionary cast, which proved an extensive blessing to successive centuries. This view only will account for their numbers in this and other empires and kingdoms, through the reign of the man of sin. Such was their procedure down to the sixteenth century, when they perceived several learned men, and also through their means, several among the unlettered of the people, were beginning to expose the darkness arising from error, superstition, and a lack of religious knowledge. They lived less retired than they had formerly done, and engaged to come forward with others, to diffuse the light of a purer religious knowledge, and to demolish the Romish superstition as much as it was in their power.[8] They did not scruple to draw many over from the Romish church in a very open way, incorporating them with themselves by re-baptization. "This re-baptizing," said Bishop Bossuet, " is an open declaration, that in the opinion of the brethren, the Catholic church has lost baptism."[9] To further the work of reform, many of the brethren itinerated through various districts, and were reproached with the name of "the wandering Anabaptists."[10] Among these Anabaptists, were Hetzer and Denck, who published translations of parts of Scripture.[1] Multitudes of minds were by these means instructed in the truths of the gospel, and many learned, enlightened, and eloquent men only waited for some opening in Providence, to advocate more fully and publicly, the gospel of Christ.[2] But, amidst all the sectaries of religion, and teachers of the gospel in Germany at this time, the Baptists *best understood the doctrine of re-*

---

[8] Mezeray's Fr. Hist., p. 618.   [9] Rob. Hist. of Bap. p. 463.
[10] Rob. Res. p. 513.   [1] M'Crie's Italy, p. 178.   [2] Lon. Ency. vol. xviii. p. 669, Reform. Jones's Lect., vol. ii. 511.

ligious liberty, to them, therefore, the peasants turned their eyes for counsel;[3] and to their immortal honour be it recorded, that *the Baptists were always on the side of liberty*. Under whatever government they could realize this boon, whether Pagan, Saracen, or Christian; domestic or foreign; that dynasty which would guard their freedom, was their government. In this respect, like the apostles, they paid no regard to its religion, civil government was their object.[4] This might be traced in all their migratory movements, from the Italian dissidents to the Rhode Island settlement[5].

1500 15. We have now detailed the history of the Puritans through several nations, and under various names, and shall by these records, have proved at the Reformation, That the Baptists' has been *the only Christian community* which has stood since the days of the apostles; and as a Christian society, which has preserved pure the doctrines of the gospel through all ages.[6] These societies we shall find perpetuated in a few years, under Menno Simon's fostering care; whose creed will speak their affinity to the Vaudois, and though many, in claiming relation to these people, have disputed some things in their practice, none ever denied that they baptized adults on a profession of faith, before they received them into their communion.[7]

16. The sectaries or Picards, in itinerating, had been successful in bringing persons of all classes over to their views and community, from the Catholic church. Their conduct in re-baptizing, awakened the anger of the Catholic priesthood, and measures were proposed to stay the growing evil. Consequently, in 1510, the

1510 clergy and bishops prevailed on the sovereign

---

[3] Rob. Res., p. 545.   [4] Id. p. 641.   [5] Id. p. 311, Cox and Hoby's Am. Bap., p. 444.   [6] Bap. Mag., vol. xiii. p. 344, A.D., 1821.   [7] Rob. Res., p. 508.

to use means equal to the danger; whereupon, an edict was made, that all the Picards, without distinction of sex, age, or quality, should be slain.⁸ The influence of some noblemen prevailed for its suspension for eighteen months, but the edict received the sanction of government at the end of that term, yet interpositions of Providence prevented its full execution. The threatening aspect of affairs in Germany, suggested to the Picards the necessity of emigrating, and Mosheim asserts, "*that the German Baptists* PASSED IN SHOALS *into Holland and the Netherlands*, and in the course of time, amalgamated with the Dutch Baptists."⁹

17. "The drooping spirits of this people," says the same writer, "who had been dispersed through many countries, and persecuted everywhere with the greatest severity, were revived when they heard that Luther, seconded by several persons of eminent piety, had successfully attempted the reformation of the church."¹⁰ Consequently, several persons with the views of the Baptists, made their appearance at the same time, in different countries; this appears from a variety of circumstances, especially from this striking one, that all the Baptist ministers of any eminence, were, before the Reformation, almost all, heads and leaders of particular and separate sects (or congregations.)¹ The Baptists occasioned little publicity, and made little noise before the Reformation, though the most prudent and rational part of them considered it possible, by human wisdom, industry, and vigilance, to purify the church from the contagion of the wicked, provided, the manners and spirit of the primitive Christians could but recover their lost dignity and lustre; and

1518

---

⁸ Clark's Martyr., p. 127.   ⁹ Ec. Hist., c. 16, § 11, p. 336.   These shoals accord with Morell's 800,000 Waldenses.   ¹⁰ Id. vol. iii. p. 321.   ¹ Id. p. 323.

seeing the attempts of Luther, seconded by several persons of eminent piety, proved so successful, they hoped the happy period was arrived, in which the restoration of the church to purity was to be accomplished, under the divine protection, by the labours and counsels of pious and eminent men.[2]

18. Many religionists, at this period, as Venner, in the days of Cromwell, were projectors of a new state of things, others were in anticipation of an unspotted and perfect church; while some, as we shall see, carried their speculations into frenzied enthusiasm.[3] These views had some encouragement from Luther and the reformers; for every impartial and attentive observer of the rise and progress of the Reformation, will ingenuously acknowledge, that wisdom and prudence did not always attend the transactions of those that were concerned in this glorious cause; that many things were done with violence, temerity, and precipitation.[4] Luther had boldly stepped forward, and set tyranny at defiance. This was known, and was differently viewed by the religionists throughout Europe, but more particularly animated those who were addressed by Luther and his associates. To further the great work, he published the New Testament in German, wrote letters to the sovereigns of Europe, broke with the pope, and propelled forward the work of reformation. To these efforts, he added a work on Christian liberty, in the German language, which was read with the most astonishing avidity, and the contents were communicated to those who could not read. In this work, Luther speaks of what he calls spiritual liberty, that is, the freedom of the spirit or mind, in matters of religion;

1519

1520

---

[2] Ency. Brit., Anabap.   [3] Mosh. Hist., vol. iii. p. 232.
[4] Id. p. 102.

and he assigns the causes of bondage, to sins, laws, and mandates, which naturally mean our sinful passions, the laws of magistrates, and the canons of the church.[5] The pope denounced Luther, and he nobly, on Dec. 10, 1520, had a pile of wood erected without the walls of Wittemburgh, and there in the presence of a prodigious multitude of all ranks and orders of people, committed to the flames both the bull that had been published against him, and the decretals and canons relating to the pope's supreme jurisdiction. By this act, Luther publicly declared to the world that he was no longer a subject to the Roman pontiff; and the man who publicly commits to the flames the code that contains the laws of his sovereign, shows thereby *that he has no longer any respect for his government, nor any design to submit to his authority.*[6] These zealous and decisive acts of the reformer, however dignified, impressed the minds of men very differently, and in the mind of the oppressed peasant, it awakened a spirit of *restless insubordination,* which only waited a suitable season to disclose the inward ferment.[7] The boldness of these measures occasioned Luther's being called to Worms, by Charles V., where he boldly and nobly pleaded his cause, but was condemned, and to prevent his sustaining any injury, Frederick caused him to be arrested, and conveyed privately to the Castle of Wartenberg, where he divided his time between writing and hunting.[8]

1521

19. One benefit the scattered brethren realized was, the translation at this period of the whole of the New Testament by Luther, agreeably to their views, and his and their sentiments concurred by his translating Matt. iii. 1, " In those days came *John the dipper.*"[9] Other

---

[5] Rob. Res. p. 540.   [6] Mosh. Hist. vol. iii. p. 40.   [7] Rob. Res., p. 540.   [8] Mosh. Hist., ut sup.   [9] Rob. Hist. Bap. p. 442.

parts of his writings were in perfect accordance with this sentiment.[10] So that Luther is charged with being the author or father of the German dippers, since some of the Catholics expressly declare they received their first ideas of it from him.[1] Also Moshovius says, that anabaptism was set on foot at Wittemburgh in 1521, among the Reformers, by Nicholas Pelargus, or Stork, who had companions with him of very great learning, as Carolostadius, Melancthon, and others; this, he says, was done while Luther was lurking in exile.[2] In pursuing this course, and practising only believers' baptism, these reformers were consistent, as they professedly took the Scriptures for their guidance. Luther's views and writings supported such a procedure, since he declared, "It cannot be proved by the Scriptures that infant baptism was instituted by Christ, or began by the first Christians after the apostles." Nearly all the reformers expressed themselves in similar language about baptism; besides, all the Puritans, whose support to the cause of reform was desirable, held these views on the ordinance. The reformers gave very considerable support to the Baptists in these measures.[3] Luther had no great objection to the Baptists in his early efforts. He encouraged the Muncer of notoriety, who was a Baptist minister, and so highly esteemed by Luther, as to be named his Absalom. Their united efforts greatly increased persons of the Baptist persuasion. When the news reached Luther, of Carolostadt re-baptizing, that Muncer had won the hearts of the people, and that the reformation was going on in his absence, he on the 6th of March, 1522, flew like lightning from his confinement, at the

1522

---

[10] Rob. Res., 542, and Booth's Pædo. Exam. [1] Rob. Res., p. 542. [2] Good and Greg., Cyclo., Anab., Ivimey's Hist., vol. i. p. 18. [3] Burnett's Reform., vol. ii. p. 110.

hazard of his life, and without the advice of his patron, to put a stop to Carolostadt's proceedings.[4] On his return to Wittemburgh, he banished Carolostadt, Pelargus, More Didymus, and others, and only received Melancthon again.[5]

20. When some of Luther's assistants went into Bohemia and Moravia, they complained, that between Baptists and papists *they were very much straightened*, though they grew among them *like lilies among thorns!*[6] The success and number of the Baptists "exasperated him to the last degree;" and he became their enemy, notwithstanding all he had said in favour of dipping (while he contended with Catholics on the sufficiency of God's word); but now he persecuted them under the name of *re-dippers*, *re-baptizers*, or *Anabaptists*.[7] One thing troubled Luther, and he took no pains to conceal it; that was, a jealousy lest *any competitor* should step forward, and put in execution that plan of reformation which he had laid out: this was his foible; he fell out with Carolostadt, he disliked Calvin, he found fault with Zuinglius, who were all supported by great patrons, and he was angry beyond measure with the Baptists.[8] His half measures, his national system, his using the Roman liturgy, his consubstantiation, his infant baptism, without Scripture or example, were disliked by the Baptists—yea, the Picards or Vaudois hated his system;[9] and *he hated all other sects*.[10] The violence of Luther sunk his cause into that of a party.[1] The reformers differed as widely among themselves about the ordinances, as they did from others:[2] and their spirit of contention subsided

---

[4] Maclean in Mosheim, vol. iii. p. 45, ch. 16, § 18.   [5] Ivimey ut sup.   [6] Rob. Res., p. 519.   [7] Id., p. 542.   [8] Id., p. 540.   [9] Id., p. 541.   [10] Neal's Hist. vol. i. p. 93.
[1] M'Crie's Italy, p. 176.   [2] Camp. Lect., p. 445.

into acts of persecution and reproach.³ But Mosheim remarks, "there were certain sects and doctors against whom the zeal, vigilance, and severity of Catholics, Lutherans, and Calvinists *were united. The objects of their common aversion were the Anabaptists.*" To avoid the unhappy consequences of such a formidable opposition, great numbers retired into Poland, hoping to find a refuge—where they formed congregations.⁴

1522   21. It is at this period the term *Anabaptism* was used among Christian brethren.⁵ The word, in its strict sense, is expressive of the practice of those who re-baptize such persons who came from one of their sects to another; or, as often as any one is excluded from their communion, and again baptized on being re-admitted into their fellowship—as Cyprian and the church of Carthage practised. If the party baptizing disallow the first ceremony as unscriptural, the repetition of the act guided by apostolic authority is not re-baptization, but Christian baptism. The word, in a loose sense, has been in use from the ascendancy of the church in 413, to distinguish those who disavowed infant baptism, and sequently, not only baptize persons on a confession of their faith, but baptize, as it were, again those persons that were in infancy subject to what they considered a pseudobaptism. The term was now familiarized from Luther's dislike to the Picards or re-baptizers.⁶ We have often used the word, not that we approve it as expressive of our practice, but as conveying the views of those who, by the word, intended fully to describe, designate, and reproach the Baptists. A *full* history of the people thus designated, is exceedingly difficult to write;⁷ since, as Mosheim admits, "the true

---

³ Rob. Bap., p. 548, 554.   ⁴ Mosh. Hist., pp. 3, 363, 293.
⁵ Good and Greg. Cyclo. Anabap.   ⁶ Ency. Brit. Anabap.
Rob. Res., p. 517.   ⁷ Rob. Bap., p. 465.

origin of the Baptist denomination, who espoused the Mennonite views, and who acquired the stigma of Anabaptists, by administering anew the rite of baptism to those who come over to their community, *is hid in the remote deeps of antiquity.*"[8] But baptism may be administered to persons who have received a rite in some community without incurring Anabaptism; as,

First. When the subject has been dipped before, he has been rightly instructed into the essential truths of the gospel, as was the case with the twelve disciples at Ephesus. When Paul reached this city, he found disciples baptized, who were ignorant of an important truth, revealed by John for all candidates to believe: viz., " *He shall baptize you with the Holy Ghost;*" but these disciples had heard nothing of the Holy Ghost, consequently here was a departure from John's views, and apparent ignorance of the Author of every sanctifying process. Scriptural views of baptism, and a knowledge of the Author of our salvation being essential to a right receiving baptism, led Paul to instruct these disciples, and then again baptize them.[9]

Secondly. When repentance and faith, the indispens-

---

[8] Ecc. Hist., vol. iii., p. 320. Their antiquity may be traced back, viz.:—1450, Picards or Waldenses, Wall's Hist., 2, 270.—1420, Hussites, Crosby, vol. i. pref. xxxiii. Ivimey, 1, 70.—1176, Waldo and his followers, Jones's Lect., 2, 486.—1150, Waldenses and Albigenses, Collier's G. Dict. Anab.—1140, Arnoldists, Facts Op. to Fict., p. 46.—1135, Henricians, Wall's Hist., 2, 250.—1110, Petrobrussians, Wall, ib.—1049, Berengarians, Facts, &c., p. 42. Mezeray, p. 229.—1025, Gundulphians, Jortin's Rem., 5, p. 27.—945, Paterines, Jones's Lect. 2, p. 254.—714, Vaudois in France and Spain, Rob. Res., 242.—653, Paulicians, Gibbon's Hist., c. 54, and Allix's Pied., c. 15, 138.—311, Donatists, Mosh. Hist., 1, 302.—250. Novatianists, Ency. Brit. Anab.—56, Ephesians, Acts xix. 2, &c. Miln. Ch. Hist., C. 1, ch. 14.

[9] Miln. Ch. Hist., C. 1, ch. 14.

able pre-requisites, have not been exercised by the subject, Matt. iii. 8—when the conscience has not chosen the duty, 1 Pet. iii. 21—and where a personal profession of faith has not existed, the service is unacceptable to God. Heb. xi. 6. Rom. xiv. 23.

Thirdly. When the ordinance, in its administration, does not bear the same analogy to its primitive design and resemblance of Christ's death and resurrection, as those did administered by the apostles, Rom. vi. 4, 1 Cor. xv. 29, it is then another baptism, and not a New Testament ordinance, since its analogy to Scripture language is lost.

Fourthly. When, from a multiplicity of ceremonies, the original design is obscured, and it ceases to *make manifest* the disciples of Christ, John i. 31, and the *cleansing properties* of his work, Acts xxii. 16, it ceases to be Christ's appointment. The earliest dissidents were guided by this view, and yet were not Anabaptists.

In this practice, two motives are apparent in the conduct of re-baptizers: first, right instruction; and, secondly, purity of communion. The first view led different bodies of early professors to re-baptize those who came over to their communion, from parties whose creed was not in accordance with their own: and the second, from a desire to maintain purity of communion, regulated many early churches. We know unauthorized rites and ceremonies were early adopted by many churches. To free the mind of the candidate from those human rites, and to maintain the ordinance in its native and simple aspect, occasioned early dissenters to require those who came to join them from other churches, to submit to the ordinance in the way they administered it.[10]

---

[10] Robins. Res., p. 212. Jones's Ecc. Lect., vol. i. p. 410.

22. Of all the teachers of religion in Germany at this period, the Baptists best understood the doctrine of civil and religious liberty: to them, therefore, the oppressed Boors, as has been observed, looked for counsel. The tyranny of the Catholics and Lutherans was equal in every thing, except extent. *Luther never pretended to dissent from the church, he only proposed to disown the pope:* but in this partial conduct, and mope-eyed device, all could not see with him. Among the Baptists, one of the most eminent was Thomas Muncer, of Mulhausen, in Thuringia. He had been a priest, but became a disciple of Luther, and a favourite with the reformed. This dear son Luther named his Absalom; and the people so highly approved of him, as to call him Luther's Curate. He appears to have itinerated and laboured principally in Saxony. While Luther was hunting, writing, and regaling himself with princes, Muncer was preaching in the country, and surveying the condition of their tenants. He saw their miserable bondage; and that, from Luther's plan of reform, there was no probability of freedom flowing to the people. He (Luther) only intended to free the priests from obedience to the pope, and to enable the officers of the state to tyrannize over the people in the name of civil magistrates. Muncer saw this fallacy, and remonstrated against it. Luther broke loose from his recluse, and dealt severely with those who dared in his absence to progress the cause differently to his plan. With Carolostadt he was severe, but *Muncer was banished for his crime of remonstrance.* Muncer now travelled into various parts, preaching doctrines highly acceptable to the lower orders. He settled at Mulhausen, and was there when the peasants rose. It is very probable he now embraced fully the sentiments of the Baptists, seeing his instruction to this people was much on the nature of religious liberty, and

illustrative of the errors of Catholicism and Lutheranism, which he represents as carrying things to the extreme, without embracing the liberty purchased by the death of Christ. His instructions conveyed, that a Christian church ought to consist of virtuous persons, and not, as Luther taught, to include whole parishes. On these principles he formed a church, A.D. 1523, and advised the members of it to make use of retirement, meditation, and prayer; to consider the several points of religion for themselves. The peasants relished his doctrine, and repaired to Mulhausen in vast numbers, to be instructed and comforted by Muncer.[1]

Here was Muncer's crime; and, as Voltaire remarks, "Luther had been successful in stirring up the princes, nobles, and magistrates of Germany, against the pope and bishops: Muncer stirred up the peasants against them. He and his companions went about addressing themselves to the inhabitants of the country villages in Suabia, Misnia, Thuringia, and Franconia. *They laid open that dangerous truth, which is implanted in every breast, that all men are born equal;* saying, that if the popes *had* treated the princes like their subjects, the princes *had* treated the common people like beasts."[2]

23. What Luther had said and censured about the pope's usurpation, he now practised himself towards these good men. Carolostadt he followed from place to place, and got him expelled wherever he settled. Thomas Muncer was driven in like manner, with others, against whom Luther set himself, in writing to princes, and publishing, by which he disturbed society, and stigmatized them as image-breakers and sacramentarians, or Anabaptists.[3] On hearing of Muncer's success, he wrote to

---

[1] Robins. Res., pp. 546-8; and Marsh's Michaelis, vol. iv. p. 542, &c. [2] Robins. Res., p. 551. [3] Id., p. 543, &c.

the magistrates of Mulhausen, to advise them to require Muncer to give an account of his call; and if he could not prove that he acted under human authority, then to insist on his proving *his call from God by working a miracle!!!* Lord, what is man! The magistrates and monks complied with this Lutheran bull, but the people considered this a refinement on cruelty, especially as coming from a man whom both the Roman court and the diet of the empire had loaded with curses, for no other crime than that of which he accused his brother.

The people now resented the insult; they expelled from the city Luther's monkish allies; and the magistrates elected new senators, of whom *Muncer was one!* To him, as their *only friend*, the peasants looked for relief under oppression.[4]

24. The tones of authority assumed by Luther, and his magisterial conduct towards those who differed from him, made it evident that he would be *head* of the reformers.[5] He and his colleagues had now to dispute their way with hosts of Baptists all over Germany, Saxony, Thuringia, Switzerland, and other kingdoms, for several years.[6] Conferences on baptism were held in different kingdoms, which continued from 1516 to 1527.[7] The support which the Baptists had from Luther's writings made the reformers' efforts of little effect. At Zurich, the senate warned the people to desist from the practice of re-baptizing, but all their warnings were vain. These efforts to check the increase of Baptists being ineffectual, carnal measures were selected. The first edict against Anabaptism was published at Zurich, 1522, in which there was a penalty of

[4] Robins. Res., p. 548.   [5] Id., p. 542.   [6] Wall's Hist., pt. 2, p. 269.   [7] Clark's Lives, and Danvers' Hist., p. 307.

a silver mark set upon all such as should suffer themselves to be re-baptized, or should withhold baptism from their children. And it was further declared, that those who openly opposed this order, should be yet more severely treated.[8] This being insufficient to check immersion, the senate decreed, like Honorius, 413, that all persons who professed Anabaptism, or harboured the professors of the doctrine, should be punished with death by drowning.[9] It had been death to refuse baptism, and now it was death to be baptized; such is the weathercock certainty of state religion.[10] In defiance of this law, the Baptists persevered in their regular discipline: and some ministers, of learned celebrity, realized the severity of the sentence. Many Baptists were drowned and burnt.[1] These severe measures, which continued for years, had the consent of the reformers, which injured greatly the Lutheran cause.[2] It was the cruel policy of papacy inflicted by brethren. Wherever the Baptists settled, Luther played the part of a universal bishop, and wrote to princes and senates to engage them to expel such dangerous men; but it was their refusing to own his authority, and admit his exposition of the Scriptures, which led him to preach and publish books against them, taxing them with disturbing the peace.[3] We have recorded that the Baptists were the common objects of aversion to Catholics, Lutherans, and Calvinists, whose united zeal was directed to their destruction. So deeply were the prejudices interwoven with the state party, that the knights on oath were to declare their abhorrence of Anabaptism.[4] The senti-

[8] Ger. Brandt's Hist. Ref., vol. i. B. 2, p. 57. [9] Miln. Ch. Hist., C. 16, ch. 16. Neal's Hist., vol. v, p. 127. [10] Rob. Bap., 426. [1] Milner, Brandt ut sup. Ivimey's Hist., vol. i. p. 17. [2] Rob. Res., p. 543. [3] Ib. [4] Mosh., 3, 362.

ments of these people, and which were so disliked by statesmen, clergy, and reformers, may be stated under five views, viz. : " A love of civil liberty in opposition to magisterial dominion; an affirmation of the sufficiency and simplicity of revelation, in opposition to scholastic theology; a zeal for self-government, in opposition to clerical authority; a requisition of the reasonable service of a personal profession of Christianity rising out of man's own convictions, in opposition to the practice of force on infants—the whole of which they deem superstition, or enthusiasm; and the indispensable necessity of virtue in every individual member of a Christian church, in distinction from all speculative creeds, all rites and ceremonies, and parochial divisions."[5] These views—to the statesman, were adverse to his line of policy with his peasants ; to the clergy, they were offensive, since it placed every man on a level with the priesthood, and sanctioned one to instruct another; to the reformers they were objectionable, since they broke the national tie, and allowed all persons equal liberty to think, choose, and act in the affairs of the soul: thus these sentiments were the aversion of all. An edict issued by Frederick, at a later period, shows how unpalatable these views were. His majesty expressed his astonishment at the number of Anabaptists, and his horror at the principal error which they embraced, which was, that according to the express declaration of the holy Scriptures (1 Cor. vii. 23), they were to submit to no human authority. He adds that his conscience compelled him to proscribe them, and accordingly he banished them from his dominions on pain of death.[6]

"This maxim is a true source of the peculiarities

[5] Robins. Bap., p. 482.   [6] Id. Res., p. 525.

of the Baptists," says Mosheim, "that the visible church was exempted from all those institutions which human prudence suggested:" but this view of religion, the state and the reformed could not receive.[7]

25. During the contentions and disputations of the reformers and others, the peasants of Suabia groaned in 1524, under their hard servitude, and resolved to seize the first opportunity to get free. In the November following, they revolted. The news flew all over Germany, and awakened restless feeling in the plebeians throughout the empire. The lords of the soil and the gentry entered into a confederacy, and agreed to suppress them; and Furstenberg, in the name of the confederates, went to inquire into their grievances. They informed him they were Catholics, that they had not risen on any religious account, and that they required nothing but a release from those intolerable secular oppressions, under which they had long groaned, and which they neither could nor would any longer bear. Others required relief from the oppression of abbots. The ensuing spring offered to others, who had more reason to complain than the preceding boors, an opportunity to leave their work, and such assembled in different provinces to the amount of *three hundred thousand men*. The doctrine of liberty had been advocated by all the reformers, while pointing out the usurped claims of the pope; but none understood or carried out this liberty into practice but the Baptists, consequently all eyes were, in this crisis, directed to Muncer, who now drew up a memorial expressive of their grievances, and which was presented to their lords, and dispersed all over Germany. It consists of twelve articles, on civil and religious

[7] Ecc. Hist., vol. iii. pp. 320, 327.

liberty. It is allowed to be a master-piece of the kind, and Voltaire says, " A LYCURGUS WOULD HAVE SIGNED IT."

These tenets, which all persons now professedly love, are still held forth in the views and writings of Pædobaptists of these times, as the damnable anabaptistical errors; but where dwelt the advocate of real liberty, and where could this boon of paradise have been found, if there had been no Anabaptists? This was the head and front of their offending, and on this ground alone they were everywhere spoken against. In this instrument there is *no heretic* but a tyrant, nothing proposed to be hated but the feudal system, and liberty is the only orthodoxy. This memorial, when compared with the creed of Ausburgh, will create feelings of reverence in the Collater for the mild justice of Muncer and his memorialists! It is the doom of the poor to be aspersed, Prov. xiv. 20. At the close of the memorial, the peasants appealed to Luther. He told them the princes *deserved dethroning*, yet their tumults were seditious, and that they had been seduced by false teachers: that it was foolish to put all mankind upon a level, and that Abraham had slaves. He *wrote* to the princes, and taxed them with having caused all the present ills by their excess of tyranny, and accuses them for saying that his doctrine had been the cause of all this disturbance, threatening them with all the vengeance of heaven if they persisted in their tyranny and cruelty. The *third* publication was addressed to both princes and peasants, advising both parties to settle their disputes, and be at peace, for the public good of Germany. These advices being disregarded, he drew up a *fourth*, addressed to the princes, in which he conjures them to unite all their force to suppress sedition, and to destroy all who resisted government, i. e. oppression and slavery. These oppressed men were consequently met by their lords with a sword, instead of redress; being defeated, they were slaughtered and reproached, the invariable result and concomitants of defeat; Muncer, their friend and chief, was put to death.[8]

26. All men condemned Luther for these murdering proposals, but in order to relieve himself, he made the devoted people the scape goat; he and his colleagues imputed the crimes of the empire to the Anabaptists, and so escaped!!! From the breaking out of the rustic war, the empire continued to be in an unsettled state. "The first rising," says Sleiden, "was among persons of the papist communion, the tumults did not originate on the subject of religion, but from secular exactions.[9] Religious liberty had been learnt by many from Luther's work, which caused many to seek both civil and religious freedom."[10] The twelve articles, expressive of their grievances, which Magna Charta they had not power to enforce, "comprehended," says Osiander, "persons of all persuasions."[1] Had Muncer succeeded in procuring liberty for the German peasants, ten thousand tongues would have celebrated his praise in different ages, devotions would have been rendered to him as to Titus. Flaminius and many historians would have vied to crown his memory with unfading honours. The site of such an achievement would have been equalled only by Runnymede, and its honours more permanent and glorious than those of Naseby field. All this occurred ten years before the affair of Munster. It was not therefore an affair about baptism, but the feudal system: it was not water, it was government that was the question, and the Baptists had the glory of

[8] Mosh. Hist. iii. p. 51, § 22.   [9] Danvers' Hist., p. 322 from Guodolius.   [10] Ib. from Spanheim.   [1] Ib.

first setting the reformed an example of getting rid of tyranny.[2] The routed and scattered remains of this vast body of men sowed, in the different provinces, the seeds of discontent, which, after keeping the empire in a feverish state for some years, ultimately led to some redress. Many new projectors were among this people, as to the nature and extent of Christ's kingdom, which ideal projects were carried out so far in succeeding years by some, as to bespeak delirium in its advocates.

1526 27. Disputations on the subject of baptism continued through this and the ensuing year; and the system of drowning those the reformers could not convert was still in prevalent use. The reformers' influence and reflection on the Baptists, with the Catholic hatred, made the situation of our brethren very critical, independent of the iron bondage many endured under their lords. From the views the Baptists held on civil and religious liberty, and the memorial of the peasants' grievances being drawn up by one of that body, and approved by all; which memorial struck at the root of the lords' tyranny, occasioned great jealousy in the minds of princes, and occasioned their attention **1527** and displeasure to be constantly directed towards them. Some emigrated to England, where their circumstances were not improved. Erasmus **1529** said of this people (1529), "The Anabaptists (in Switzerland), although they are very numerous, have no church in their possession. These persons are worthy of greater commendation than others, on account of the harmlessness of their lives. But **1532** they are oppressed by all other sects." When Frederick, in 1532, conferred privileges on the

---

[2] Rob. Res., p. 544, &c.

German protestants, he excepted the Baptists.
1533 In 1533, a reward of twelve guilders was promised to any person who should apprehend any anabaptistical teacher, and all harbouring them was forbidden.³ "They were," says Dr. Robertson, "this year, 1534, watched so closely by the magistrates as to find it necessary to emigrate into other quarters."⁴ Their religious liberties being destroyed, their views under the greatest reproach, their lives and property liable to injury, before Munster affray, will show their critical situation, and account for their succumbing conduct to the reformers at this period. It only wanted some local commotion to involve such suspected subjects in ruin. The brethren in different parts had sent to the reformers, desiring *their countenance and support.* Erasmus genteelly declined. Luther did not like them; he reproached them with anabaptism. They made the best apology they could, admitting they had always rebaptized such as joined their churches, but they said, so had Cyprian in early ages. Learned men were to confer with them on this point. This year seems to
1533 have been taken up in forming a more unreserved intercourse between the brethren and the reformers. By intercourse and compromise, and a negociation of some years, and after a vast deal of trouble, a conjunction was effected. Some of these societies had altered and amended their creed eight times in a quarter of a century, and now with the last edition presented to Luther, they confessed they had studied the subject of church government and discipline more diligently, in which also they had been assisted by some eminent divines, they had concluded with the

---

³ Mezeray's Fr. Hist., p. 597. Brandt's Hist. of the Reform. vol. i. p. 60.   ⁴ Hist. of Charles V., b. 5, p. 73.

reformers, that there was no need to re-baptize, and they had now left off the practice, and moreover, had unanimously agreed never to re-baptize in future, nor ever, with Luther and his friends, to call re-baptization baptism, but ANA-BAPTISM.[5] Thus what the Moravian and other brethren long sought for, they at length obtained,—a comprehension in the establishment. To their creed which had been so frequently improved, the last of which met the reformers' approbation, Luther wrote a preface; observing, that he had formerly been prejudiced against the brethren called Picards, though he had always admired *their aptness in the Scriptures.* He admitted they had not the advantages of learned languages, and had expressed themselves obscurely, the confession, however (of his colleagues' amending), was *such a learned performance*, that it had no need of his recommendation! It is evident Luther brought many of the old Baptists to his terms, while every circumstance in the empire combined to force these people under Luther's wing, or out of his jurisdiction. The imperial edict was published, the bells were rung, and the reproach of Picardism or Anabaptism was professedly rolled away from these conformists, and our only surprise is to find such multitudes in succeeding years not comprehended. "Their quiet became carnal security, their liberty glided into licentiousness, and," says Comenius, " the pious wept."[6] The year previous to this conjunction, Calvin appeared as a public teacher, and his views of truth, on being known, were preferred, and found to be more in accordance with the Baptists' views than Luther's; consequently "many of the Waldenses, or Sacramentarians," says Mezeray,

1535

---

[5] Robins. Res. p. 506. [6] Id. p. 507.

"united with the reformed churches."[7] It is easy to perceive the vestibule to these national churches was Pædobaptism.

28. The city of Munster, in Westphalia, became the site of great tumult and disorder. One Bernard Rotman, a Pædobaptist minister of the Lutheran persuasion, assisted by other ministers of the reformation, began the disturbances at Munster in opposing the papists (1532).[8] Spanheim and Osiander say, that the first stir in this city of Munster was about the protestant religion, when the synod and ministers opposed the papists with arms, before any Anabaptist came.[9] While things were in a confused state in this city, many persons of a fanatical character came into Munster. "They gave out that they were messengers from heaven invested with a divine commission to lay the foundations of a new government, a holy and spiritual empire, and to destroy and overturn all temporal rule and authority, all human and political institutions." Confusion and uproar immediately prevailed in Munster. These frenzied people began to erect a new republic, calling it the New Jerusalem. Now what must have been the state of this city, previous to these madmen's arrival? Would a few fanatics have destroyed the order of a well-governed civic body? The subversion of Munster by so few frenzied individuals, proves its previous perversion by some tumultuous proceedings. Venner's rebellion is in close affinity with this affair, yet London was easily rescued from similar disorders.[10] The Bishop of Munster, assisted by

---

[7] Fr. Hist. p. 597. [8] Mosh. Hist. C. 16, p. 2, § 7. note q, by Maclaine. Ivimey's Hist., vol. i., p. 16, from Budneus. [9] Danvers' Hist. p. 324. [10] Ivimey's History, vol. i., p. 306—313.

1535 German princes, besieged the city in 1535, when the enthusiastics were all subdued, taken, and put to death in the most terrible and ignominious manner. This disorderly and outrageous conduct of a handful of Anabaptists with others, drew upon the whole body, who was previously under ban, heavy marks of displeasure from the greatest part of the European princes.[1] Cassander, a papist, declares that many Anabaptists in Germany did resist and oppose the opinions and practices of those at Munster, and taught the contrary doctrine.[2] Nevertheless, as they were, to a man, for civil and religious freedom, and at the same time opposed to Luther's articles, the severest laws were enacted against them the second time, in consequence of which, the innocent and the guilty were alike involved in the same terrible fate, and *prodigious numbers* were devoted to death in the most dreadful forms.[3] In almost all the countries of Europe,

1536 *an unspeakable number of Baptists preferred death in its worst forms*, says Mosheim, *to a retraction of their sentiments*. Neither the view of the flames that were kindled to consume them, nor the ignominy of the gibbet, nor the terrors of the sword, could shake their invincible constancy, or make them abandon tenets that appeared dearer to them than life and all its enjoyments.[4] "It is true, indeed," says the same writer, "that

---

[1] Mosh. Hist., vol. iii. p. 78. [2] Ivimey's Hist., vol. i. p. 309. [3] Mosh. Hist., vol. iii. p. 79. [4] Id., p. 326. "And when they shall have finished their testimony, the beast shall kill them—and the same hour a tenth part of the city fell," Rev. xi. 7—13. It is rather remarkable that, while these witnesses were suffering in every province from Catholics, Lutherans, and Calvinists, in the same hour or period Henry VIII., by an act, 1536, separated England, the tenth part of the pope's dominion, from his authority.

many Baptists suffered death, not on account of their being considered rebellious subjects, but merely because *they were judged to be incurable heretics;* for in this century, the error of limiting the administration of baptism to adult persons only, and the practice of re-baptizing such as had received that sacrament in a state of infancy, were looked upon as most flagitious and intolerable heresies. Those who had no other marks of peculiarity than their administering baptism to the adult, and their excluding the unrighteous from the external communion of the church, ought to have met with milder treatment.[5] Many of those who followed the wiser class of Baptists, nay, some who adhered to the most extravagant factions, were men of upright intentions and sincere piety, who were seduced into fanaticism by their ignorance and simplicity on the one hand, and by a laudable desire of reforming the corrupt state of religion on the other.[6]

---

[5] Mosh. Hist., vol. iii. pp. 326-7.

[6] Id. 325. A combination of circumstances led to this unhappy affair. An anxious and laudable desire for the extension of Christ's kingdom was evident before the name of Luther was known. The wiser sort of Baptists tried to effect this by human prudence (Ency. Brit.). The groaning condition of the rustics led them to cherish every sound of liberty; and some, in their frenzied enthusiasm, carried out their views to a new Jerusalem state of things, and Munster fanatics involved our denomination in disrepute. Pædobaptists dwell on the plenitude of the sin, to divert the mind from the originators of the affray, and by blackening the Baptists, they leave a happy comparison for the excesses of their favourites. Had no Baptists been mixed up in this affair, *no such people would have been allowed to exist at the time;* but the incredible numbers of our persuasion rendered it impossible for any commotion to take place about religion in these provinces, without involving the continental Baptists. This affair at Munster is often repeated and recorded; but one reason is evident, *it is*

29. While the terrors of death, in the most awful forms, were presented to the view of this people, and numbers of them were executed every day, without any distinction being made between the innocent and the guilty, those who escaped the severity of the sword were found in the most discouraging situations that can well be imagined. On the one hand, they saw with sorrow all their hopes of liberty blasted by the ravages of Munster; and, on the other, they were filled with the most anxious apprehensions of the perils that threatened them on all sides. In this critical situation, they derived much comfort and assistance from the counsels and zeal of MENNO SIMON.[7]

30. It is now evident, that many persons of the Baptist persuasion and views existed on the Continent long before the affair of Munster blackened their escutcheon; and the characters of these people have awakened admiration in men of distinguished parts, and who have left testimonies of their piety, which may be brought into comparison with any denomination of the present age. Among their admirers may be found the names of Commenius, Scultetus, Beza, Cloppenberg, Cassander,[8] Erasmus, Heyden, Hoornbeck, Cocceius, and Cardinal Hossius. The latter says, "If the truth of religion were to be judged of by the readiness and cheerfulness which a man of any sect shows in suffering,

the only slur which stands against the denomination! If repartees were allowable, we could pay our accusers with compound interest, by inquiring, Who martyred our early brethren, the Donatists, the Paulicians, Albigenses? *Who cut off the ears and virilia of the French' clergy?* Who planned Venner's rebellion? &c. &c. &c. Ans. Pædobaptists!!! Do they repudiate these things? So do Baptists the *single affair* of Munster. See preface to Crosby's History of the Baptists.

[7] Mosh. Hist., C. 16, s. iii. p. 2, § 7.   [8] Danvers' Hist., pp. 308—12.

then the opinions and persuasions of *no sect can be truer or surer* than those of the ANABAPTISTS; since there have been none for *these twelve hundred years past*[9] that have been more grievously punished."[1] Father Gretzer, and Professor Limborch we have quoted in the Waldensian section.

31. The venerable MENNO SIMON was born at Witmarsum in Friesland, A.D. 1496. His education was such as was generally adopted in that age with persons designed to be priests. He entered the church in the character of a minister in 1524. He had no acquaintance with the sacred volume at this time; nor would he touch it, lest he should be seduced by its doctrines. At the end of three years, on celebrating mass, he entertained some scruples about transubstantiation; but attributed the impression to the devil. No moral change was yet effected: he spent his time in dissipating amusements; yet he was not easy in his mind. He resolved, from the perturbed state of his thoughts, to peruse the New Testament. In reading this volume, his mind became enlightened; and, with the aid of Luther's writings, he saw the errors of popery. Menno was generally respected; and all at once became a gospel preacher, without the charge of heresy or fanaticism. This is accounted for, by his being courted by the world, and still continuing in alliance with it. Among the thousands that suffered death for anabap-

---

[9] Cardinal Hossius was chairman at the council of Trent. His acquaintance with history is indisputable. This statement of the Baptists' sufferings 1200 years, from 1570, carries our denomination back to 370, the very year in which we have the first record of a child's baptism. So that our witnessing and suffering are coeval.

[1] Bap. Mag., vol. x. p. 401, and vol. xviii. p. 278, from Brandt's History.

tism, was one *Sicke Snyden*, who was beheaded at Lewarden. The constancy of this man to his views of believers' baptism, preferring even an ignominious death to renouncing his sentiments, led Menno to inquire into the subject of baptism. Menno could not find infant baptism in the Bible; and, on consulting a minister of that persuasion, a concession was made, *that it had no foundation in the Bible.* Not willing to yield, he consulted other celebrated reformers; but all these he found to be at variance, as to the grounds of the practice:[2] consequently he became confirmed, that the Baptists were suffering for truth's sake. In studying the Word, convictions of sinfulness and of his lost condition became deepened; and he found God required

---

[2] Austin and his coadjutors, in the infant rite, washed the child, to remove the stain of original sin. (Wall's Hist., pt. 1, c. 15.) Austin had never heard of any Christian who did not give it on this ground. (Id. p. 303.) And Wall asserts Calvin only disturbed this foundation (pt. 2, p. 165, &c.); but faith was required in the candidate. So the ancients asserted children had *the faith of the sacraments*;—the Papists said that they had *the faith of the church* (Danv. Hist., p. 183);—the Lutherans affirm, that children had a *proper and peculiar faith,* to entitle them to baptism (Id. 147); that baptism is necessary to salvation; that God's grace is conferred thereby (Confess. Id. 146);—Calvinists affirm, they have *no faith,* but ought to be baptized by virtue of the *faith of the parent* in covenant (Id. 147);—the English church baptizes on a *promised faith,* supported by a vow of the sponsors; Mr. Richard Baxter, a Presbyterian, says they have *a justifying faith* (Danv. Hist., p. 184); while others practise it from the promise made to a believing parent, though John denied baptism to the children of that promise. (Matt. iii. 9.) Some confer the rite, from the holiness of the seed; and thus deny the universal corruption of man. (Ep. ii. 3.) Others bestow it from the covenant of circumcision; yet these give the rite to females, but withhold it from servants, and make every parent of such practice a federal head to a covenant; so as to be equal with Abraham and equal with Christ. Such are a few of the Proteus forms of this national bond.

sincerity and decision. He now sought new spiritual friends, and found some, with whom he at first privately associated, but afterwards became one of their community. Menno was baptized by immersion; as he confessed that "we shall find no other baptism besides dipping in water, which is acceptable to God, and maintained in his word."[3]

1536 After passing a year in studying and writing with this small but faithful band of Christians, he received an unexpected call from a church of similar faith and practice. He felt the difficulty of deciding: he was conscious of inability and ignorance; and the times were exceedingly difficult, since deaths were presented, in the most awful forms all around, to all persons of the Baptist persuasion; yet the excellency of the people who had invited him had some consideration. After prayer and meditation, he saw it was his duty, in the face of every danger, to accept their invitation. He laboured hard, endured great trials and privations, the times compelling him often to remove from one province to another with his wife and family. But wherever he went, his ministry was very remarkably blessed.[4]

32. Menno drew up his plan of doctrine and practice

---

[3] This view is supported by Luther and Calvin. Luther says, that in times past it was thus, that the sacrament of baptism was administered to none, except it were to those that acknowledged and confessed their faith, and knew how to rehearse the same; and that it was necessary to be done, because the sacrament was constituted externally to be used, that the faith be confessed and made known to the church. (De Sacrament, tom. iii. p. 168.) Calvin observes, " Because Christ requires teaching before baptizing, and will have believers only admitted to baptism, baptism does not seem to be rightly administered, except faith precede." In Harm. Evang. Com. Matt. xxviii. 19.

[4] Bap. Mag., vol. x. p. 381. 1818.

entirely from the Scriptures, and threw it into the form of catechisms. His system was of a milder nature than had been adopted by the perfect class of ancient Baptists. He retained, indeed, all those doctrines commonly received among them, in relation to the baptism of infants, the millennium, the exclusion of the magistrate from the Christian assemblies, the abolition of war, the prohibition of oaths, and the vanity as well as the pernicious effects of human science.[5] Their churches are founded on this principle, that practical piety is the essence of religion, and that the surest and most infallible mark of a true church is the sanctity of its members. It is at least certain, says Mosheim, that *this principle* was always and universally adopted by the Baptists.[6] They admit none to the sacrament of baptism but persons that are come to the full age of reason. They rebaptize such persons as had that rite in a state of infancy; since the best and wisest of the Mennonites maintain, with their ancestors, that the baptism of infants is destitute of validity: they therefore refuse the term of Anabaptist, as inapplicable to their views.[7] It was in 1536, under Menno, that the scattered community of Baptists were formed into a regular body and church order, separate from all Dutch and German Protestants, who at that time *had not* been formed into one body by any bonds of unity. Some of the perfectionists he reclaimed to order, and others he excluded. He now purified also the religious doctrines of these people.[8] As in the early, so among these modern Baptists, two classes are found, at a later period distinguished by the terms of rigid and moderate. The former class observe, with the most religious accuracy,

---

[5] Mosh. Hist., vol. iii. p. 320, § 9.   [6] Hist. ib. § 13.
[7] Id. vol. iii. 318, note.   [8] Bap. Mag., vol. xiii. p. 344.

veneration, and precision, *the ancient* doctrine, discipline, and precepts of the purer Baptists. The latter are more conformed to Protestant churches.9

33. The Mennonite Baptists consider themselves as the real successors to the Waldenses, and to be the genuine churches of Christ. It is apparent the gospel was introduced into the Netherlands, Flanders, &c. during the eleventh century, by some disciples of Gundulphus, who were arrested while on their visit of mercy. In 1181 the persecuted Waldenses sought refuge in the Netherlands, bringing with them Waldo's translation of the New Testament. In the ensuing year, some of these people suffered death for rejecting infant baptism.10 The churches formed at this early period were branches from the great body of Albigensian and Waldensian Antipædobaptists,1 which were preserved through successive ages, retaining much of their original character and creed. They are said to have lived as peaceable inhabitants, particularly in Flanders, Holland, and Zealand; interfering neither with church nor state affairs. Their manner of life was simple and exemplary. They, like their ancestors in the valleys, sought to regulate their conduct by Christ's sermon on the mount.2 When the Mennonites assert that they are descended from the Waldenses, Petrobrussians, and other ancient sects, who are usually considered as *witnesses of the truth*, in the times of universal darkness and superstition, they are not entirely mistaken, says Mosheim; for before Luther and Calvin,

---

9 Mosh. Hist., vol. iii. p. 335.   10 Bap. Mag., vol. xiv. p. 53, note. Jones's Lect., vol. ii. p. 428.   1 See the works of Herman Schyn, Mehrning, D. T. Twiscke, T. V. Braght, &c. Reiner con hæeret, civ. Hossius' works, p. 212. Hist. Mennon. by Schyn, in Bap. Mag., vol. xiv. p. 51. Mr. Gan in Bap. Mag., vol. xiii. p. 429.   2 Bap. Mag., vol. xiv. p. 50, &c.

there lay concealed, in almost all the countries of Europe, many persons (a multitude of minds prepared to receive reforming doctrines, and many learned, enlightened, and eloquent men, to advocate its claims[3]), who adhered tenaciously to the doctrines of the Dutch Baptists.[4]

1536   34. So soon as Menno had formed his society, and rose, as a parent, to reform and patronize the Baptists, those who abstained religiously, as many of this ancient people did, from all acts of violence and sedition, following the pious examples of the ancient Waldenses, Henricians, Petrobrussians, Hussites, and Wickliffites, adopted the doctrine and discipline of this apostolic man: all which will be allowed, says Mosheim, without hesitation.[5] Shoals of Baptists, who had hitherto resided in Germany, now left their native country, and passed into Holland and the Netherlands, to enjoy their religious privileges.[6] The success of Menno awakened the displeasure of the state parties; and in 1543 the emperor offered a reward for his apprehension; but a watchful and interposing Providence always opened a way of escape. In these harassing times, Menno found a refuge and patron in the lord of Fresenberg and Lubeck, to whose territories great numbers of the Baptists repaired. Churches were formed, and pastors were settled over them, and here Menno carried some of his plans into execution, by erecting a printing press, and defending the denomination against the reproaches of their enemies.[7] To preserve a spirit of union and concord in a body com-

1540

---

[3] Lon. Ency., vol. xviii. p. 669.   Jones's Lect., vol. ii. p. 511.
[4] Mosh. Hist., vol. iii. p. 320, § 2. Bap. Mag., vol. xiv. pp. 50-54.
[5] Hist. vol. iii. p. 333, note.   [6] Id. vol. iii. p. 336, § 11.
[7] Bap. Mag., vol. x. p. 361. 1818.

posed of such a *motley multitude* of dissonant members, required more than human powers; and Menno neither had, nor pretended to have, supernatural succours.[8] The sanctity of character aimed at by the old Baptist interests among "the perfect class," from the earliest days, and the imitation of them by the Mennonites in discipline, occasioned some divisions among this people.

1552   A warm contest, concerning excommunication, was excited by several Baptists. These brethren carried the discipline of excommunication to an undue rigour. Their austerity went into the social ties (1 Cor. vii. 5), which was opposed by many of the community; and now two visible sections formed the body of the Dutch Baptists. Menno employed his most vigorous efforts to heal these divisions, and to restore peace and concord in the community; but when he perceived his attempts were vain, he conducted himself in such a manner as he thought the most proper to maintain his credit and influence among both parties. Perhaps Menno acted in the wisest way for the interest at large, though the propriety of his conduct in this affair has been questioned. The parties were now distinguished by the terms of *rigid* and *moderate*. The rigid live in Flanders, and are called Flandrians, or Flemingians; the moderate reside in Holland, and are termed Waterlandians.[9]

1555   35. No sooner had the enthusiasm among these brethren subsided, than all the members of the different sects agreed to draw the whole system of their religious doctrine from the holy Scriptures; consequently, they drew up confessions, in which their views of religion were expressed, in phrases of holy writ. "These confessions," observes Mosheim, "prove as great a uniformity among the Mennonites, in relation to the

---

[8] Mosh. Ec. Hist., vol. iii. pp. 333-4.   [9] Id. p. 336.

great and fundamental doctrine of religion, as can be pretended to by any other Christian community."[10] About this period, a severe decree was issued against the Baptists. In this instrument, it was forbidden to unite with them. In 1560, this prohibition was put in force in Hamburgh, with this further injunction, " that no re-baptized persons should be taken into employment, or exercise any profession." Notwithstanding these severe measures they increased, though some were driven into different provinces, as was Menno. It is said of these persecuted people this year, " that most of them do show signs of a pious disposition ;" " and it seems to be rather by mistake," says Dr. Wall, " than by any wilful wickedness, that they have departed from the *true sense* of the Scripture, and the uniform agreement of the (catholic) church. They seem worthy rather of pity and due information, than of persecution or being undone."[1] Their steadfast piety and consistent conversation, created respect among those clergy who were strict Lutherans, these made a public declaration of " their most heartfelt regard for the Baptists, and of their affection for them as their much-beloved brethren." These Christian spirits increased considerably in the middle of the sixteenth century. And at this period some were numbered among them, who were learned and pious.[2] Their increase is illustrative of " the more they afflicted them, the more they multiplied and grew." Menno continued to labour with indefatigable industry, until the ensuing Jan. 15, 1561, when he died at Wustenfelde, and was buried in his own garden.[3] " Menno had," says Dr. Mosheim, " the inestimable advantage of a natural and persuasive eloquence.

---

[10] Mosh. Ec. Hist., vol. iii. p. 336. [1] Hist. of Inf. Bap. pt. 2, p. 275. [2] Bap. Mag., vol. xiv. p. 58. [3] Ib. vol. x. p. 361.

He appears to have been a man of probity, pliable and obsequious in his commerce with persons of all ranks and characters, and extremely zealous in promoting practical religion and virtue, which he recommended by his example as well as his precepts. During the space of twenty-five years, he travelled from one country to another, with his wife and children, exercising his ministry under pressures and calamities of various kinds, that succeeded each other without intermission, and constantly exposed to the dangers of falling a victim to the severity of the laws. East and West Friesland, together with the province of Groningen, were first visited by this zealous apostle of the Baptists; from thence, he directed his course into Holland, Gelderland, Brabant, and Westphalia, continuing it through the German provinces that lie on the coast of the Baltic sea, and penetrated so far as Livonia. In all these places, his ministrations were attended with remarkable success, and added to his denomination a prodigious number of proselytes.[4]

36. The severity of the enemy's measures compelled Menno, with others, to migrate the year before his death. It is very probable some of his afflicted brethren visited England about the same time.[5] Those who continued in the Netherlands became very numerous, and realized at length liberty for religious worship.[6] This liberty granted to the Baptists in Hol-

1568

---

[4] Hist. vol. iii. p. 330, § 8.   [5] Fuller's Ch. Hist., C. 16, p. 164.   [6] Wall's Hist., pt. 2, p. 286. Bap. Mag., vol. xv. p. 389. Mosh. Hist., iii. 346. At this period, 1577, Socinus visited Poland, (Rob. Res., p. 603.) He found all the Baptist churches *strict* on the terms of their communion. He disapproved of the narrowness of their policy, and showed them *the innocency of mental error*, and the necessity of a wider charity. He succeeded to commune without immersion, and infant baptism, with every other pernicious error, ensued to all the churches in this

land, would point out to the suffering brethren under Elizabeth's iron hand, a suitable and providential asylum from English ignorance and tyranny; consequently, we find several Englishmen of note, and a congregation of our countrymen enjoying the advantages, at the conclusion of this century. Among those who realized this boon, was a Mr. Smith. He had been a disciple of Robert Brown, and was associated with him in 1592. Being harassed by the English High Commission Court, he removed to Holland, with others, and settled at Amsterdam, in 1606. Here a division took place, Mr. S. differing with his brethren on infant baptism. He settled at LEY with some brethren, where it is said he baptized himself. His Arminian views might have prevented his uniting with the Mennonites. While in Holland he published a work on infant baptism,[7] see English Baptists. The liberty realized by our brethren in Holland, allowed in time a difference of opinion to arise on the mode of baptism.[8] Some of the Mennonites introduced pouring,

---

kingdom. This is *the first record* of mixed fellowship in Baptist churches. The general Baptist churches in England, pursuing the same open system, realized corresponding results. Where are our large city interests, which formerly assembled in Pinner's Hall, Collier's Rents, Petticoat Lane, Currier's Hall, Bridewell Lane? Where are the many interests, once Baptists; leaving the Pseudo-Presbyterians, as Trowbridge and others? Let us come to within fifteen miles of my domicile; who has Newport Pagnell, Old Bedford, Wollaston, Malden, Cotton End, &c., who from being allowed to mix at the table, are now striving to subvert Keysoe and Thurleigh interests? We say, these interests are now under the control of *independent ministers with their endowments and pecuniary resources;* and other interests are, from the same constitution, in a regular way for transmigration! See Reasons for Strict Communion, by the Author. Verbum sapienti sat est. [7] Crosby's Hist., vol. i. pp. 3, and 265. [8] Bap. Mag., vol. xv. p. 390.

and pleaded that it virtually contained baptism;[9] while the greater part retained *dipping* and were called *immergenten*.[10]

37. The visits of the English established a slight correspondence between the brethren of our denomination; and the severity of Elizabeth's measures having exiled all Dissenting ministers, they found it necessary to send "to Holland for a regular administration of believers' baptism, as other denominations had for ordinations."[1] Hearing that regular descendent Waldensian ministers were to be found in the Netherlands, they deputed Mr. Blount, who understood the Dutch language, to visit Amsterdam. He was kindly received by the church in that city, and their pastor, Mr. John Batte.

1633 On his return, he baptized Mr. Samuel Blacklock, a minister, and these baptized the rest of the company, fifty-three in number.[2] The Socinians, with their pernicious charity, infected and divided these

1658 remaining Mennonite churches,[3] and on their ejection from Poland, they flowed into this region of liberty, and impregnated the waters of the sanctuary with the wormwood of their doctrines;[4] consequently, the Mennonites, to a great extent, have departed in various respects from the principles and maxims of their ancestors, and their primitive austerity and purity is greatly diminished, especially among the Waterlandians and Germans. Their opulence relaxed their severities, and they now, with others, enjoy the sweets of this

1750 life, and are as censurable as any Christian community.[5] From the ascendency of a rational religion

---

[9] Rob. Bap., p. 549. [10] Bap. Mag., vol. 15, p. 390.
[1] Neal's Hist., vol. i. p. 308. [2] Ivimey's Hist., vol. i. p. 143. [3] Lon. Ency., Art. Collegiates. [4] Wall's Hist., vol. ii. p. 278. [5] Mosh. Hist., vol. iii. p. 341.

and love of the world, divisions arose in the seventeenth and eighteenth centuries, which present the interests at this period in a humbling aspect. The gold is become dim! Those who retain the name, and we hope, the piety of their ancestors, are calculated, says Mr. Ward, at 30,000.[6]

1820

38. We have thus endeavoured, though feebly, to trace, in all ages of the Christian church, *the footsteps of the flock.* Emotions of a mixed nature have arisen within our bosoms, during our progress in this beaten path. Yet the unquestionable piety of the people, whose lives we have essayed to delineate; their consistent purity and integrity; their ardent and evident attachment to the laws of Zion; their firm and stedfast conduct in upholding truth; their open, bold, and consistent manner of witnessing, through successive ages, for the Redeemer, in the midst of surrounding darkness, wretchedness, vice, danger, and death; have so far raised our admiration and gratitude, that our pleasures, in our mental travels, have far exceeded our griefs. Their perpetual preservation through so many ages, in the face of every opposition which could be raised by men or devils, is a pleasing feature of the *veracity* of THAT BEING, on the truth of whose word our hope is supported. Let us devoutly adore Him for the display of such care and tenderness towards these people, while our gratitude should be additionally enlivened, if He has permitted us to have *a name—a place* among the successors of such followers of the Lamb!

[6] Bap. Mag. vol. xii. 99, and vol. xiii. p. 392.

INDEX

Ærius' efforts, 122.
Africa, Baptists in, 62.
Albigenses, rise of, 54, 135, 159.
    Views and practice, 162, 163, 167, 192, &c. 219, &c.
    Soundness in doctrines, 169, 170.
    Resuscitated, 172.
    Order of their churches, 184.
    Numbers, 183.
    Sufferings, suppression, extermination, § ix.
Alexandrian School, 63.
Ammonius Sacco's plan, 66.
Anabaptists, See German Churches.
Apostles' Unity of practice, 7.
Armenia, Baptists in, 122, 124.
    Christianity early planted in, 121, 124.
Arnold and Arnoldists, efforts and success of, 145, 146.
    Sentiments, 148, &c.
Associations, origin and design, 28, 107.
Augustin, rise, character, and efforts of, 88.

Baptism, import of, 2, 101, 117, 123.
    Evidences of, 46.
    Importance of, 1.
    Instituted by God, 2.
    Refused by the Rabbis, 3.
    Proselyting unknown, 4.
    Test and Qualification for discipleship, 5.
    Given to all converts, 6.
    How administered in the first century, 13, 14, 101.
        Second century, 25.
        Third century, 35, 80.
        Fourth century, 38—44, 117.
    Views of Barnabas, 12.
        Hermas, 12.

INDEX.

Baptism, Views of Clement, 13, 25.
                 Justin Martyr, 22.
                 Irenæus, 24
                 Tertullian, 31, 67.
                 Origen, 34, 72.
                 Dionysius, 34.
                 Arnobius, 34.
                 Hilary, 38.
                 Athanasius, 38.
                 Ep. Syrus, 38.
                 Jerom, 38.
                 Basil, 39.
                 Chrysostom, 41.
                 Siricius, 41,
                 Cyril, 41.
                 Gregory, Naz., 42.
                 Gregory Nys., 42.
                 Ambrose, 43.
                 Epiphanius, 43.
                 Augustin, 44.
       Enforced by counsels, 44—46.
       Did not supersede circumcision, 103.
       Of believers' children, 47.
Baptisteries erected, 37, 56, 150.
Baptists, History difficult, pref. 6, 335.
       in the 1st century, 8, 12, 63, 101, 157, 222.
            2nd cent. 23, 25, 64, 106, 158, 247.
            3rd cent., 31, 50, 68, 110, 159, 310.
            4th cent., 37, 38, 56, 82, 116, 136, 22
            5th cent., 44, 59, 90, 160, 248, 310.
            6th cent., 61, 98, 138, 162.
            7th cent., 124, 138, 164, 248.
            8th cent., 132, 138, 164, 254.
            9th cent., 133, 139, 166, 223, 255.
            10th cent., 134, 140, 167, 312.
            11th cent., 135, 141, 171, 256, 313.
            12th cent., 145, 176, 224, 259, 314.
            13th cent., 151, 200, 227, 262, 318.
            14th cent., 228, 266, 322.
            15th cent., 230, 267, 324.
            16th cent., 224, 273, 329.
            17th cent., 281, 362.
            18th cent., 363.
            19th cent., 364.
Baths abound in the East, 16.
Baxter, R., quoted, 78.
Beghard's rise, 313, 316.
       Character, 317.
Berenger, Efforts of, 173.
          Sentiments on Bap., 175.
Bernard's Lamentation, 180.
Bohemia described, 222.

Bohemia, Baptists in. 223.
Bogue and Bennett, 35, 306.
Brethren, United, rise of 240.
               Comprehension, 245.
Bruys and Petrobrussians, efforts of, 176, 260.
                       Sentiments of, 177.
Bulgaria, Baptists in, 132.

Calixtines, a mixed body, 242.
Calvin, doctrines same as Baptists, 286, 287.
      Views of baptism, 355.
Children employed in churches, 79.
Christianity, its progress, 14.
      Sophisticated, 22.
Church at Jerusalem, 6, 101.
            Of whom composed, 8, 9, 14, 15.
            Its government, 6, 21, 30, 108.
   Catholic, awful state, 144, 146, 147, 164, 326.
Churches, character of the first, 19.
      Purity of early, 18.
      Independent, 21, 30, 108.
      Bond of union, 21.
      Terms of Communion, 23, 53, 163.
      Baptists, in order, 6, 8, 35, 85, 125.
      Abuses early, 10, 31, 52.
      In Rome, 37.
Circumcision annulled, 10 102.
           Not superseded by Baptism, 102.
Claude of Turin, 254.
Communion, open, its rise and influence, 307, 361, note.
Constantine the Great, character of, 56, 116.
Covenant with Abram and Jews broken, 10, 11.
Creeds, rise and use, 64.
Crusaders, rise and character, 203, 204.
Cyprian, Bishop of Carthage, 73.

Dissidents, 31 50, 109, 119.
Dissenters, John, Jesus, and apostles were, 51.
Domitian, his persecution, 12.
Donatists in Africa, 84
      Sentiments and order, 85.
      Sufferings. 90.
Donatus dissents, 83.
Dutch churches, 309.
    Baptists, 325.

Epistles, general use, 8.

Fides inquires for pædobaptism, 76.

Gaul, churches in, 157.

Germany described, 309.
 Christianity early planted in, 310.
 Churches and order, 309.
 Practice of, 314.
 Persecution of, 321, 323, 330.
 Divisions of the Empire, 326.
 Baptist reformers there. 327.
  Proscribed, 329.
  Dispute with Luther, 340, 343, 346.
  Persecuted and drowned, 346, 347.
 Revolution in, 349.
  Causes of, 351.
 Character of the Baptists there, 348, 352, 360.
Grecian churches, 100, 315.
Gundulphus, rise, efforts of, 141, 256.

Henry of Toulouse, efforts of, 179.
  Followers of, 181.
  Views of baptism, 182.
History, its importance, 1.
Holland, churches in, 357, 358.
 Shoals of Baptists arrive in, 330.
 Baptists persecuted there, 358.
  Obtain liberty in, 361.
 English visit, 362.
 Visited by Mr. Blount, 363.
 Churches degenerated, and extent in, 364.
Huss, rise, character, and efforts of, 229, 230, 323.

Immersion, see Baptism, and 2, 3, 13, 23, 25, 33, 35, 41, 43, 101, 117, 118, 122, 123, 124, 161, 166, 312.
Inquisition, 265.
Italy, Baptists in, 31, 50, 136.

Jews' war with the Romans, 11.
 Distinction removed, 11.
Jerome of Prague, rise, character, trial, martyrdom of, 232, 233, 234, 236.
Jones's valuable History, pref. 8, 196.

Liberty, Baptists friends to, 249, 329.
  Best understood, 328, 339.
Lollard, W., rise and views, 322, 323.
Luther, rise, 330.
 Remained a Catholic, 330.
 Zeal and boldness of, 331, 334.
 Views of, on baptism, 332, 333, 355.
 Violence, 333.
 A persecutor, 339.
 Murdering advice, 344.
Lyons, city of, 159, 208.

INDEX. 369

Lyons, Peter of, or Waldo, rise, 185.
      Efforts, 185, 189, 225, 262, 315.
      His followers, 186, 262.
      Character, 187.

Manes, and his system, 113.
Manicheans, sentiments of, 113.
Martyr, Justin, apology, 22, 106.
Menno, Simon, rise, 353, is baptized, 355.
    Efforts, 358.
    Character, 360.
    Sentiments accord with early Baptists, 357.
Mennonites, numerous, 357, 361.
   Character of, 360.
   Divide, 359.
Ministers chosen by Christ, 7.
   Corrupt ones, 29, 74, 118, 144, 146.
Minor baptism, rise, 64, 66, 68.
Montanus, rise and efforts of, 65, 112.
Muncer, rise, character, and efforts of, 338.
    Friend to civil and religious liberty, 340.
    Persecuted by Luther, 338.
    Drew up the peasants' memorial, 343.
    Defeated and executed, 345.

Nero a persecutor, 11.
Noble lesson, 261.
Nonconformists' rise and extent, 110.
Novatian, dissents and efforts, 52, 55, 120.
Novatianists, character of, 55.
    Order of Churches, 54, 85.

Officers in the early churches, 27, 107, 128.
Optatus quoted, 87.
Origen, 34, 72.

Pædobaptism unknown, 13, 35, 42, 88.
    Its rise, 36, 38, 60, 68, 76, 78, 93, 96, 120, notes.
    Confined to national churches, 144, 145, 305, 308.
    Its advocates, 45, 74, 77, 89, 95, 96, 144, note.
    First rule for, 46.
    First law for, 46, 311.
    Grounds of, 73, 77, 93, 95, 96, 354, notes.
    Aids infidelity, 15, 40.
    With filthy practices, 144, 145, note.
Pædobaptists divided on grounds of the rite, 354.
    Partial course, pref. 7.
Paterines, name whence, 138.
   Sentiments and practice, 139, 142.
   Number and character, 142, 143.
   Emigrate largely, 144, 152.
   Sufferings and obscurity, 155.

INDEX.

Paulicians, rise and sentiments, 124—127.
        Order and discipline, 127, 128.
        Numbers, 128.
        Sufferings, 131, 133.
        Emigrate into France, 135, 167.
        Italy, 143.
Peasants in Germany, condition of, 326.
        rebellion of, 343.
Persecutions, causes of, 19.
Picards, origin of, 189, 225, 315.
        Views of, 227, 318, 324.
        Efforts of, 327, 329.
        Comprehended by imperial law, 348.
Piedmont, Description of, 246.
        Churches of, 246—248.
        Early and puritanical, 251.
Pyrenées, description of, 161.

Raymond VI. supports Puritanism, 202.
        Excommunicated, 203.
Re-baptizing, 75, 92, 336, 347.
        When lawful, 336, 337.
Reformed churches, 277, 281.
Reformers, Baptists :
  Tertullian, 30.
  Novatian, 52.
  Donatus, 83.
  Montanus, 112.
  Manes, 113.
  Ærius, 122.
  Constantine Sylvanus, 124.
  Simon, 131.
  Gundulphus, 141.
  Arnold, 145.
  Hinchmar, 166.
  Leuthericus, 173.
  Berenger, 173.
  Valdo, 175.
  Peter de Bruys, 176.
  Henry, 179.
  Peter of Lyon, 185.
  Jerome of Prague, 223.
  Hetzer, 328.
  Deuck, 328.
  Muncer, 338.
  Menno, Simon, 353.
Rhantism and Pouring, rise of, 98, 106.

Spain, freed of dissenters, 199.
Sprinkling, heathenish custom, 106.
Stephen's death, 8.

Spanish churches, 161.

Temple destroyed, 11.
Tertullian quoted, 31, 67, 112.

Unity among Baptists, pref. 7.

Voltaire quoted, 339.

Waldenses, origin of, 104, 247.
    In France, 161.
    In Piedmont, 246.
        Early existence, 248.
        Church order, 249.
    Views of baptism, 250, 260, 261, 279, 286, &c. &c.
    Character of, 251, 273.
    Ministers among the, 253.
        Itinerate, 255—257.
        Manner of teaching, 258.
        Success, 259, 265, 267.
    Writings of the, 178, 261.
    Persecuted, 268.
    Degenerated, 275.
    Comprehended in the state, 277.
    Scattered, 285.
    Modern, not Puritans, 286.
    Not Pædobaptists, 286, appendix.
    Not open in their communion, 306.
Waldo, Peter, see Lyons.
Wall, Dr. W., quoted, 39, 48, 73.
"What is Antichrist?" 178.

P.S. Distance from the press, with other circumstances, rendered it inconvenient for the author to receive the proof sheets. In perusing the work, he has discovered some few things which he wishes his readers to correct.

Page 38, line 6, from the top read *Valens* for *Valeus*.
    51 — 15   *devised* for *derived*.
    71 — 9   (leave out *to*.
    71 — 14   *He* for *It*.
   113 — 15   *Mermo* for *Merino*.
   119 — 3   *became* for *and*.
   124 — 1   bottom   *in* for *to*.
   155 — 2   top   *destruction* for *instruction*.
   187 — 18   take out *of*.
   194 — 18   *in* for *to*.
   201 — 20   *Raux* for *Baux*.
   219 — 23   *such* after *support*.
   224 — 4   bottom   *her* after *to*.
   227 — 6   *titles* for *tithes*.
   248 — 11   . top   *Antoninus* for *Antonius*.
   288 — 11   bottom .   *of* after *Christian*.
   308 — 7   top   *sanctioned* for *sanction*.
   318 — 17   *re-baptizing* for *rebellion*.

Published by the Author, and may be had of G. Wightman.

THE INSEPARABLE CONNEXION BETWEEN GRACE AND GLORY. Price 6*d*.

TEN REASONS FOR STRICT COMMUNION, with *Nine* Objections to Open Communion; and the Arguments of the Open Advocates considered under *thirteen* particulars. Price 6*d*.

Also preparing for the press,
A CONCISE HISTORY OF ENGLISH BAPTISTS.

In this work, their rise, character, extent, and influence will be shown; with detailed accounts of the American, Welch, Irish, and Scotch churches; also, the origin and progress of their various missionary stations: chronologically arranged from their establishment to the present day.

J. Haddon, Castle Street, Finsbury.

www.ingramcontent.com/pod-product-compliance
Lightning Source LLC
Chambersburg PA
CBHW062005180426
43198CB00037B/2410